20:21 VISION

Bill Emmott

20:21 VISION

The Lessons of the
20th Century for the 21st

ALLEN LANE
an imprint of
PENGUIN BOOKS

ALLEN LANE
THE PENGUIN PRESS

Published by the Penguin Group
Penguin Books Ltd, 80 Strand, London WC2R ORL, England
Penguin Putnam Inc., 375 Hudson Street, New York, New York 10014, USA
Penguin Books Australia Ltd, 250 Camberwell Road, Camberwell, Victoria 3124, Australia
Penguin Books Canada Ltd, 10 Alcorn Avenue, Toronto, Ontario, Canada M4V 3B2
Penguin Books India (P) Ltd, 11, Community Centre, Panchsheel Park, New Delhi – 110 017, India
Penguin Books (NZ) Ltd, Cnr Rosedale and Airborne Roads, Albany, Auckland, New Zealand
Penguin Books (South Africa) (Pty) Ltd, 24 Sturdee Avenue, Rosebank 2196, South Africa

Penguin Books Ltd, Registered Offices: 80 Strand, London WC2R ORL, England

www.penguin.com

First published 2003
2

Set in 10.5/14 pt PostScript Linotype Sabon
Typeset by Rowland Phototypesetting Ltd, Bury St Edmunds, Suffolk
Printed and bound in Great Britain by Clays Ltd, St Ives plc

ISBN 0-713-99519-X

Contents

Acknowledgements

This book's origins lie in an essay I wrote for *The Economist*, to mark the end of the twentieth century, called 'Freedom's Journey', which was published on 11 September 1999. Stuart Proffitt at Penguin spotted the essay and convinced me that it was a foundation on which a book could be built. He commissioned the book, nurtured it and offered countless suggestions and criticisms of several drafts. He also convinced Jonathan Galassi at Farrar Straus Giroux to publish the book in America, and Jonathan provided many useful ideas too. Elizabeth Stratford was an efficient and skilled copy-editor, for editors, above all, also need to be edited. My literary agent, Arthur Goodhart, was as encouraging and professional as ever, and went far beyond the call of duty in reading and offering comments on what must have seemed an interminable number of drafts. Mark Doyle checked every fact he could find, and even some opinions, and was responsible for numerous improvements both to the data and to the text. Peter Drucker, in California, gave generously of his time and attention by reading and commenting upon the final draft.

The benefits of being editor of *The Economist* arise not merely from the publication itself. They arise also from the chance to be stimulated and educated by working with some of the world's best journalists; from the chance to travel all over the globe; from the support we get from our readers and advertisers; and from the work of my fourteen predecessors as editor in giving the publication the shape and standing it has today. I am grateful to all, for their inspiration and influence. Unlike *The Economist*, however, this book is the work of one person, and all criticism of it should be directed only at me.

The burden of all that travel and of my year-round obsession with news and global affairs falls most heavily on my wife, Carol. She nevertheless encouraged me to write this book, tolerated the extra incursion thus imposed on our time together, imposed some further discipline on my work when such discipline was needed, and yet continued to provide the love and laughter that are the essence of life. My principal thanks go to her.

Bill Emmott
Wiltshire,
September 2002

I

20:21 VISION

There are many wonderful things about being a journalist. The excitement of responding to, and trying to make sense of, the flow of news. The challenge of trying to sort out the wood from the trees, the important from the unimportant, the honest from the dishonest, the reasonable from the hyperbolic. The independence of mind and of spirit, the accompanying sense of the ridiculous, that are available to an outsider, an observer of rather than participant in events, processes and organizations. The fact that so many people read or hear what you have to say, and that some of them even pay heed to it. The privilege of being able to, and actually being paid to, write or broadcast what can fairly be described as a sort of first draft of history, albeit with all the foibles and frailties that performing that task typically implies.

Yet that is also where the limitations of journalism begin. Our perspective is always a fairly short-term one. Our readers want to know how something that happened today might be connected to something that happened yesterday, or last month. Furthermore, our preoccupations are for ever vulnerable to the fads and fashions of instant hopes, fears and worries. Writing in a weekly such as *The Economist*, with a global, highly motivated readership and a clear analytical mission, this journalist is insulated against some of that vulnerability. But it is still necessary to write about the issues and events that preoccupy people, even when such preoccupation is not really justified and when the journalist's main role is simply to say so. And, like all instant analysts, the journalist is constantly at risk of over-interpreting the short-term and under-rating or under-interpreting the longer-term trends. Something that did not seem to matter at all yesterday becomes, tomorrow, the only thing that seems to matter.

Thus it was that on 10 September 2001 international terrorism by religious zealots was not thought to be an especially important topic. It was just one fear among many on the standard lists of present and future threats, but not a very immediate one. After 8.46 a.m. American Eastern Standard Time, on the following day, such terrorism was, for a time, transformed into the only topic that mattered.

That shift in perspective was entirely understandable, given the magnitude, drama and horror of the events of that day, and at the time it was also entirely appropriate. Everyone's attention was transfixed by what had happened, their minds filled with possible explanations for it and with possible ramifications. Yet the truth about that particular episode, as can already be seen with the benefit of hindsight, is that neither the view on 10 September nor that on the 12th was correct.

The threat of international terrorism by the sort of groups that devastated the World Trade Center in New York and the Pentagon in Washington, killing thousands of civilians, was already real before that infamous day. It had been the subject of many worthy reports, conference papers and articles, whether the expected terror was in the form of low-tech warfare as in those attacks or, more worrying still, in the high-tech form of nuclear, chemical or biological weapons of mass destruction. But, being chiefly theoretical as one danger among many, it was not given a high priority either by pundits or by policy-makers, even though several attempts at such terror attacks had been thwarted already, including in the United States itself. Had these succeeded, they could have delivered a shock comparable to that of 11 September. But they did not, and so international terror was not the talk of any town.

By the same token, in the days and weeks after those attacks on 11 September, and after the ensuing war in Afghanistan, the danger of international terrorism was by no means the only danger to the peace and prosperity of the West, nor was it the only important political force at work in the world. Even so, for quite a while, it was the only threat being talked of in most Western capitals and on the editorial pages of much of the Western media. On one day, furthermore, two of the world's great civilizations were assumed to be ignoring each other, living separate lives; on the very next morning, it was widely believed that those civilizations, Islam and the Judaeo-Christian West, were in fact engaged in a mighty, epoch-making clash.

A very big event was thus given an even greater significance than it deserved. This was a telling example of one of journalism's biggest weaknesses, that of jumping to conclusions. The events of 11 September did have the *potential* to become world-shattering, era-dominating, overshadowing all other candidates for that role, yet that was only ever one possible outcome. It is unlikely that in years to come we shall see 11 September as insignificant, but nevertheless it remains far too early to say whether this will in fact be the most important occurrence during the first decade of the twenty-first century. The more common examples of this weakness, though, are of journalists allotting a misleadingly high significance to quite minor events. These may just be misjudgements, or they may be efforts to create drama and hence to sell newspapers, for the news media are, after all, only a branch of the entertainment industry. Whatever the reason, the draft of history that journalists write is not just frail and full of foibles but inevitably flawed.

Instant judgements are not all bad judgements; indeed, some can be very sharp. What gets lost, however, is a sense of perspective, a sense of the relative weight of different events, tendencies, ideas or people. It gets lost because of the hurly-burly of news and the cacophony of competing voices. It gets lost because the half-life of an idea or a theme in today's world can be measured in months, weeks or even days. But it also gets lost for the simple reason that we do not actually know what is going to happen next.

Compared with the historians who will be writing about the same event in fifty or a hundred years time journalists face two crippling disadvantages. One is that, to a historian, a decade is a blink of an eye amid a broad theme or movement, the events within it just detailed evidence for or against a wider thesis. To a journalist even a year seems an eternity, and a month can seem to change everything. A trend, to some commentators, is something that will last until their next show or column. We are forced, both by our readers and by ourselves, to be short-sighted.

The other disadvantage is that we lack the most crucial thing that is necessary to evaluate an event properly: knowledge of what happened next, or later, as a consequence of the event about which we are writing. Our 'first draft of history' always contains, along with known facts, a huge amount of speculation about the future context within which the particular event will in the end be judged, either implicitly or explicitly. The anarchist who shot Archduke Franz Ferdinand of Austria and his wife on a visit to the Bosnian capital, Sarajevo, on 28 June 1914 may have thought he was simply striking a blow in a regional struggle over power and autonomy. That would indeed have been a reasonable interpretation at the time. Only later was it possible to interpret this event in a rather different context, that of the struggle between old empires and new that generated two world wars during the ensuing four decades.

It is banal to say it, but it is true: what is needed is a longer view. We need a longer view simply in order to understand the present: how we got here, what are the most important forces in today's world for good or for ill, and what are the reasons why some people are rich and some poor, some at peace and some at war, some content and some in despair. We need a longer view in order to put current events, issues and preoccupations into their appropriate contexts. But what everyone also wants is for that longer view to be clairvoyant, laying out a good sketch of what the future will hold. Once you have such a sketch in hand, it ought to be possible to plan for that future.

The trouble, of course, is that clairvoyance is not possible. In the whiskery words of Sam Goldwyn, 'Never prophesy, especially about the future.' No one knows what the future holds, and those who claim to know, at least beyond quite a short perspective, are charlatans. Just as a weather forecast is inherently unreliable beyond a few days, and an economic forecast is unreliable beyond a few months, so a broad forecast of future political, economic, technological and social events is unreliable beyond a very few years – and it generally does not pass muster for even that long. Futurology should be seen just for what it is, namely enjoyable speculation. It cannot be more than that.

This is awkward, to say the least. It also flies in the face of human nature. For not only are we all curious about the future, but we also carry an implicit set of expectations about it around in our heads. We are all prisoners of some idea of the future that is inherent in our view

4

of the present. It is there in our beliefs and disputes about current issues, in life, in politics, in economics, in science, in religion. It is contained in our beliefs about the security of our jobs, about the sort of education that it is desirable to have, in our choices about where and how to live and work, in our decisions, by omission or by deliberation, on how best to save or invest for retirement or for rainy days. All these are, in effect, bets we are constantly placing about what the future might hold.

Similarly, our view of tomorrow can be found in the topics we choose to protest about or, more mildly, the causes we try to help through our donations. It is contained in the allegiances and alliances that we consider acceptable for our countries to enter into or maintain, in the sort of relationships our political leaders affect to strike up with the leaders of other countries, most of which reflect not personal 'chemistry' but a more established set of assumptions about national and international interests, priorities and relationships. And many of our decisions, especially those made by big organizations or by governments, could themselves end up altering the very future about which we are all wondering: by polluting more or polluting less, by encouraging hard work or by discouraging it, by restraining corporate activities or by fostering them, by stimulating financial volatility or dampening it down, by making war or making peace, by having babies or by not having them.

*

The future matters, in other words. It cannot be avoided or ignored just because we are necessarily ignorant of what it will bring. So what can we do? The best answer is to avoid making a conscious effort to look forwards and to understand the future by looking backwards instead. That sounds paradoxical, and it is. But it is the best way to understand the present, as well as to gain a sense of the forces that really matter in determining what lies ahead. We cannot use the past to make predictions, of course. But we can use it to help set our priorities, to assign a more appropriate set of weights or levels of importance to our current preoccupations. Such a claim can give rise to scepticism. In that case, listen to one of the twentieth century's greatest men. Winston Churchill, as well as being a politician, amateur painter and wartime prime minister of Britain, was also a popular historian. Churchill once said: 'The further backward you look, the further forward you can see.'

That is the spirit of this book, and also its purpose. The aim is to step back from the short-term preoccupations of the journalist, and to try to take a longer view. It is a view, first and foremost, about what the past tells us matters most today and will matter most in the future, a future which for convenience can be called the twenty-first century. Whether the view is of a hundred years or fifty or just twenty-five does not matter very much, for it is a view about the sweep of future history, and only the arbitrary dictates of the calendar associate such a sweeping view with the whole of the century that has just begun. The view of what will matter most is itself derived from history, a history which for similar reasons of calendrical convenience can be called that of the twentieth century, whether or not that relevant past can, in truth, be held to have lain strictly or only between 1900 and 2000.

This book's longer view is also, however, a view about the issues in today's world that are especially relevant to those broad, future-shaping topics, and about what past experience, the long-term perspective, has to tell us about those contemporary issues. Thus, even if you do not happen to accept the book's overall hypothesis about which are the big, future-shaping questions, you will at any rate find here an exploration of what the present author considers to be the biggest issues of our time, of how history and principle meld together to suggest the real importance of those issues, and of what factors will be important in determining how they evolve.

*

What, then, were the big, life-determining issues of the twentieth century? And why should they continue to shape our lives in the twenty-first? Can't we move on? The answer is that we can't. One of the two big issues that shaped the twentieth century was really of an eternal nature, made more important and apparent by the onward march of technology; it will also, in one form or another, shape the twenty-second and twenty-third centuries. The other big issue, which began to emerge as long ago as the nineteenth century, is one that continues to dog us. Despite an apparent denouement a decade ago, this issue is not, in reality, settled. Quite probably it never will be, given the nature of modern life and an essential contradiction at the heart of humanity.

All this may sound rather enigmatic. What are these two issues? Well, the first of them can begin to be glimpsed by the observation that, above all other things, the twentieth century was shaped by war. This is despite the fact that it was a century in which, for human beings in general, the most notable development was a big rise in life expectancy, thanks to a combination of improvements in medical technology, better diet and better sanitation. Someone born in 1900 could expect, at that point, to live for an average of 45–50 years if they were lucky enough to be born in a richer, developed country, or 20–40 years if they were unluckier and lived in the poor world. By the end of the century those averages had risen to 75–80 years in the rich countries and 50–60 in the poorer ones. Such figures measure quantity of life, not quality. Something else besides sheer chance helped to determine whether or not a particular life enhanced or impaired those averages, and whether it was lived in peril or in some semblance of stability: whether the person's country, or region, was at war. And the nature of that life was also determined by whether the country was ruled by a dictatorial government that killed its own citizens or was a democracy that avoided such atrocities.

All centuries, all periods of human history, have felt the heavy influence of war and other forms of violence. But although the twentieth century did not differ in kind, it differed in degree. It was the first century to feature a truly world-spanning conflict, one involving countries from opposite sides of the globe. And, as if to emphasize the point, it featured not just one such world-wide conflict, but two.

Some historians like to suggest that the two world wars were in reality just one, interrupted by an interlude of peace. That idea may contain some truth for the European powers, but it under-rates the much greater geographical spread of the second war, and the fact that one of the crucial participants in that war, Japan, had been on the opposite side during the first conflict. China's condition today, more-over, was shaped crucially by the war that began on its territory in 1931 and did not in reality end fully until the communist takeover in 1949. Nevertheless, some historians even extend their definition of the twentieth century's single world war to include the 'cold war' of

1947–91 between the Soviet Union and the United States, despite the fact that in both the conventionally defined hot wars of the century Russia and America were formally on the same side. The conclusion of the second war, however, crystallized a basic rivalry between the two. And the post-war settlement of 1945 froze some countries in the unsatisfactory state in which they had found themselves as the war ceased, with Eastern and Central Europe mostly under Russian occupation, for example, and the Balkans given the artificial unity of Tito's communist Yugoslavia. Even if we disagree that the whole period should be seen as a single conflict, it is surely true that the world did not properly start to shake off even the medium-term effects of these successive wars until the 1990s.

The twentieth century's wars and dictatorships did not merely innovate by geography. They innovated by the sheer, appalling size of the death-toll they caused. The table shows estimates, derived from a 1994 book, *Death by Government*, by an American academic, R. J. Rummel, of the numbers of people killed in wars, the direct consequences of wars or by governments; the figures have been updated to include conflicts in the final years of the century. Such figures will always be estimates, and controversial, for nobody during these killings sat ticking off names in a ledger, and many of them occurred in the jurisdictions of dictatorial governments with a strong interest in falsifying such records as did exist. The estimates may be wrong in their specific magnitudes, but they offer a good indication of the horror and general scale of what occurred. The category of deaths 'associated with' war involves civilians who were slaughtered by their own governments (for example, by Germany's Nazis) or by occupying governments (for example, Germany's Nazis) in or near wartime; or who died in civil conflicts exacerbated by an international war (for example, China in the 1930s); or (a large category) those who died in famines resulting from war. For this last group, it should be noted that famines rarely occur because of sheer lack of food; they typically occur because of disruptions to the distribution of food, generally caused by war or government action.

Government action explains the final and largest category of all, the 97 million estimated here to have died in the Soviet Union and communist China as a result of unnatural causes. These numbers are especially controversial: plenty of studies can be found that claim that

People killed in war and by the most murderous
governments in the twentieth century

1. Deaths in declared wars:

International	29m.
Civil	5m.
Sub-total	34m.

2. Civilian deaths associated with wars, or in undeclared wars:

Germany (1933–45)	21m.
China (Kuomintang 1928–49)	10m.
Japan (in China, 1936–45)	6m.
Sub-total	37m.

3. Civilian deaths directly or indirectly caused by governments:

Soviet Union (1917–91)	62m.
China (1949–)	35m.
Cambodia (1975–9)	2m.
Turkey (1909–18)	1.8m.
Sub-total	100.8m.
Ungrand total	171.8m.

either or both of them is either too high or too low. For this purpose, however, it does not really matter whether the total ought really to be 60 million or 140 million. As Stalin himself said: 'One man's death is a tragedy; a million deaths is a statistic.' These statistics give a terrible sense of what occurred. Some deaths were direct, official killings, some were in labour camps, some (in China especially during the 'Cultural Revolution' of 1966–76) occurred amid government-inspired anarchy. The largest numbers of deaths, though, were probably caused by famine when, in both the Soviet Union and China, at different times, the central government brought about chaos in food production and distribution either because of misplaced ideas or for brutal political ends.

The list of individual countries and perpetrators could have been much longer, of course. Cambodia is included in the table because Pol Pot's Khmer Rouge slaughtered an extraordinary percentage (about 30 per cent) of that country's population in just four years. But more than a million people were killed in Vietnam, too, for reasons outside the direct conflict between North and South, and with America. Indonesia's brutal suppression of a supposedly communist uprising in the 1960s could have added 600,000 or more, as could the Rwandan genocide of the 1990s. No one knows what number should be included for North Korea, as a result of official killings, labour camps or famines. But these details would not have altered the basic point: the twentieth century, a century of enormous progress in medical, agricultural and other technologies, was nevertheless one in which governments working alone or in wars managed to kill somewhere in the region of 170 million people, a figure equivalent to more than 10 per cent of the world's entire population in 1900.

Why? There are many explanations: ideology, ambition, greed, fear, insanity, the legacy of colonial empires, among others. Two, however, stand out as being important for today and for the future. The first, simplest and most enduring is technology.

Developments in the second half of the nineteenth century and in the early decades of the twentieth in electronic communications and in transportation made it possible not just to be a dictator but to exercise far greater control over more people and across much larger areas. Dictators existed before, but it was hard, perhaps impossible, for them to be 'totalitarian'. The electric telegraph and the telephone made it possible to send and receive commands and other information instantly over huge distances, serving military, intelligence and propaganda purposes. Railways, motorized vehicles and aircraft similarly enabled power to be deployed or projected over huge areas. Add the increasing destructive power of weaponry, especially in armoured tanks, machine guns and bomber aircraft, and the result was the potential for powerful despotisms, cowed populations and mass slaughter.

Those technological underpinnings of dictatorial brutality continue to exist and develop today. In one sense, though, recent technological change has weakened governmental control. The even cheaper long-distance communication that is possible through computers, telephones, satellites and the Internet has made it harder to maintain a monopoly of knowledge, harder to bamboozle a population. George Orwell's 'Big Brother', manipulating people's minds in his novel *1984*, became, in the Britain of 2000, merely the name of a tawdry television game show. That change needs, however, to be weighed against others more sinister. It may be easier to find out that your government consists of knaves or fools, and easier to organize resistance movements, but that resistance would now face even more overwhelming odds than in the past. The ability of governments to detect dissidents has been improved by the same new information technology that helps the dissidents, and military firepower continues to become more efficiently destructive. China's dictatorship has so far seen off the Tiananmen Square protests, the Falun Gong religious sect, and Internet-based organization and dissemination. It has proved adaptable in many aspects of life and economics, but not in terms of its political control.

This also helps to explain why a group of American gun activists once published an advertisement in their magazine making the remarkable accusation that the present author is in favour of genocide. *The Economist* had published an article advocating greater governmental control of the availability of guns in the United States. According to the gun activists' logic, when it is made harder for a citizenry to possess and bear arms the balance of power is tilted in favour of the government; and in history, genocides have occurred only when a population has been unable to resist its government. Such logic has half a point, though it does rather over-rate the probability that the United States might descend into dictatorship any time soon. Nevertheless, it is true that a dictator such as Saddam Hussein in Iraq, who is willing to use chemical or biological weapons against his own lightly armed or unarmed people as well as powerful conventional means, can be very hard to dislodge.

In the long run, the real limits to dictatorship are chiefly economic: the ability of a government to continue to harness resources sufficient to maintain military control at home or to satisfy ambitions abroad.

Those resources can come from the sale of natural commodities such as oil, but generally, and especially over the longer term, they come from the wider economy. That, in the end, is what brought down the Soviet Union: the contradiction between a weak economy and large military or totalitarian aims. In the long run, dictatorships generally fall if, or rather when, they fail to maintain their countries' economic capacity, for they then become vulnerable to overthrow or military defeat. But, to paraphrase Lord Keynes, in the long run, many more citizens would already be dead.

*

The potential for dictatorship, with associated deadly brutality, is undimmed. The main limiting factor is economic: centralized control has proved to be a poor way to build a wealthy, modern economy, and wealthy economies are those most able to afford the latest offensive, defensive or repressive technologies. Modern, wealthy economies have developed when economic power has been dispersed to a wide population and when individual enterprise has been given its head. Such developments make dictatorship harder and repression costlier. But it is far from impossible to sustain a dictatorship, over long periods of time, as the Chinese Communist Party has shown. And the importance of the economic sacrifice entailed by centrally directed regimes is essentially relative: it is the growing wealth of other countries, operating in an open, market economy, that makes it harder for a dictatorship to restrain the economic expectations of its own citizens and to keep up with other countries' military technology and resources. But if other countries' economies become depressed, life for the dictator could well become easier.

An open, global market economy is not, moreover, an inevitable by-product of the modern world. To the degree that it exists (for it remains incomplete) it is a by-product of the existence of a general state of peace that seems sufficiently reliable or durable for companies and individuals all over the world to feel willing to engage in international trade and investment, and of the existence of a state of trust between most countries that is sufficiently reliable or durable for that trade and investment to take place according to a more or less agreed set of laws and financial arrangements.

This brings us to the second important explanation for why the twentieth century was characterized by so much violence and war. It is that, for the century's first forty or forty-five years, there was no guarantor of such a state of peace, no keeper of the balance between nations, no preserver of that trust and that rule of international law. There was, in other words, no hegemon, no dominant power, until the United States of America emerged to take on this role in 1945.

After 1945, America competed with the Soviet Union for the role, but soon did so with greater acquiescence from the subjects of its dominance and with much less need for military control. It does not even feel quite right to call the United States a hegemon today, now that the Soviet Union has gone, though many of America's opponents and critics use the word. Similarly, it is probably too simple to describe Great Britain as having been the hegemon of the nineteenth century, even though that was the period when 'Great' appeared to be a significant part of the country's name. Still, Britain built a world-wide empire, an empire on which 'the sun never set', an empire that meant that British schoolchildren's maps appeared to be covered with pink. The empire was built on naval power; like Britain's large and effective army, it was built on the foundation of her early industrial revolution and relatively rapid economic growth. Although it has not, since the loss of Calais in the sixteenth century, occupied or otherwise ruled any substantial part of continental Europe (the sole exception is Gibraltar), Britain has acted and intervened to keep the balance of power in Europe, to prevent any other country there from becoming dominant and thus a potential rival. For the half century following Britain's defeat of France's Napoleon in 1815, Britain had no political or military rival on the Continent. The British empire suffered a great defeat in 1776 when its most promising colony of all, America, declared its independence. But it made up for that loss by expanding its imperial territories to the east, in India, and to the south, in Africa. The most important thing of all was that the former colony itself exhibited no desire to rival Britain around the globe, preferring to concentrate on its own development and on its closer foreign interests in its own hemisphere.

After 1815, the nineteenth century was a relatively peaceful period, with few clashes between the great powers around the globe. Although France, Germany, Italy and even young (1830) Belgium had sought by the end of the century to establish small colonial empires of their own, especially in the uncharted territory of Africa, none felt it worthwhile to confront Britain head-on, or at least not for long. Russia expanded its contiguous empire to the east and south, and came to rival Britain on the fringes of both countries' empires, notably in Afghanistan, but never in such a way as to pose a durable or broad-based challenge. The result was that an international system of communication, trade and capital flows developed, led and generally designed by Britain, and chiefly policed by the British navy. There was nothing perfect about this outcome, and it was one that depended on Britain maintaining occupying forces and administrations in a large number of countries, governing large numbers of people. But it endured, more or less peacefully, for many decades because it was accepted or at least acquiesced in by other countries.

That acquiescence was disappearing as the new century was born in 1900. The spread of industrial technology and trade was enabling other countries to catch up with Britain, and leading them to expect a commensurate influence over world affairs as well as their own colonial empires. Old, smaller empires – the Austro-Hungarian empire of the Habsburgs in Central Europe, the Ottoman empire in the Middle East – were decaying, as nationalist feelings among their various component states combined with rivalrous pressures from outside to undermine them. In place of clear British dominance over a world in which other powers were either feeble or balanced against each other, the new world of the twentieth century was one in which several powers – Britain, Germany, France, Russia, Japan, the United States, Turkey – were strong but in which none commanded sufficient resources or technology to dominate or to deter the others. A fateful blend of ambition and insecurity led to war, and to the fracturing of the old British-led system of international trade, payments and investment.

Any system based chiefly on force, especially the force of a small island economy off the coast of Europe, was bound to collapse eventually. The trouble was that nothing – or rather nobody – was ready to replace the system or to repair it. The first half of the twentieth century is best understood as a story of the decline of empires, of the rise of new powers as technology and wealth spread, but, most of all, as the story of a power vacuum. Only after 1945 was the vacuum truly filled, as the United States of America took on the mantle of world leadership (albeit in rivalry to the weaker Soviet Union) that had been forfeited by Britain. In effect, the most important story of the century, at least in hindsight, was not one of Germany rivalling its European neighbours, or communism rivalling capitalism, or even of Soviet Russia rivalling others, but that of the United States taking over from Britain. It had long been capable, in principle, of doing so. But it had not wanted to adopt an international role commensurate with the size and strength of its economy, and Britain was not yet weak enough to yield the vestiges of its own pre-eminence voluntarily. The Second World War altered America's wishes, as well as enfeebling Britain.

The result was seen in economics as well as politics. The second half of the twentieth century was far more prosperous than the first for most people in the world. The annual growth rate of output, per head of population, doubled in what are now the rich member countries of the Organization of Economic Co-operation and Development (OECD), a rich-country club originally set up to manage and monitor America's economic aid to Western Europe in the late 1940s. The OECD members' growth rate rose from a 1.3 per cent annual average in 1900–50 to 2.6 per cent, but that rate meanwhile soared in populous Asia (from a miserable 0.1 per cent to a life-changing 3 per cent). Although there were wars aplenty – Korea, Vietnam, Afghanistan, India–Pakistan, Israel, Iran–Iraq, Congo, Angola, Ethiopia, former Yugoslavia, to name but a few – this period was on the whole more peaceful than the century's first half. Fewer people died in war, although many continued to be killed by their governments. Wars destroy economies, peace builds them.

There was no new colonial empire to explain the post-1945 peace. Britain's empire was dismantled during the three decades after 1945, but none rose to take its place. America maintained military bases abroad, in Japan, South Korea, the Philippines, Germany, Britain and elsewhere, but always with the consent and even at the request of the host country. The rules for trade were agreed in the General Agreement on Tariffs and Trade (GATT), signed up to by twenty-three countries in 1947. A new framework intended to maintain financial stability was superintended by two institutions, the International Monetary

Fund and the World Bank, which were also set up in 1946 and which now have 183 member countries.

For the West European countries and for Japan, it may be that the exhaustion of war partly explains why after 1945 they accepted international rules and conventions of conduct, and avoided military conflict. In general, though, there is one explanation alone for the relative peace and prosperity of the past fifty years: the existence of a dominant power, in economic, technological and military matters, namely the United States of America. This power, moreover, has been willing to exert its dominance across the globe whenever there was a serious threat to the general peace, and has been willing to exert leadership whenever there was a serious threat to prosperity.

During the first few decades after 1945, this point was obscured by the existence of a rival, nuclear-armed superpower, the Soviet Union. During the 1950s the legacy of war combined with ignorance of the truth led some to believe that the USSR might even overtake its capitalist opponent. But that truth was that America was always the stronger power, and knowledge of that fact (for it knew about its own weaknesses) restrained the USSR. Moreover, while America led a trading and financial system adopted by much of the world, the USSR's rival system was adopted only by a modest number of countries.

America's behaviour during this period was far from perfect, and it blocked the emergence of fully-fledged international institutions on several occasions itself (for example, GATT's proposed evolution into an 'International Trade Organization' in 1948, and the creation of an International Criminal Court in the late 1990s). Its willingness to engage in international disputes and problems was and remains patchy. But the important point is that America will, *in extremis*, intervene in disputes, attempt to quash threats to global peace and stability, and work to maintain the existence of international economic institutions, and this knowledge serves to deter others from letting ambition or insecurity lead them into military adventures. America is not a true hegemon, in the sense of a power that seeks to impose its will on all and sundry. Nor is it a true policeman, patrolling the globe. But it is like a giant elder brother, a source of reassurance, trust and stability for other weaker members of the family, and a source of nervousness and uncertainty for any budding bullies.

For that reason, the biggest geopolitical question for the twenty-first century must be whether that American leadership, that American role as a giant elder brother, will endure, or whether it will go the way of Britain in the twentieth century and decline. America could forfeit its role in one of three ways: by becoming weaker; by becoming unwilling to exert itself outside its own borders; or by being challenged by other newly strong powers. In principle, America's loss of leadership may prove to be only a matter of time: a country of 280–300 million people ought not to be expected to lead forever a world whose population is already twenty times its size, and which by 2050 could be about twenty-five times its size. Yet, to all of us, time is of the essence. What matters to us is whether America's dominance is going to last merely another thirty years or for a further century or more. That is what the first part of this book explores.

*

The second part of the book concerns itself with the other issue that dominated the twentieth century, and which promises also to matter hugely in the twenty-first. It is an issue that began to emerge during the nineteenth century, as the industrial revolution forced agriculture-based feudalism into an accelerated decline and replaced it in the most advanced countries with a new, urban, industrial capitalism. What began at the time when Karl Marx and Friedrich Engels wrote their *Communist Manifesto* in 1848 and when Charles Dickens was sketching out the misery and dislocation of modern London between 1835 and 1870, was a struggle between not just two ideas but two parts of human nature itself: on the one side, man's inherently competitive, selfish, acquisitive instincts, and on the other his frequent intellectual or moral distaste at the consequences of his own selfishness.

This struggle took on a systemic, ideological, geopolitical flavour after 1917, when the Bolshevik revolution overturned the provisional government in Russia and the world's first communist regime was proclaimed, with the declared ambition of helping to spread communism around the globe. From then until 1989–91, capitalism and communism were said to be engaged in a battle for supremacy, a battle to prove which set of ideas offered a superior way to organize an economy and a country and a superior insight into the true nature of human instincts and motivation. With the fall of the Berlin Wall in

1989 and the collapse of the Soviet Union itself in 1991, this battle was, not surprisingly, considered to have reached a denouement. Capitalism had won.

Yet, understandable though that conclusion was, given the political history of the century and especially of the cold war, it was at best short-sighted, at worst somewhat blinkered. What had undoubtedly come to an end was the cold war between the United States and the Soviet Union. What had also undoubtedly been made clear by the preceding decades was that central planning is a poor way to run a modern economy. It can occasionally work well in a simple, primitive economy, but it is unable to deal effectively or efficiently with the complex range of activities and needs of a more diverse, sophisticated state. However much political or military power he possesses, no planner has sufficient knowledge either to produce or to execute his plans in an economy that is at all advanced. Central planning failed. But did capitalism therefore succeed? It fared better than did central planning. But that is not saying much.

To say more, it is as well to ask oneself why this battle occurred in the first place. Communist ideas did not, in truth, arise in a vacuum, as a rival set of ideas to capitalism, springing out of nowhere. They arose because the true battle lies within capitalism itself. The twentieth century, which experienced the most rapid and widespread economic development in history, was also a century in which capitalism engaged in a series of struggles with itself, with its inherent weaknesses. It was those weaknesses that gave rise to communism, and in particular to its appeal to a wide range of people. That appeal was for a time identified with communism's particular (and supposed) implementation in the Soviet Union and in China, but it went far beyond that association.

Chief among its weaknesses is capitalism's very instability, the way it veers wildly from boom to bust and back again. As well as wealth, productivity and innovation, capitalism produces insecurity, of jobs, of housing, of pensions, of welfare, even of family unity. Any economic system that can allow the Great Depression of the 1930s, with falling incomes and appalling unemployment, is bound to raise doubts and cause dissent. Although the extremes of the 1930s were of a sort that has occurred at most once a century, evidence of capitalism's continuing instability can be seen in any decade. In the 1990s alone there was Mexico's trauma in 1995; there was the East Asian financial crisis of 1997–8, in which currencies, companies and countries slumped, seemingly overnight, putting millions out of work and giving rise to a popular revolution in Indonesia; there was the extraordinary boom in American financial markets, especially those dealing in high-tech companies' shares, followed by an equally extraordinary bust; and there was a long stagnation in Japan, which followed a similar story of boom and bust in Japanese shares and property. Some may argue that modern economies have 'built-in stabilizers' in the form of government spending and borrowing, which prevent such instability from proving disastrous, or that central banks have learned enough from history to deploy their own stabilizing mechanisms. That may well be true. Yet collapses still occur, and the bookshops periodically fill up with works explaining why another huge crash could be just around the corner.

At least, you might say, instability hurts everyone. But it doesn't: during a crash or recession the already poor and vulnerable are invariably hurt more than the rich and powerful, both within countries and when comparing richer countries and poorer ones. That inequality of resources and power is another inherent weakness within capitalism. Indeed, one of capitalism's main motors is the very desire to create inequality, an inequality between those who succeed and those who fail. It is a competitive system. The incentive to create wealth, to build successful businesses, is an incentive to become unequal. While a well-functioning capitalist economy does tend, over time, to make everyone better off, it also tends to make some people better off than others. Among those who do less well, it is probably inevitable that at some points and in some circumstances resentment will build up, and that minds will be drawn towards alternative ways of organizing things, or new ways to adapt a capitalist economy. Politicians often like to describe the aim of such thinking as 'social justice'. It is a telling phrase, as it implies that the outcome of capitalism is somehow unjust, simply because it is unequal.

The richer the country, the more likely it is that even those who have profited from capitalism will find a further reason to dislike it: the environment. All economic activity alters the natural environment, whether under the label of capitalism or communism. Many of the worst examples of pollution and other environmental damage occurred when Soviet or Chinese communists were directing economic activity. The fact that capitalism proved cleaner than its twentieth-century rival does not rescue it from criticism, however: it may be less bad, but that does not make it good enough. In so far as industrial capitalism consists of taking the resources of the earth and processing them into new forms, it will always alter the earth and will distribute its residues to places where such materials did not exist before. It will always, therefore, give rise to awkward and controversial choices, between those who would prefer the earth (or, generally, their part of the earth) to be left unchanged and those who would prefer to have the jobs, incomes and profits that arise from change. And, as the world's population grows from 6 billion now to 9 billion at some point in the twenty-first century, the pressure of such choices is likely to grow and to spread to more and more places around the globe.

Capitalism is what brought, directly or indirectly, the improvements in human welfare that were seen during the twentieth century. Its resources and incentives produced the technological developments that altered our lives, from antibiotics to MRI scans, from telephones to computers, from motor cars to jet airliners, from oil refining to air conditioning. In countries that enjoy such developments, capitalism has paid for education, health care, welfare support, holidays and pensions. For most of the second half of the twentieth century, especially the 1980s and 1990s, the lure of those benefits proved strong enough to make most people accept capitalism even if they could not bring themselves to love it.

Moreover, the phenomenon that has come to be called 'globalization' is in truth simply the spread of this open, trading capitalism to more and more countries around the world that previously sought to shut themselves away from it. China, Vietnam, the Soviet Union and its Eastern European satellites shut themselves away because they were communist; most of Latin America shut itself away because it wanted to be self-sufficient; India shut itself away because of a mixture of socialism and the urge for self-sufficiency. During the past twenty years, the governments of countries containing around 3 billion people – half the world's population – have sought either to adopt a basically capitalist economic system or to connect their existing domestic capitalisms to international trade and capital flows by opening up their borders. Globalization is simply the voluntary adoption of international capitalism.

It is not necessary to be a professional economist to realize that this voluntary process is controversial, however. Protests against globalized capitalism have erupted in many cities around the world, generally at times when international institutions (and thus the media) were holding their annual get-togethers. In domestic politics, too, trade unions and corporate bosses campaign for restrictions on imports or on foreign competition when their own sales are suffering badly. This happens especially frequently in Europe and America in old industries such as steel, textiles and agriculture. Environmentalists meanwhile seek restrictions on capitalism everywhere, regardless of whether the firms involved are domestic or international ones, and whether the environmental damage is domestic (for example, pollution or new dams) or international (for example, global warming).

Since all the progress that has been, and will be, seen in technology and in general welfare has arisen from capitalist activities, and since no alternative set of ideas has emerged to give hope to poorer countries that they can match the rich world's progress by adopting anything other than capitalism, it might seem reasonable to assume that capitalism is likely to be simply a given for the twenty-first century. One way or another, it will be a feature of life during the next hundred years. That is surely true. But all the difference in the world, and for the world, is contained in that phrase, 'one way or another'. How much technology develops, how it develops, how well off we become in material terms, how big a problem the relative poverty of the under-developed world will pose for the developed countries, how the planet's environment serves to limit or enable our activities and circumscribe or enhance our lives – all these questions depend on the way capitalism develops, or rather the way it is allowed to develop.

This, too, like the role of leadership in preserving peace, is probably an eternal question. Our feelings about capitalism have always been and probably always will be mixed. Capitalism works. It appeals to the inherently competitive instinct in man, the instinct that to survive and thrive one must compete, and that to compete one must take risks. Man, however, has other instincts. We are social animals, seeing both pleasure and benefit in co-operation. Capitalists combine competition with co-operative ventures. It is not just dog eating dog. But we also have what Adam Smith, capitalism's greatest economic thinker, described (approvingly) in the eighteenth century as 'moral sentiments': emotions, feelings about fairness, compassion. Such sentiments can be, and often are, affronted by capitalism. The losers, the less successful, are always likely to think of fighting against the outcomes of capitalism. Yet even the winners, the more successful, feel a clash between their selfish instincts and their moral ones. It makes them worry about capitalism, seek to modify or mollify its nature and, at times, even to repress it altogether. It leads them sometimes to enter into alliances with the losers. It means that capitalism is forever under challenge, forever being questioned. How that challenge takes place and is met will make all the difference in the twenty-first century.

*

This book's argument is beguiling in its simplicity. It is that from the morass of issues, problems and solutions that we might envisage as having a bearing on our futures, only two questions really matter when we are thinking about our future in the twenty-first century. These are the questions that have mattered most in determining how we stand now, in the present, because they also determined the shape of the twentieth century. One is whether capitalism will survive, thrive and retain the current, unusual allegiance that it commands around the world. The other is whether the United States of America will continue to keep the peace around the globe, making the world safe for capitalism to spread, by retaining its current clear pre-eminence as a political, military, economic and cultural power, and by retaining the desire to exercise its power as a force for peace and progress. Simple indeed: just two questions. If only it were as simple to provide the answers.

PART ONE

PEACE CHALLENGED

2

American Leadership

As with so many things, Winston Churchill had a quip to sum it up, one that was affectionate and pointed at the same time. 'The Americans will always do the right thing,' he said, '. . . after they've exhausted all the alternatives.'

What did it sum up? It summed up the essential faith of a British leader, especially a wartime leader, in America's power, ability and moral purpose. It also, however, summed up a constant European prejudice about America: that, compared with those sophisticated, old world types, with their centuries of culture and diplomacy, the new world was a rather bumbling, vulgar, inexperienced sort of place, which did not really know how to conduct itself on the world stage.

John Maynard Keynes, the greatest British economist of the 1920s and 1930s, echoed those sentiments when he visited Washington in 1941 to negotiate the terms of America's financial support for Britain's war effort. According to his biographer, Robert Skidelsky, Keynes was taken aback by the apparent incompetence of American government, with poor bureaucratic procedures, open divisions between departments, incomplete authority and lack of clear leadership. He was also disturbed to find that the capital seemed to be overrun by lawyers. Admittedly, this was Keynes's first visit to Washington since 1934, so he was a bit out of touch. Even so, Lord Skidelsky records what Keynes wrote to a friend: 'I always regard a visit [to the United States] as in the nature of a serious illness, to be followed by a convalescence.' So much for Britain's closest political and military alliance, one that later British politicians would come to call 'the special relationship'.

Ignorance and the effects of distance ought by now to have dissipated. Yet it remains common, all over the world, to hear American government described as bafflingly sclerotic and indecisive, to hear laments about the excessive number of lawyers in Washington, to hear criticisms of American diplomacy as being ham-handed, ignorant, arrogant, simplistic, absolutist, short-sighted, selfish, over-politicized . . . and countless variants of such adjectival accusations. Factoids are quoted about how few American congressmen have passports (the true number in 2000 was 93 per cent, according to a survey by the *New York Times*) and how little most Americans know about the rest of the world. Foreigners note with horror or disdain that ambassadorships in important capitals (at least, capitals that are considered so by their self-important residents) are given not to diplomatic professionals but to political appointees who are not diplomats at all, generally golfing partners to a new president and whose other main qualification is that they contributed money to his election campaign. That is, if the posts are filled at all, since many are left vacant for months at a time, awaiting a decision from the White House on whom to send, and then approval from a capricious Senate on whether to allow that person to go. Laws with an entirely international purpose, such as the payment of dues to the United Nations, become laden and obstructed by amendments covering domestic issues such as abortion.

Europeans still look down their noses at these seemingly shambolic activities in much the same way as Churchill did. Meanwhile some, especially those with French accents, hope that through their continent's own unity and economic integration they might in future create a 'counterweight' to the pesky superpower with whom they are in alliance. Among the Europeans, the British governing élite tends to be sympathetic to America's point of view and ways of operating, but the general public and the media are often more sceptical, as are many continental governments. President Ronald Reagan became a favourite butt of European scorn after he described the Soviet Union as 'an evil empire' in the early 1980s. In January 2002 President George W. Bush's state-of-the-union address provided a new focus for European derision, thanks to his identification of Iraq, Iran and North Korea as 'an axis of evil'. Naturally, such scorn and derision could also be heard inside the United States itself against both these Republican presidents.

But the difference is that domestic critics see such presidents merely as being foolish or simple-minded by historical American standards; foreign critics tend to see them as confirmation that American standards are themselves foolish and simple-minded.

The criticism glides smoothly from sneering to resentment. Many Russians still see any gain to America as inevitably meaning a loss to themselves. Chinese officials read more or less from a standard script condemning American arrogance, interference and 'hegemonism'. The Japanese have become more sheepish since the 1980s, when a right-wing politician, Shintaro Ishihara, came together with one of the country's best-known businessmen, Akio Morita of Sony, to publish a bestselling book, *The Japan That Can Say No* (by which was meant '... to America'), but this sort of sentiment remains widely held. Financial officials there seem to think that any Japanese proposal (e.g. that for an Asian Monetary Fund in the late 1990s) is automatically blocked by the American Treasury. Some in the older generation still resent America's occupation of Japan in 1945–51, and its imposition then of what they see as a demeaning constitution.

South Koreans are divided between those who think America is their saviour, using its bases there to deter invasion from the communist North, and those who blame America for the Korean peninsula's very division. Every country that is host to an American military base – and at the last count there were 725 bases outside the United States and its territories, of which 17 were large installations, defined as those with facilities worth $1.5 billion or more – has citizens with reason to resent it, for its noise, its land-hogging, its associated sex industry, its occasional crimes by servicemen. The leaders of Malaysia and Singapore, while fiercely opposed to each other, are united in their exposition of the need for 'Asian values', which they mainly define as being not American. Arabs in many countries in the Middle East think America rides roughshod over their interests, cares little for their fate and supports corrupt regimes that rule over them. Most crucially, they believe that America's backing for what they see as the brutal Israeli regime that occupies Palestinian land means that America has double standards.

World-wide, there is a basic fact arising from a half century of American leadership and international engagement: more people live in countries that have been bombed or otherwise attacked by America during that period than have been attacked by any other country. It is little wonder that some critics think America interferes too much overseas. Yet many others think it callously ignores the rest of the world and should do more. And a further group think it simply interferes clumsily.

To be criticized in so many places, and in such incompatible ways, is in truth a sort of compliment, a tribute to America's overwhelming power and its unusual nature. For three points are hard to dispute. One is that America did take over leadership of the world from Britain in the twentieth century, and did so without encountering, or causing, any gigantic obstacles. Given its supposed incompetence, the outcome was a remarkably successful one. The second is that the gap between America's military power and that of any other country is greater than has been the case for any previously dominant world power. Sheer money sums it up: at more than $400 billion a year, America's defence spending plans for the first decade of the twenty-first century are ten times larger than those of any other country and exceed the spending plans of the next fourteen largest defence spenders combined. It is the mightiest colossus, in both absolute and relative terms, that the world has ever seen. The third, though, is in apparent contradiction to this: it is that America, the mighty colossus, is the first world power to have exercised dominance without building any formal empire, in other words without occupying and subduing other countries by force or systematically arranging things to its own direct advantage.

It can be argued that this third feature is merely a consequence of the times and of technology. There have not been many previous world powers in the past; before Britain in the nineteenth century, only sixteenth-century Spain and the Rome of two millennia ago could really be defined in that way, and even the Romans in reality had only a regional influence, albeit one spanning from the north-western tips of Europe well into the Middle East and Central Asia. Communications and transport technology simply did not permit those empires – or their spheres of influence – to extend widely around the globe. That changed in the nineteenth century as new inventions in communication and transport enabled Britain to exert its influence even in the parts of the world that it did not conquer, such as Latin America, especially once its trade and investment grew in global importance. Yet Britain still felt the need to control many areas through force and possession.

America's post-1945 dominance has been non-imperial by design, but that non-imperial character has been made possible by telephones, satellites, jet aircraft, long-range missiles and fast ships – and by the sheer magnitude of its military superiority. Power can be exerted and felt in many ways: direct military action, the threat of military action, economic pressure, diplomatic pressure, and even the softer influence of ideas, culture and aspirations. It may not have a formal empire, but America still meets an informal definition of that term, since its ability to influence others' behaviour extends far and wide – indeed, far further than was the case for nineteenth-century Britain.

Even so, it can be claimed that America is the first world power to have exercised its dominance by and large in a benevolent manner. Many would dispute this. But it is certainly defensible in *relative* terms: Britain's period of dominance depended far more than America's on the repression of the peoples over which it ruled, and on the overt twisting of the trading relationship between the home country and its colonies in the direct favour of British firms. America has not, typically, told countries or their leaders what to do; nor, typically, has it invaded them or rounded up groups of their citizens to imprison them or shoot them (as the British were known to do). It has mainly, when it has deemed it necessary, simply told them what not to do. When it has acted brusquely or pre-emptively, as in Grenada during the 1980s or Iraq in the 1990s and more recently, it has sought to do so in a wider interest than merely its own national goals. That end is often disputed by others, as are the means used. But the fact remains that such actions are not those of a classic imperialist.

In *absolute* terms, however, the claim does require that qualifying phrase 'by and large', since America has certainly been selfish at times, and has violated principles and values abroad that it would not dream of violating at home, sometimes defending dictators, subverting democracy or turning a blind eye to abuses of human rights. Britain did the same in the nineteenth century, seeing itself at home as the upholder of liberty, governed by the mother of parliaments, while abroad acting as an often ruthless dictator, quelling liberties and killing rebels or ordinary citizens whenever they threatened British interests. Britain was a gentler imperial power than other colonialists of the time, but it was still brutal by today's American standards. For the most part America has since 1945 built a co-operative empire, one that is intended to be mutually advantageous to virtually all its members, rather than a coercive one. Why? In part because of America's own democratic and liberal values, which have long had a more universalist, utopian cast than did nineteenth-century Britain's; but also for a more pragmatic reason: in principle, a co-operative empire is a lot cheaper to maintain than a coercive one.

Another decidedly unusual nature of the American empire, indeed, is that most Americans did not really seem to want an empire at all, during most of the twentieth century. As an immigrant nation, its people or their forefathers had chosen to flee from the rest of the world, so they were not keen on returning to that world to repress it; many believed, along with the Founding Fathers, in America's 'manifest destiny' in establishing itself as different to and separate from the old world. Some, such as Andrew Bacevich, professor of international relations at Boston University and author of *American Empire*, say that this idea of the 'reluctant superpower' is a myth; that for well over a century there have been important Americans who sought to expand the country's influence overseas. The country itself is a sort of empire, consisting as it does of territory acquired by settlement, purchase or force.

That is all true, but two things are different about America: first, that since the end of its expansion into its own contiguous territory and some limited adventures at one time in Cuba and the Philippines it has not in fact sought to conquer an overseas empire; and, second, that the pressure from those wishing to expand the country's influence overseas has been balanced by pressure from those who want no such thing, or want it expressed in different ways. The country's constitution is designed to achieve exactly that sort of check on decisive, executive action. The result is that since 1945 the American empire has been characterized by a rather unusual effort to try to make its subjects, in Europe, Asia and elsewhere, stronger and more able to act independently – as long, of course, as such actions do not threaten the interests of the United States.

The question before us, though, ought not to be whether the American empire is admirable or detestable. There are really two main questions that are relevant for the twenty-first century. First, what will America do with its current dominance? And second, will the dominance last?

*

The first of these questions seemed easy to answer during the cold war from 1947 to 1990, rather hard to answer in 1990–2001, and then again much easier to answer after 11 September 2001. It is unclear how long this last answer will endure, but the best bet is that it will last for at least a decade and perhaps longer. And the broad shape of one of the main challenges beyond that point is also apparent.

What is evident, at least with the benefit of a great sweep of historical hindsight, is that the world suffered badly during the first half of the twentieth century from the lack of any dominant, or even leading, world power. By 1914 the big European powers were evenly balanced in economic and military power, and the task of fighting against Germany then stripped Britain of the ability either to command its world-wide empire or to extend it. The 'Great War' of 1914–18 came to an end only when the protagonists were exhausted and when America joined in on the British and French side. With their resources and economies gravely damaged, and their credibility burnt, the European powers could not then steer the international economy after 1918 either, as they (led by Britain) had done before the war. America made a series of big loans and interventions, but without the clout or the commitment to bring about the stability required for economic revitalization. And again, in the Second World War, it was the entry of America at the end of 1941, along with Hitler's decision to invade the Soviet Union, that determined the ultimate outcome. After 1945 America then led the effort to win the peace, just as it had led the winning of the war, wresting leadership away from an enfeebled Britain, helping to set up institutions to protect financial stability and free trade – and, most important, putting its own by then huge clout and commitment behind them.

In retrospect, the purpose of American policy from the beginning of the cold war (which is generally dated from 1947) until the fall of the Soviet Union was also pretty clear. It was to prevent communism from spreading around the globe and threatening the capitalist democracies – and in particular from threatening the United States itself. Associated with that objective was the desire to ensure that the conditions that had led to the Second World War were not repeated – economic instability, the isolation of countries from each other, the spread of totalitarian ideas. Both these points can be expressed in a different, more selfish way, as an effort to ensure that America was the leading superpower and was not usurped by the Soviet Union, but it comes to much the same thing.

Such clarity of purpose had some great virtues. It brought allies to America's side, and kept them there, for fear of a common enemy. It helped to muster and then sustain support among the American public for high levels of military spending, for a high degree of American military deployment overseas, and for frequent American intervention in international economic affairs. The threat of the Soviet Union in Europe helped to focus European minds on both defence and the maintenance of good relations between the European democracies. And in overall terms it was a success: communism was contained and, in the end, collapsed in its home country, the Soviet Union.

However, it also brought some vices. Chief among them was the fact that seeing the world through a single prism – in that case, the containment of communism – can blind policy makers to the ultimate truth of whether a particular engagement or problem really fits that neat categorization, and can then give rise to embroilments that last a lot longer than was originally intended or expected. The Vietnam War is a classic case. America entered that conflict with the best of anti-communist intentions, but left it, more than a decade later, with more than 47,000 of its own servicemen dead, 1.4 million Vietnamese dead (a million on the northern side and 400,000 on the southern), its reputation and confidence shattered, and its munitions littered all over Indochina. It may well be that communism would have spread through South-East Asia (by the domino effect) had America not intervened in Vietnam. But it is also possible that a more limited intervention could have served the task of containment just as well.

A related, secondary vice was that containing and combatting communism provided cover for people and institutions to act in brutal, hubristic or plain manipulative ways. In the American case the excellent anti-corruption checks provided by the constitution risk being overridden or neutralized when policy is viewed through a single prism.

During the cold war, such acts may – or in some cases may not – have been performed with good intentions but many of the results were not good. Examples include the toppling of the Allende regime in Chile in the 1970s, or interfering with the governments of sundry Central American countries, or the sale of arms to Iran in the mid-1980s and the use of the proceeds to finance the Nicaraguan 'Contra' rebels. One which it may still be too soon to judge dispassionately is America's clandestine support for the *Mujahideen* militias that fought against the Soviet occupation in Afghanistan in the 1980s. Was this a necessary and in the end effective way of weakening the Soviet Union by trapping it in a long and costly war in Central Asia, which helped to bring the USSR down in 1989–91? Or was it an interference that merely laid the path towards Afghanistan's chaos in the 1990s, giving rise to the extreme fundamentalist Taliban regime there, which provided shelter for Osama bin Laden and his al-Qaeda terrorists? Most historians in future are likely to fall in with the first supposition rather than the second, because the Afghan War did indeed weaken the Soviet Union, and its fall followed shortly afterwards. But that could change if al-Qaeda proves to be more successful in the longer term than at present appears likely.

Another way of looking at the outcome in Afghanistan is that the country was especially unfortunate because America's intervention there straddled two different periods of American foreign policy: one, from 1947 to 1990, in which the superpower had a clear purpose; and another, in which it lost its sense of purpose along with the end of the cold war, and flailed around rather aimlessly at the same time as it reduced some of its international engagements. During the 1990s America's foreign policy lost its coherence, and became dominated by the fighting of fires here and there, and by well-meaning if rather selective efforts to boost democracy and defend human rights. Aid budgets were cut, the US Information Agency (the main propaganda channel) was closed, and Congress became less interested in foreign affairs and sometimes actively hostile towards them. In such a climate, Afghanistan ceased to matter, as did quite a few trouble-spots.

No longer. The attacks on 11 September 2001 suddenly brought about a new era in the attitude and role of the world's dominant power. Afghanistan mattered again. But it mattered again, in particular, because there was once again a clear purpose for the use of America's dominance, a single prism through which to see the world. The definition of the prism is not quite as simple as it was during the cold war. It was initially described as a 'war on terrorism', but that soon proved inadequate. In reality it is a war on threats to global security, which encompass threats to American security. They arise principally from two separate quarters: from international terrorist groups such as al-Qaeda, who are ready and willing to commit atrocities across the globe, such as the destruction of the World Trade Center in New York; and from the efforts of unpredictable dictators to secure or develop weapons of mass destruction. These are separate issues, which require different sorts of policies. But they combine to produce the sort of fear and sense of urgency that a single prism requires if it is to be maintained for long. One special nightmare is for an overlap between these two worries: a terrorist using nuclear, chemical or biological weapons, with or without help from an unpredictable dictator. The world's trouble-spots are no longer just an irritant or embarrassment: they are, and are seen to be, direct and potentially highly destructive threats to America itself.

Is this single prism too simple? As during the cold war, it cannot and will not be the only game in town as regards foreign policy. There are too many other things to preoccupy America, as well as the rest of the world, some of them with a link to the war on threats to global security, but others not. A potential dispute with China over Taiwan could also pose a big threat, for example, either auguring the arrival of another world superpower or perhaps, as Chapter 3 will argue, reflecting political instability inside China. And financial or economic instability in big, pivotal countries – Japan, Brazil, Indonesia, Russia – could also bring about political changes that pose threats that need to be responded to or prevented from developing in the first place. But while these other important worries will undoubtedly loom large in America's areas of concern, the single prism is nevertheless likely to be the biggest influence on American policy for the foreseeable future. And it does, after all, exemplify why the world needs the leadership of a dominant power such as America: because in human affairs, disorder is capable of spreading like a contagion across the globe, as it often did during the first half of the twentieth century; and because modern technology makes that disorder capable of truly frightening feats of destruction.

This single prism brings with it, however, the same virtues and vices as did the cold war prism. The vices will certainly become apparent, though their magnitude and significance cannot be predicted in advance. In following a policy of pursuing and eliminating inter-national terrorism as well as seeking to contain dictators' efforts to develop weapons of mass destruction, it is quite possible that a military engagement may be entered into in haste, under pressure from that policy, and then be regretted at greater if painful leisure, as it was in the case of Vietnam. It is even more likely that smaller acts of subver-sion and manipulation, at home and abroad – by the CIA, the National Security Agency, the FBI, or mainstream American forces – will take place. There is also a new vice, already evident in both Israel and India: that other countries may seek to use the simple notion of a war against terror as justification for their own actions.

And the virtues? One is clarity of purpose and determination: during the 1990s domestic interest in foreign affairs was fading, but the terrorist attacks suddenly united Americans behind their country's engagement overseas in defeating terrorists and other threats to global security. Moreover, as during the cold war, fear of a common enemy immediately brought allies to America's side after the 11 September attacks. The al-Qaeda terrorists are a common threat, for they have proved willing, in the course of a decade, to mount deadly attacks in many countries around the world, killing anyone who happened to be standing in the way. The common thread between the attacks has been America itself – its embassies, its warships, its World Trade Center. But non-Americans have died too. And many of the terrorists who have been involved or detected have been resident in countries outside America – Britain, France, Germany, Italy, Singapore and many more.

The difficulty posed by this threat is, however, precisely that it is widely dispersed. Unlike a threat from a state, such as the Soviet Union, it will always be hard to know whether the threat has increased or diminished, whether efforts to combat it have been successful or not. The result is that the alliance-creating virtue is likely to wax and wane, along with varying perceptions of the threat. Already during 2002 there was friction between Americans and Europeans which can largely be explained by differing perceptions about the danger of fresh terrorism. One fortunate aspect of messianic or Islamist terrorism is that the potential alliance against it is much larger than was the case for the Western alliance during the cold war: as well as the European Union countries and Japan, it stands a good chance of including Russia, a large number of developing countries (many of whom during the cold war declared themselves 'non-aligned') and, for some purposes, China. Moreover, whenever the terrorists commit an attack, the alliance against them will be strengthened again. Against that stands the fact that all these allies will differ at times in their view of whether this single prism should dominate policy, or whether it should be just one goal among many, to be traded off against the others.

Such differences of opinion also occurred during the cold war, but the diffuse and hidden nature of the terrorist threat is likely to make them greater, this time round. The same point applies, perhaps even more strongly, to the effort to control rogue states and weapons of mass destruction. Members of the alliance will disagree about which states are actually dangerous rogues, and which are merely misguidedly seeking to bolster their own security by obtaining such weapons. In 2002 President Bush drew special attention to three: Iraq, Iran and North Korea. At other times countries such as Pakistan and Libya might have been included in the list. The allies will also disagree about the best method of dealing with such states, about the best combination of diplomacy, economic pressure and military pressure to deploy, and about which other countries may be considered fellow warriors against terrorism. In 2002 both Israel and India posed a divisive challenge to America's alliances, for the allies disagreed about whether these countries should be supported in their fight against terrorists, or pressured to enter peace talks with those deploying the terror (Palestinians and Pakistanis, respectively) but with whom they had territorial disputes.

What this means is that America will have to strike a balance between preserving and nurturing its alliances in order to make its task easier, and sometimes simply acting decisively on its own, as it sees fit, and unhindered by dissent or alternative views. The 'hegemon' will have to decide how hegemonic it wants to be. Past behaviour would suggest that it is most likely to talk hegemonically, but to act rather more in concert than its words imply. Furthermore, this issue will be complicated by the need also to deal with other international concerns: global warming, trade liberalization, financial stability, poverty in the third world, the rise of China, wars in Africa. The hegemon will have to decide whether, as after the Second World War, helping to deal with these issues will help with its narrower task or hinder it. There will be trade-offs to be made.

One risk for America is that its actions (or, on these wider issues, inaction) could lead other countries to gang up against it, a trend that might, in turn, affect the willingness of Americans to remain engaged internationally. Another is the impact of this effort on America's economic strength: might a new military build-up, and a new accretion of responsibilities abroad, in time sap America's strength, as it has done for previous world powers? For, finally, there is the most important question of all: what can America actually achieve, in dealing with this turbulence and terror? Will the colossus pacify the globe once more and contain the terrorists and dictators? Or might the effort actually expose the limits of what any military power can achieve, showing the impotence, even of the most potent country the world has ever known, against such threats?

*

These consequences and risks will form common threads running through the rest of this book, especially during the next four chapters. One, however, must be addressed immediately: the question of whether America's economy will be able to bear the strain of greater military involvement overseas and greater military spending, without its own strength being sapped. In other words, will the dominant military power also remain the dominant economic power?

During the 1980s, after all, it was already popular to argue that America was losing its economic pre-eminence. The oil shocks of the 1970s, combined with the inflationary effects of financing the Vietnam War, had slowed the growth of output and productivity, and had begun to make America's businessmen, and thus its economy, look a spent force. It built up a big balance-of-payments deficit, its government fell into debt, and foreign investors were buying up American corporate and property assets. All this occurred while the United States was still conducting an expensive contest with the Soviet Union over armaments, operations and influence all around the world, one in which President Ronald Reagan had even raised the stakes, with missile programmes abroad and ideas of a 'star wars' missile defence system at home. Professor Paul Kennedy, a British historian by then based at Yale, looked at this combination of economic sloth and ambitious military obligations and pointed out in 1988 in his book *The Rise and Fall of the Great Powers* that such 'imperial overstretch' had brought down previous great powers and could well bring about America's demise too.

Moreover, other analysts argued that, unlike the clever Japanese, Americans were sticking to an out-moded idea of economics. Americans, they said, seemed unable to understand why governments needed to guide companies by using an industrial policy, why they needed to protect workers from the social disorder caused by hiring and firing, why their financial markets needed to shed their obsession with short-term, quarterly earnings and leave managers to invest for the long term. Analysts queued up to count the months and years before Japan would overtake the United States as the world's biggest economy. And even if that did not happen quite on schedule, Japan had taken over from America as the world's biggest creditor nation, the country with the biggest stock of financial assets overseas, while America had become a huge debtor, owing large sums to others, most notably Japan. That sort of change, from debtor to creditor and vice versa, had lain behind America's usurpation of Britain's pre-eminent position in the first half of the twentieth century, so in that sense, too, history was simply repeating itself. And Japan would not be the only country to exceed the United States in sheer economic size: China looked set to do the same, a decade or two later.

By the second half of the 1990s, things looked completely different. On Professor Kennedy's measure of 'imperial overstretch', the fall of the Soviet Union led to a considerable reduction in military spending as a proportion of GDP (gross domestic product), from 6 per cent in the mid-1980s to 3 per cent by the late 1990s, and to some cuts in America's obligations overseas. Meanwhile, as the stretch diminished, the economy's ability to bear it increased. Some of the economic measures thought of by the 'Japan-is-taking-over' school as sins began to be celebrated as saintly. Foreigners continued to buy up American companies and securities, but this now showed their confidence in the

American economy rather than their plans to devour it. The deficit on the current account of the balance of payments remained huge, as the country imported capital and goods, but this meant that Americans were showing their own confidence by spending beyond their incomes. Growth accelerated, and productivity surged. In the wake of the Internet and other developments in information technology, financial markets boomed, companies invested heavily in new computers and software, and a 'new economy' was proclaimed.

Thus, America again looked a world leader, as its firms dominated the new market for all sorts of computer software, recaptured the valuable parts of the semiconductor trade from the Asians, and sharpened up their management in older sectors too. Far from needing governmental guidance, a flexible economy was now evidently what a modern country needed, with the freedom to hire and fire, and spared the dead hand of industrial policy. Equity markets were now thought to be better than banks or other lenders at giving managers the discipline and the incentives they needed. To support this line of thinking, it helped greatly that by this time Japan was in the second half of a stagnant decade, following its financial-market crash of 1990, and the European Union, too, was having a sluggish time. So, compared with those losers, America looked a clear winner.

Since the heady days of 1999 and 2000, some of the shine has come off America's economic prowess. Companies have gone bankrupt, frauds have been exposed, unemployment has risen, share prices have fallen and/or stagnated, confidence in the integrity of companies and their bosses has been dented. Although the first decade of the twenty-first century does not look like being a repeat of the Great Depression of the 1930s – which followed the 'jazz age' industrial boom of the 1920s – the weight of debt on corporate and household shoulders looks likely to make the economy a rather more subdued affair than in the 1990s. New regulations will be brought in to try to clean up the corporate abuses, but investors and company executives are all likely to act more cautiously and nervously for some years to come. Technological innovation – in computing, telecoms, biotechnology, energy and other fields – will continue to stimulate both investment and consumption. Other factors, particularly debt and industrial over-capacity, will hold things back.

Fortunes, and perceptions of fortunes, fluctuate from year to year. But this book aims to look beyond the short term and find the basis for a longer-term view. Such a view could be one of America's relative strengths, as well as its absolute vitality. But such comparisons are often misleading. China was the world's largest economy in the early nineteenth century but neither derived nor sought any global influence from the fact. America overtook Britain as the world's wealthiest large economy, measured by GDP per head of population, in the first decade of the twentieth century, but did not take over Britain's leadership role until fifty years later (by which time its GDP per head was 50 per cent larger than Britain's). What matters is not just sheer size or wealth, but the ability and the willingness to deploy it abroad.

A paradox must also be kept in mind. It is that the very nature of America's 'imperial' role, that of attempting to preserve global peace while facilitating world-wide economic development through open trade and capitalism, is designed, in effect, to reduce America's economic pre-eminence over time. The more peace there is, and the more open that trade can be, the likelier it is that other countries will catch up with America's wealth and productiveness.

This is just what has been happening since 1945 inside the small coterie of countries that make up the developed world. The end of the Second World War was the apogee of America's relative economic position, when the economies that had been large before the war, those of Western Europe and Japan, lay in ruins. In 1950 America's GDP per head was twice as big as the West European average and five times bigger than Japan's. By 1992, however, America's GDP per head was 1.2 times that in Western Europe and only 1.1 times that in Japan. The gap had narrowed, to great mutual benefit, and with considerable assistance from America's initiatives in promoting trade and democracy. Many countries that had had dictatorships in the 1930s – Germany, Italy, Japan, Spain, Portugal, Greece, even finally Russia – were democracies by the 1990s. American policy in the 1940s and 1950s was directed expressly at the rehabilitation rather than the punishment of defeated countries, as America led the effort to establish world-wide free trade through the General Agreement on Tariffs and Trade (GATT), and to set up international institutions to protect financial stability, including the International Monetary Fund (IMF) and the

World Bank. It also initiated its own lending programmes such as the Marshall Plan.

In the next half century, as later chapters in this book will argue, as long as the world remains open for trade and cross-border flows of capital, the most likely outcome – and certainly the best goal – is a repeat of that achievement in some parts of the wider developing world, enabling countries such as India, China, Nigeria, Mexico, Pakistan, Indonesia, South Africa and others to narrow the huge gaps between their economies and the wealth of the United States, even as America itself retains its own economic vibrancy. As in 1945–2000, America's own growth and development will be greatly helped if there is sustained growth in the poor world too.

*

American relative economic pre-eminence ought to diminish, if all goes well. But what of its ability to use its economic power for political objectives? To examine that, we should think about two economic dimensions: the vitality of the American economy, and the level of global obligations and interests that the vitality may need to support – in other words Professor Kennedy's idea of imperial stretch. Focusing, for now, on American economic vitality, we need to work out what will be the magic bullet that will sustain it, so that we can predict whether it will be used. But there isn't one, of course. We cannot know in advance how well macroeconomic policy will assist, or impair, the country's growth. Past experience shows that it can do either, depending on the whims and errors of politicians and officials. But what can be observed is a crucial American peculiarity compared with the economies of other countries, one that does reflect some of the perceived virtues of the 1990s and which makes the prospects look good.

America's great peculiarity is its relative lack of concern about the ills of what critics call 'unregulated market capitalism' and fans just call 'capitalism'. Capitalism consists of cycles of what Joseph Schumpeter, an Austrian economist, called 'creative destruction': the trashing of the old and the failed, through bankruptcies, closures, job losses, sales and acquisitions, and the redeployment of resources to new areas, new firms, new technologies, new ideas. When Schumpeter was writing, in the first half of the twentieth century, he predicted that these 'gales' of destruction would lead to socialism. Yet in America, where the gales have blown a lot more freely than elsewhere, this hasn't happened, despite some fierce bouts of labour conflict during the first half of the twentieth century. Trade unions in America do oppose closures and job cuts, regulations do restrict hiring and firing, and minimum wage legislation does alter the terms of the employment contract – all as a socialist might demand. Legislation on such matters as health and safety and environmental control is tight, both directly and through case law in tort litigation. Compared with other countries, however, these drawbacks offer only a weak obstacle to enterprise. Entrepreneurs can go bankrupt with little or no stigma, companies can hire people this year and fire some of them next year when they realize they have made a mistake. The result is an extraordinary capacity for innovation and reinvention, for the pursuing of new opportunities and new fortunes.

That has long been an American advantage relative to other rich countries. Nevertheless, from the late 1970s successive governments helped to accentuate this capacity by a series of deregulatory reforms which were rarely matched either in extent or speed by other developed countries. Arguably, those reforms laid the ground for the country's economic revival in the 1990s, together with tighter control of inflation by the Federal Reserve Board. Will this capacity survive in the future? Specialists can produce all sorts of detailed views on that question, sector by sector, technology by technology, state by state. In the end, though, it boils down to some quite simple points.

One, which is part symptom and part cause, is a social question. Will ordinary Americans continue to tolerate these gales, this form of capitalism which some Europeans consider unacceptably brutal? The answer, for now, is that they show no obvious signs of rejecting it. There is no gathering movement for greater social protection, although there are always local and sectional pressures for protection against competition from imports, as was shown by the steel and agriculture industries in 2002. Despite fierce resistance to changes in Social Security and Medicare, the reduction of welfare support implemented by the Clinton administration in the 1990s failed to stimulate any serious opposition. A further piece of evidence is that there is a continuing supply of would-be Americans seeking to join this bracing environment. If America's lack of 'social protection' were such a terrible thing, would so many people want to go to live there? A European might retort that the would-be immigrants tend to come from countries where life is even worse. They do, but current, well-established Americans could leave if they wished to. There has been no sign of large-scale emigration either in the doldrum years of 1975–90 or, naturally enough, in the boom years of the 1990s.

Other social problems have brought torment in the past, and could do so again in the future: the race riots of the 1960s and 1970s; the troubled, crime-ridden inner cities of the 1980s; illegal drugs and consequent gang wars; the poor relationship between black and white. It was those, rather than the brutality of capitalism, that gave rise to the main post-1945 bout of social legislation, Lyndon Johnson's 'Great Society' programmes. Only Roosevelt's 1930s 'New Deal' has really treated capitalism's vagaries as a big, agenda-defining problem, and that was in the exceptional circumstances of the Great Depression. Moreover, unless those other social problems come in future to loom so large that they threaten the overall social and political stability of the country, they look unlikely to affect America's long-term economic prospects. They are important in their own right, but they have no direct bearing on the economy.

Their only bearing is as part of a second, simple point. It is that America's biggest potential source of long-term weakness is its education system. The aforementioned social problems both result from this weakness and help to perpetuate it. Education is also one of America's strengths, for its institutions range from the dismal to the brilliant. The country has a poor record in its public schools, especially in the bleaker areas, delivering an unusually wide variation in test scores in maths, literacy and other subjects between the best and the worst graduating pupils. But America is home to what are easily the world's best universities, in any subject you can think of. It also has an excellent system of mid-level tertiary education, ranging from state universities to community colleges, which prepares able and eager young people well for a wide range of vocations.

We should bear in mind one lesson from history, and then pay attention to two risks. The lesson from history is that Britain, too, had the same sort of educational imbalance, with excellence at the top and under-performance at the bottom, during the nineteenth century. This did not matter for a long time, but Britain was eventually caught up and then overtaken in educational standards by Germany's superior high schools and scientifically advanced universities. The first of the two risks is that poor education for ordinary people could put a brake on productivity growth, preventing American firms from beating cheaper overseas competitors through greater efficiency and sophistication. One of the puzzles of the productivity boom of the late 1990s was that industry seemed to be employing more and more unskilled labour which had previously been considered educationally unfit, and yet still achieved rapid growth in productivity. The answer is probably that the productivity growth was in part a mirage.

The second risk is of a future degrading of the top universities, such as Stanford, Harvard, Yale, Princeton, Cornell, Caltech and the Massachusetts Institute of Technology (MIT). If that were to happen, it would be time to speculate upon America's future decline. Such a disastrous outcome could occur if the universities' teaching, research and entrepreneurial spin-offs were to become subverted by some other political goal, such as social policy or foreign propaganda. If, for example, inequality were to become a top political issue, perhaps because of social unrest, one tempting remedy might be to alter the tests students must pass in order to enter university, thus making access 'more equal', but the universities less meritocratic. This would, in other words, extend the already damaging and controversial efforts at 'affirmative action' for racial minorities. A better solution would be to pay greater attention (including investment) to the primary and secondary schools that have failed to equip people to learn more and earn more, and which thus lie behind the inequality in the first place. Political impatience may press towards the bad sort of remedy, for it could be implemented more quickly. But if inequality remains a secondary issue rather than an election-determining one, the more patient, and better, solution would be likelier.

In recent years, the inequality debate has tended to remain in that secondary, and more patient, category. For Americans have a far greater tolerance for inequality than do their equivalents in other developed countries. This is another way of describing their willingness to live and work in a society with weak social protections against unemployment and poverty. But it is also a reflection of a further point, simple but important for America's future. Inequality is tolerated – even welcomed – in America because of its association with economic mobility and meritocracy. The idea that an entrepreneur or chief executive can earn many millions of dollars, or even billions, does not cause political ructions if people think it possible that they could have been in the same position, or – more likely – if their daughters or sons could achieve the same good fortune in future. Compared with Britain, France or Germany, America has long had a mobile society – or at least the clear feeling that it is or can be mobile. This is crucial for America's continued vitality during the twenty-first century, because it underpins the country's ability to permit creative destruction to take place.

What of the other sort of threat, that the burden of America's world role could itself become so large as to distort and divert the country's economic course? This is, in part, what happened in the 1970s when the financing of the Vietnam War contributed to rapid inflation, which in turn depressed corporate investment and economic growth. Such a thing could certainly happen again, if efforts to contain terrorism or the spread of nuclear weapons give rise to lengthy wars.

Two mitigating points need to be borne in mind, though. The first is that it took a long time and a truly exceptional event – Vietnam – for this to occur during the cold war. In other words, the American economy has a very large load-bearing capacity before the strain begins to be felt. The second is that today's less regulated, more flexible economy, operating in a world with freer trade and thus more international competition, is less prone to inflation than America's economy was in the 1970s. Moreover, the Federal Reserve Board should have learned from the experience of the 1970s and so, as long as that memory lasts, should now be better able to control inflation. These points do not guarantee that the economy will be unaffected, and new damage could in any case occur in new, as yet unforeseeable, ways. But they do suggest that we should not expect America's economy to be an imminent obstacle to its foreign policy – or vice versa.

*

Such simple points – tolerance of capitalism's harshness, educational quality, meritocracy – do not and cannot amount to an economic forecast. But they are the broad factors that have made America the exceptional economy that it has been for the past century and which will determine its fate in the next one. And they are reasons for optimism. That exceptional character, moreover, is vital to America's self-image. In crude terms, settlers and later immigrants came to the United States to escape the rest of the world, to set up a society that was better than those they were leaving. A paradox of the twentieth century is that their descendants ended up going back out into the world to clean it up, to restore it to order.

They did so remarkably successfully. But will their descendants continue to be willing to offer such leadership? Will they, in President Kennedy's famous words of 1961, be willing to 'bear any burden, pay any price' for the sake of liberty and peace? Before 11 September 2001 the answer looked clear: they would not. The benefits to Americans of sorting out the world's problems looked too small or elusive to make the effort worth the risk and expense, especially in terms of military casualties. After those attacks brought a new simplicity to the threat facing America and a new sense of urgency about the task of dealing with it, the answer changed: now Americans were again willing to bear burdens and pay prices.

That, at least, is the conventional reading of events. In fact, Americans have long been willing to bear a great deal: even by the end of the 1990s after the post-cold-war 'peace dividend', their annual defence spending of over $300 billion was more than 50 per cent higher than all their NATO allies combined, and was five times larger than that of all the Pacific allies, too. China officially spends around $15 billion a year on defence; even if you double or treble it to cater for hidden spending, it is still no more than a sixth of America's level. This was despite the fact that, until 11 September 2001 there had been no major attack on American soil since Pearl Harbor in 1941.

Notwithstanding all that spending, it was widely assumed during the 1990s that Americans opposed military intervention overseas. This was, on the face of it, an odd view. After all, with 725 military installations abroad, and a further 88 in US territories outside the fifty states, America's 'forward deployment', as the military specialists call it, is extensive, and there has been no public clamour to reduce it. The only substantial public opposition to American forces being based overseas has been found in the host countries, not at home. When

America closed its huge naval base at Subic Bay in the Philippines in 1992, it was because of local hostility, not concern among Americans.

There is, however, the crucial question of casualties. The real issue for an American is whether his forces abroad are in danger. Some have proved to have been so: 19 American soldiers died in a terrorist bombing of their Khobar Towers building in Saudi Arabia in 1996; 241 marines died in their barracks in Beirut in 1983; 18 Rangers died on active service in Somalia in 1993. The table puts these into the context of all American deaths in combat in the past hundred years or so.

American deaths in combat

First World War (1917–18)	53,513
Second World War (1941–5)	292,131
Korean War (1950–53)	33,870
Vietnam War (1964–73)	47,072
Beirut (1983)	241
Gulf War (1991)	148
Somalia (1992–3)	18
Saudi Arabia/Khobar (1996)	19
Kosovo War (1999)	0
Afghan War (2001–2)	approx. 20*

Sources: Walter Russell Mead, Special Providence;
Department of Defense
* As of August 2002

The numbers of combat casualties have declined, markedly (other servicemen have died in accidents, though such deaths can occur at home, too). Technology has advanced, enabling more bombing and less use of ground troops; and the nature of the wars in the 1990s was rather different from Vietnam or Korea. But might the public, also, have become less willing to accept casualties? Opinion polls provide little direct evidence of it. A study called the 'Program on International Policy Attitudes' (PIPA), produced by a special centre at the University of Maryland, combed through the poll data following all the combat deaths of American servicemen that took place during the 1990s. The researchers found that after the deaths in Somalia, all the polls taken in the succeeding week showed only a minority favouring withdrawal. In polls taken by CNN/USA Today, ABC and NBC respectively, 55 per cent, 56 per cent and 61 per cent actually favoured sending even more American troops in response to the killings. The Gulf War was a simpler case, although the balance of opinion about intervention and casualties was in fact closer than in the Somalia results. After the 1996 terrorist bombing in Saudi Arabia, the only poll with a direct question on the issue, produced for *Newsweek*, found 55 per cent of respondents believing America should retain its military presence there despite the deaths.

A reasonable conclusion is that the American public is proud of having its troops overseas and is pleased when they achieve military and political success. That is what PIPA's poll data suggest; they even suggest that the public is quite gung-ho for such success, and favours a tougher response following casualties. The policy élite and the politicians, though, seem to take a different view. They became more afraid of failure after Vietnam, and in a televisual age such failure becomes plain very rapidly and painfully. The public may like success, and be willing to countenance continued risks being taken in pursuit of it, but politicians fear, quite reasonably, that failure will be punished severely in the voting booth – as when Jimmy Carter lost the presidency in 1980 after a failed raid to free American hostages in Iran.

More generally, policy-makers are ever-conscious of the fact that intervening abroad is a complex affair, since it is often not possible in such actions to define clear objectives and clear points at which America may be able to withdraw its troops and its political involvement. The doctrine named after General Colin Powell, chairman of the Joint Chiefs of Staff during the Gulf War and George W. Bush's secretary of state during the Afghan War, is a natural reaction to this: it says that America should not intervene unless it is willing to deploy overwhelming force and can define a clear exit strategy. Taken at its word, this would rule out almost all interventions, since such clarity is rarely obtainable. It is, however, better taken simply as a general symptom of a considerable military and political caution, one which technology is unlikely to eliminate altogether. It is the generals who do not want their men to be killed, not the public; and it is the politicians and diplomats who most fear the consequences of failure, either in humiliation at home or damaged credibility abroad.

The events of 11 September changed that, however, because they changed the public expectations under which those politicians and diplomats have to operate. As long as there seems to be a clear and present danger of further terrorism or of the further spread of weapons of mass destruction into dangerous hands, it is likely that American politicians – and indeed generals – will fear the political consequences of inaction rather more than action. They will fight on in Central Asia and get involved in other conflicts if there is a risk that terrorists might gain from them. And after 11 September they felt an almost irresistible pressure to attack Iraq in order to depose Saddam Hussein, to enforce United Nations resolutions of 1991 and thereafter against Saddam's weapons programmes and, not least, to try to begin the long process of reforming the Arab world and removing the need for America to be involved in supporting or policing dictatorial Arab regimes. The generals will remain voices of caution, as they were in Afghanistan in 2001–2. But they will carry out the politicians' orders. How long will this feeling of clear and present danger last? There is no way of saying, for it will depend on future terrorist attacks or on intelligence about the threats of them.

*

Americans do, no doubt, like being thought a force to be reckoned with around the world; they like being the world's greatest power. Does this mean that in future they will act alone or at least stand aloof, disregarding the views of others? That is a common European accusation, or perhaps fear. The interesting point about the many multilateral institutions that America helped to set up after 1945 is that one effect of such bodies as the International Monetary Fund, the World Bank, the United Nations and the World Trade Organization is to limit America's ability to boss others around. Most irksomely, they also have the effect of making it more possible for others to boss America around, if they can gang up on her.

Theorists of international relations are especially fond of this idea of ganging up. One tenet of traditional international relations studies is that the world tends to move towards a balance of power rather than sticking with a situation of overwhelming predominance by one country. If that is correct, then other countries can be expected to react to American power by forming alliances against it.

In general, though, this is unlikely – and it certainly does not seem to be happening. America's array of allies has been increasing since the end of the cold war, not shrinking. Faced with such a strong power, most countries seem to want to ingratiate themselves with America rather than confront it, especially as its international aims and values appear not to be threatening. In broad economic terms, moreover, the trend in the past few decades has been one of convergence towards the American way of doing things rather than opposition to it, amid an increased dependence on trade with the United States itself. There is an exception to this story, however.

When pundits argue about the merits of multilateralism or of unilateralism, about whether America should go it alone or work with its allies, it may often seem as if they are talking about military matters. If so, they shouldn't be. In military matters, the superpower is always likely to take the dominant role, for its forces and technology are far superior to those of others, and co-operation always complicates the already tricky task of war. Unless it is near to its own shores, however, it is unlikely ever to operate entirely alone, for both geography and diplomacy are likely to lead it to seek logistical support from others. But in the big international institutions and treaty negotiations things are different. It is in these institutions, and in the conflict between national sovereignty and multilateral co-operation, that the real debate lies about how America should – and will – conduct itself.

Multilateralism, after all, implies rather more than simply garnering support: it implies submission to a process of collective decision-making which you will not always be able to control. Such a process is much harder for a superpower to stomach, for world leaders like to get their way. That process is, however, exactly what the United States submitted itself to when it pushed for the establishment of the IMF and World Bank in 1947, and when it signed GATT in the same year. It is also integral to the operations of the broader United Nations institutions that were set up at the same time, though at least there America, along with the other 'permanent five' members of the Security Council, retains a veto over UN resolutions and actions.

Typically, the executive branch of government (that is, the White House) has been more willing to sign up to multilateral processes than has Congress, which has often subsequently voted them down. Examples of administration deals rejected by Congress include American membership of the League of Nations in 1919, the proposal to turn GATT into the more powerful International Trade Organization in 1947, and the Kyoto Protocol on global warming (rejected by the Senate in a unanimous vote in 1997, well before President George W. Bush withdrew from international talks over it in 2001). Treaties require ratification by a two-thirds vote in the Senate, a majority which is hard to obtain. As a result many post-1945 administrations have preferred, when Congress allows them, to sign so-called 'executive agreements' with other countries instead, since these require only a simple majority of both houses.

The effect of this difference of opinion is multiplied by – or perhaps simply encouraged by – the fact that under America's constitution domestic law has primacy over international treaties. In most countries, it is the other way round. Congress can alter the terms of any international treaty entered into by the administration, and all treaties need to be implemented through domestic laws. Not only is it wrong to imagine that America is a single, unified actor, it is also the case that the constitution was expressly designed by the Founding Fathers to prevent such a single actor from emerging. The various elements are supposed to check and balance each other, deliberately limiting the ability of government to be effective. In international affairs that makes America especially difficult to deal with, since countries are accustomed to dealing with each other as sovereign governments, empowered to negotiate. The American system does its best to prevent the White House from being able to negotiate freely.

That background makes it all the more remarkable that America's formal emergence as the world's leading power in 1945 was marked by the setting up of so many multilateral bodies and processes. It was an act almost of self-denial. In economics, this act was understandable, for it reflected a by then prevailing liberal view that in economic matters decentralized, dispersed decision-making according to an agreed set of rules or laws is in the best interests of all, including the United States. Although Congress did not want an International Trade Organization making rulings against American firms, and thus voted the idea down in 1948 (just as it does not like the idea now of the World Trade Organization – set up at last in 1995 – doing the same), it accepted after the experience of the 1930s that free trade would be to America's benefit. GATT was a good way to begin to create it, since other countries would not see it as an American attempt to direct trade itself. Similarly, the IMF and the World Bank can be seen as a solution to the international financial instability of the 1920s and 1930s. A solution was in America's interest; others would accept it more readily if they had a voice in how it worked; and these institutions removed a large potential burden from America's shoulders. In economic affairs, this argument still holds: the IMF and the other entities take pressure away from America, while its financial and economic power mean that it still has the biggest single influence over what they do.

In other activities, multilateral institutions do not seem to suit America so well. In ventures such as the international law of the sea and the new international criminal court, America has helped a multilateral effort to get going and has often shaped it, but has then stayed outside its formal parameters. It is having its cake and eating it: designing the global rules and processes, often following their dictates *de facto*, but retaining the ability *de jure* to ignore them, to act differently and to avoid sanctions.

This debate between unilateralists and multilateralists, then, is a question of degree, not kind. By and large, this varied approach has worked well, both for the world's interests and for America's. There is, however, a prospect of choppier waters ahead. For there is a good chance that events and American moods might in the future conspire to push more topics along the spectrum towards unilateralism – just at a time when the world is evolving in the opposite direction.

If globalization is allowed to continue, then more countries should be able to grow and develop, and – as argued earlier in this chapter – will narrow the gap with the United States. That may not hold true in military terms, for America's lead there both in spending and in technology is so great as perhaps to deter others from even trying to catch up, but it ought to do so in economic terms. Even if not all countries achieve such growth, many will be likely to do so. As and when that occurs, not only will those countries carry more weight in the world economy, but they will also demand more say in international institutions. Such an evolution could be considered a big success for the United States – and it may even be defined as a goal by one or more administrations during this period. Yet it will also make multilateralism a more demanding business for the United States itself. Its superiority will have been eroded, and the central disadvantage to the superpower of multilateralism – that other countries can, if they wish, gang up against you – will have been enhanced.

Such economic convergence did not lead to much ganging up on America during the cold war, because all the economically successful powers felt an overriding need to stay together. Since the end of the cold war, however, there has been plenty of ganging up on America, in trade arguments and over the environment in particular. On questions of trade and of global warming, the combined importance of the European Union and Japan exceeds that of the United States. With America's presence and America's culture so apparent all over the world, the superpower is an obvious target for criticism, sneering and scapegoating. This has irked many Americans, who see their country as the model towards which everyone should be seeking to converge, and who anyway naturally prefer to have things their way. Americans, moreover, are not immune to hubris, and interest group lobbies are bound to try to bend international policies in their own direction. Add that to the bias in America's constitution against full participation in international treaties and institutions, and the result is a recipe at least for friction, but more likely for a drift towards unilateralism by America and towards ganging up on it by other countries.

In the seemingly benign and certainly plush world of the international, acronym-laden institutions like the IMF and the World Bank, that drift may not be disastrous. It would certainly be inconvenient, however, and could hamper those institutions from responding properly during a crisis. In trade such a drift would be more damaging, since it could hamper economic activity directly and might even lead to a partial reversal of globalization.

In international treaties on nuclear proliferation or against biological weapons, this drift could become very serious indeed. Such treaties are essentially exhortations and promises, in which the crucial ingredient is trust that the other signatories will actually do what they have promised. Conformity with these treaties is hard to verify and enforce even in extreme situations, as the UN found in its weapons inspections in Iraq and North Korea during the 1990s. If the world's leading power essentially detaches itself from the treaty process, hoping others will comply but not wanting to make commitments itself, it is likely to encourage non-compliance. These treaties will not be worth the paper they are written on. They will become an irrelevance, and could actually end up promoting the very activities they are designed to deter.

That prospect may act to deter America from turning unilateralist in this area of international affairs. The Bush administration's pressure on Iraq has been largely unilateral, though in defence of multilateral aims. On the basis of a successful change of regime in Iraq, the best outcome would be if America then convened an international conference to come up with new multilateral measures to enforce the anti-proliferation treaties. With Russia now much friendlier to America since 11 September, and with other great powers such as China also feeling vulnerable to terrorism or to weapons proliferation, the prospects for success at such a conference ought to be good. If, that is, America can put aside its growing distaste for treaties.

*

America is, and will continue to be, willing to use its military forces abroad, and even to accept casualties. Since 11 September 2001 it has found a clear, single prism through which to view foreign policy, a clear purpose for the use of its power. That purpose will help concentrate the minds of its allies, but with a strength that may wax and wane over time. America will retain the ability to afford its international commitments, and is likely to remain economically vibrant. But its recent drift towards unilateralism is quite likely to continue, as other countries increase their economic weight in the world and the disadvantages to America of multilateralism increase. American leadership will persist, and offers a crucial hope to the rest of the world. But there will be frictions.

Such gentle predictions come strolling out of the garden, but then find themselves caught in a bracing wind. That wind is the reality of the outside world. America is willing and able to use its power. But can its use of its power be effective? In a conventional war, the answer is clearly that it can. But the suicide hijackings of 11 September showed that opponents may well respond to America's manifest superiority in unconventional ways.

The challenge moves on to the sheer number and range of unruly, unstable countries in the world. Anyone who thinks that one mighty country can achieve anything it likes need only glance in the direction of Israel and Palestine, where America simply lacks the levers with which to influence events decisively; or in the direction of India and Pakistan, where threats of conflict, perhaps even nuclear combat, have been constant in recent years. Meanwhile, the tectonic plates of geopolitics are already moving as if in an earthquake, as the world's most populous country, China, shakes itself from a centuries-long torpor and becomes richer, stronger and, in time, more ambitious. Even dealings with the other great powers, the Europeans and the Japanese, look likely to be far from plain sailing for their American leader.

The world would be even more difficult and disorderly without American leadership. In that respect, the twenty-first century begins with better prospects than did the twentieth. With American leadership, especially in security matters but also in economics, there is a good chance that the threats of terrorism and of weapons of mass destruction can be subdued, though never eliminated, and that the prosperity-enhancing process of globalization will continue. The twenty-first century nevertheless remains in the shadow of a further question: how orderly can even America make it?

3

Chinese Ambition

Whenever a scholar, a political analyst or any other sort of Western pundit is assembling a list of possible threats to world peace during the twenty-first century, of possible challenges to the dominance of the United States, of possible sources of change in the geopolitical balance, China is invariably high on the list. Before the terror attacks of 11 September 2001, it was generally top of most people's lists, and was certainly considered by many senior officials in the new Republican administration in Washington to be their trickiest long-term challenge. It is a mark of the way in which the terror attacks gripped the imagination and concentrated minds that China suddenly seemed a much less important challenger on 12 September than it had just a day or two earlier.

Mainly this was because of the way short-term, immediate analysis and projections tend to blind us to longer-term trends and priorities. However, it was also because China was one of the countries that offered a surprising amount of support, or at least acquiescence, to the United States in its battles against Osama bin Laden and his associates. It even stood silent as Japan exploited the Afghan War to break its constitutional taboo on sending military forces to assist in a far-off war. Perhaps China, too, felt threatened by terrorism? In reality it is more likely that now and in the near future it prefers co-operation to confrontation as it seeks to achieve economic growth and to raise the standard of living of its people. After all, in the autumn of 2001 it had achieved another co-operative goal: following many years of negotiations, it finally joined the World Trade Organization, a moment which signalled the coming of age as an international capitalist of this former bastion of central planning.

This celebration of an emerging companionship is too sanguine, however. The pundits were right to put China high on their lists of possible challenges, and nothing that happened in the autumn of 2001 could have changed that. In the short run, China is probably not a threat (or even a challenge); it is simply too poor for that, and will have too great an interest for many years to come in obtaining help and advantage from the outside world. But in the longer run, both the lessons of history and the logic of current developments suggest that China will indeed pose the biggest challenge of all to the current status quo in the world – which therefore means to the leadership of the United States of America.

*

Admittedly, history and contemporary experience pull in confusing directions. China is the last of the two communist superpowers of the post-1945 world. Frequently, an alarming parallel is drawn with Germany at the start of the twentieth century. Germany then was a rising power, which had fairly recently shaken off its old fragmentation by means of a political unification, and which felt by turns dissatisfied with and nervous about its status, circumstances and security, at first within its region but also in the world as a whole. In history, such new powers have always, it is said, eventually had to be accommodated, either peacefully or more often through war. Those descriptions certainly apply to China now, with its expanding economy but acute sense of past humiliations, with its history of fragmentation that came to an end in 1949, with its array of territorial disputes with its neighbours, with its sense of historical destiny, and with its feelings of vulnerability, given that it shares its borders with fourteen other countries.

Yet that idea is also, on the face of it, odd – or, at least, highly premature. In all dimensions except its population of 1.3 billion and the size of its territory, China today is a modest country at best. Even in population, India is rapidly catching up and if present trends endure will overtake China in the next couple of decades. China is now gaining renown as an exporter, and yet its share of world merchandise exports (about 3.9 per cent in 2000, excluding Hong Kong's own exports) was roughly the same as that of the Netherlands, a country with a population of a mere 16 million, or just 1.2 per cent of China's people.

Only in 1993 did China's share of world trade reach its pre-1939 peak. Its economy, thanks to that huge population, is now the world's sixth largest, but that still places it well below Britain's, which is the fourth largest and which normally thinks of itself, slightly mournfully, as a second-rank power.

Despite enclaves of wealth and traffic jams of Mercedes cars in coastal cities, the country's people are largely poor, many of them abjectly so. In terms of GDP per head of population, according to the World Bank, in 2000 China ranked 141st in the world, with an annual GDP per head of a mere $870, excluding tiny but wealthy Hong Kong, which had a GDP per head of $22,180. That ranked China as roughly equal to Sri Lanka and just behind the Philippines, while the former British colony of Hong Kong on this measure matched France and Belgium. Boosters of China prefer to cite figures for GDP or GDP per head adjusted for 'purchasing-power parity' (PPP), that is, taking account of the fact that prices in China are much lower than in the rich world, so that small amounts of money stretch rather further. This measure makes China's economy look bigger than Japan's and a mere half of America's total, and makes its income per head rise to a figure comparable now to those of Ukraine or Bulgaria. But that still leaves it behind modest little Thailand, for example, and less than a quarter that of South Korea.

China's economic statistics are in any case thought to be extremely dubious, so that it may even be that the country's economy is rather smaller than it claims, and thus that its people are even poorer than the official figures imply. That point applies just as strongly to the figures adjusted for PPP, since those numbers, too, are based on the country's dodgy GDP figures as well as on price data which can themselves be wobbly. In any case, if the aim is to compare national strengths, PPP is less useful than conventional figures as it measures domestic purchasing power rather than international clout.

China is, to be sure, one of the world's select (but decreasingly select) band of nuclear powers. But so is India, a country that is far less often on the pundits' lists of future trouble-makers or (to put it more neutrally) budding great powers. And China's armoury of inter-continental ballistic missiles, the sort that are capable of threatening the United States or Western Europe, numbers only about twenty (according to the International Institute of Strategic Studies), whereas both America and Russia have thousands. Those missiles could do a lot of damage, and could even intimidate lesser countries, but they are not going to give China clout when dealing with the world's great powers. Its armed forces are large – about 2.5 million people, plus 1.1 million in the paramilitary People's Armed Police and about 600,000 reservists – but are poorly trained and equipped. China's official defence budget, at $14.5 billion in 2000, is less than a third as large as Japan's. This figure is generally thought to underestimate true spending, which may in fact roughly match Japan's. Yet that simply means it matches a country that restricts its defence spending and responsibilities tightly according to a post-war constitution which forbids all military action except straightforward self-defence. It means, as was pointed out in Chapter 2, that China's spending is barely a sixth of America's. And even this effort puts a big strain on the economy and public finances of what is a poor country.

Companies do tend to lick their lips at the thought of doing business in the world's most populous country (and one of its last large untapped markets), but they have done so for hundreds of years. Yesterday's dream of riches through 'adding an inch to the shirt-tail of every Chinese' has its modern equivalent in dreams of selling cars, or films, or soft drinks to all those people – poor though they actually are. Precious few foreign companies have made much profit in China, and most have made none at all. Still, China was easily the developing world's biggest recipient of foreign direct investment (FDI; that is, investment in factories, bricks and mortar) during the 1990s; its inflows of $40 billion or so a year in 1995–2000 were larger than flows to the rest of Asia combined. Yet even that figure is apt to get people rather over-excited. An annual FDI inflow of $40 billion roughly matches the 1999 inflow into France, is a third less than that into Sweden in the same year, is half that into Britain, and pales into insignificance compared with the flow in 1999 of $275 billion into the United States of America. The idea which is often put forward, that FDI flows into China suggest that the world's manufacturing industry is all going to move there in search of cheap Chinese labour, is simply nonsense. China's figure is in any case somewhat exaggerated since it includes some money that is really domestic capital, which has been taken out of the country only to return in order to exploit preferential tax treatment.

So China matters a lot less than might be thought. It is nowhere near becoming a true world power, nowhere near becoming either an economy or a military force for the big league to be afraid of. Its strength at the outset of the twenty-first century is not yet comparable to that of Germany at the beginning of the twentieth, which actually overtook Britain on many industrial and economic measures in the late nineteenth century. China is several decades away from overtaking America in terms of any important measure. If a historical comparison is what is needed, China today has a position that is rather closer to that of Japan in the early 1900s. Japan had then been modernizing since the 1860s, importing foreign ideas, technology and capital, and adapting them to its own uses. It could pack a punch, as it showed when defeating China in the war in 1894–5 and then Russia in 1905. But at that point it was neither strong enough to take on Britain, Germany or the United States, nor did it have the desire to. It was still importing ideas from what it saw as the world's three great powers, and was still somewhat dependent on them.

On a short- or medium-term view, that comparison is reassuring. China is not strong enough to take on the bigger powers in a direct conflict, and remains too dependent on foreign trade and capital to want to risk a rupture with the West. On a longer view, however, it is just the opposite: by the 1930s and 1940s, after all, the previously dependent Japan was posing a huge threat to regional and even global peace. As it grew stronger, ambitious and, at times, desperate to protect its new strength, Japan's behaviour and strategy changed. The same could well happen eventually with China.

*

China's 'threat' must thus be kept in proportion. It is not and will not soon be a rival to the United States on a global scale. But it is, even so, a strong candidate for rocking the boat in its region, in a way that is bound to drag in and affect the world's real global powers. Japan's path in the twentieth century helps to explain why. Yet it is also worth looking at the differences between Japan then and China today.

Two stand out, though they are related to one another. The first is that the challenge of China could arise not merely because, like Japan in the 1900s, it is gaining in strength. In fact, its challenge is just as likely to arise because of its weakness, or rather its fragility, in the face of the ebbing and flowing of economic strength. China's political system (that is, the Communist Party) has long since lost its ideological glue and has failed to evolve alongside the development since the early 1980s of a more market-based economy in which the old methods of control no longer work. Economic failure, or even disappointment, could lead to the party's demise or fracture. This possibility is more important than it would have been for Japan in the early 1900s: if Japan's political system had collapsed at that time, it would not have mattered much to anyone else, except possibly Taiwan and Korea, which Japan had turned into colonies. In the next few decades a Chinese collapse, or a descent into internal disputation, would hold big dangers for the Asian region and for the world. The strong risk would be that such an internal power struggle would lead to a rise in Chinese nationalism, producing aggressive actions against its neighbours and, most particularly, against Taiwan.

That risk and the associated uncertainty leads, in turn, to the second difference, which is that China's communists already feel that they have reason to resent or even fear the world's leading powers in a way that Japan did not develop until the 1920s and 1930s. They feel beleaguered, they have no allies and they resent the dominant presence in the Asian region of the United States. At a pinch, whether caused by internal strife or by external circumstances, China's leaders might thus be tempted to throw their weight around in order to remedy these resentments, in the Asian region in general or, more likely, over the 'renegade province' of Taiwan in particular.

In detective stories, sleuths typically look for three things in their potential suspects: means, motive and opportunity. Although China's strength is modest by global standards, its economic growth in the past two decades and potential growth in the next few imply that it will in future gain the means to provoke geopolitical change, at least on a regional level. Its armed forces may be modest, but compared with, for example, those of Saddam Hussein's Iraq they would nevertheless already pose a serious threat. Anyone wishing to take them on, or simply to face them down, would have to think hard about the matter. Opportunity? Such a word implies that China's leaders might be inclined to exploit a moment of weakness in the leading powers to pursue their aims, for example over Taiwan. They might, although it is likelier that China would be provoked to seek change more by its internal disputes and nationalistic impulses than by something external. And motivation? That can be found in the nationalism likely to be stirred up in those possible internal disputes. And that arises chiefly from history – fairly recent history, indeed.

*

Most Westerners think of Europe as the anvil on which the twentieth century's greatest tragedies were hammered out – two continental-scale wars, Hitler's Holocaust, Stalin's slaughters and famines – as well as being the producer of another world-changing twentieth-century phenomenon, the fall of empire. Yet China has at least an equal claim for the first and most undesirable of those titles, and it sat right in the middle of the battles over the second. And, with a dictatorship still ruling over more than a billion people, who 'celebrated' its fiftieth anniversary in 1999 (and in 2001 the eightieth anniversary of the Communist Party's foundation), it stands today as a violent slap in the face for those who have already proclaimed the victory of liberal democracy and the 'end' of history. To Tibet certainly and even to many in its western province of Xinjiang, China is one of the world's remaining empires.

Looked at through a long telescope, the story of China is one of an extraordinary decline over hundreds of years, in absolute terms at least from 1820 until 1952 and still in relative terms up to 1978, followed by a so far brief economic revival. Early technological advancement plus the size of the country's population – estimated at 380 million in 1820, compared with 170 million in the whole of Europe – meant that China was the world's biggest economy in absolute terms until it was overtaken by the United States in the 1880s. It had even been the richest, per head of population, in the first half of the millennium until overtaken by several European states.

With a population now of 1.3 billion, its natural rank ought again to be as the world's largest economy, perhaps vying with India for that title. That could be achieved with quite moderate levels of growth, if sustained over a few decades. For even if its income per head could reach merely as much as a quarter of the American level, then given that its population will then be at least three times larger than America's, it would begin to approach the United States' absolute level of annual GDP. Indeed, if the trends seen since 1978 continue it will do just that, overtaking America as the world's largest economy sometime in the second or third decades of this century.

That event, if it happens, should thus be seen as the restoration of China's natural position. To the world, it ought to be a welcome sign that poverty is being reduced substantially in one of the globe's largest countries and for long one of the poorest. Commentators often describe China's development in the 1990s as extraordinary, even disturbing. Yet what would be genuinely disturbing would be if China failed to achieve its natural position as the world's largest economy, at least in the first half of this century. For this would almost certainly mean that there had been some sort of economic breakdown, which would probably mean that there had also been a political breakdown. A great opportunity would have been lost, but it would not be the first time. Such breakdowns would, alas, be a return to the normal pattern of China's recent history, for they are, after all, what explains or at least describes China's fall from pre-eminence in the century and a half before communism took hold there.

Like pre-nineteenth-century Japan, for centuries China did its best to shut out foreign influences, ideas and pressure. Unlike in Japan, however, its rulers were bureaucrats whose highly centralized, often arbitrary rule prevented a sizeable merchant or entrepreneurial class from emerging. Indeed, they saw such a thing as a threat. And while Japan reacted to the increasing evidence of Western technological and economic superiority in the mid-nineteenth century by deciding that it had to adopt and adapt Western ways if it was to survive, China still tried to keep foreigners at bay. Some in China favoured an opening-up, but they were overruled.

The result, directly or indirectly, was increasing weakness, a civil war (the Taiping rebellion in 1850–64) that was far more devastating than the internal strife Japan suffered at the same time, and then successive military defeats by foreigners, including most notably by Japan itself in 1895. In economic terms, the result was declining income per head, even during a long period (the hundred years or so up to 1914) when the rest of the world economy was growing strongly.

Then, and since, China has been a case study of all the generalizations that economists use to explain why poor countries have not, as a rule, narrowed the gap with rich countries' standards of living. It was also a case study of why a decision to reject globalization, as street protesters at world summits today would advocate for all countries, would be so devastating. That case study can be summed up in four points. Rather than importing technology, China banned foreign contacts; rather than establishing the rule of law, with clear property rights, successive regimes failed to do so or became arbitrary confiscators themselves; rather than letting farmers make enough money to buy consumer goods, it squeezed farmers to try to help town-dwellers and industry; rather than ensuring that there was peace, it succumbed to, or even fostered, war.

This last was especially important. One part or another of China was involved in a military conflict of some sort from 1895 until 1952. Japan used it as its principal colonial adventuring ground, perhaps on the view that if it was going to have an empire to match those of the Europeans, it might as well suppress its traditional regional rival at the same time. So it took Taiwan in 1895 and southern Manchuria (from Russia) in 1905, snuggled up to China's borders by taking Korea in 1910, and seized the rest of Manchuria in 1931 before launching a full-scale invasion of China in 1937. Those last two actions were, in effect, the true beginning of what became the Second World War.

No one knows the exact death-toll from the Japanese army's slaughter of civilians and soldiers in China: estimates range from 1.5 million to more than 6 million, to which can be added 10–15 million more who died of starvation and disease. Meanwhile, however, China's own government, the nationalist Kuomintang led by Chiang Kai-shek, was matching the Japanese death for death. Through its efforts to establish its authority from 1928 onwards, and ultimately in its civil war with Mao's communists, it is thought to have killed up to 10 million Chinese.

*

That terrible, and terrifying, background may help to explain some of the behaviour of Mao Zedong's communists after they seized power in 1949, but also the strangely sympathetic view that was held of them in the West even as, over the next thirty years, the communists managed to kill at least as many of their own countryfolk as had Japan and Chiang Kai-shek added together.

It helps to explain not only Mao's own brutality but also his surprisingly severe policy of isolation from the outside world, although that did serve his brainwashing campaigns, too. Foreign powers had caused mayhem in China for decades, and even Soviet Russia had for a time given support to Mao's opponents, the Kuomintang: so it was felt that it would be better to keep them all away, which Mao did after breaking with the Soviet Union in 1959. The sympathy held by some in the West arose initially from the romantic idea of Mao's Long Marches as a resistance or liberation movement against the Japanese and the very bloody Kuomintang, and later from the equally romantic notion that his rural communes and efforts at mass organization were evidence of a true and even successful alternative to Western capitalism. But Mao also began with a lot of idealistic supporters at home, men with an egalitarian, let's-roll-our-sleeves-up-and-build-China spirit, women with that view as well as delight at their sudden apparent equality and liberation from a cloyingly feudal and patriarchal society.

This helped to cover up an initial slaughter of 1–2 million landlords in 1949, as well as dissent about the collectivization of agriculture in the mid-1950s into huge communal units, which the late John King Fairbank, America's leading China scholar of recent decades, called 'a modern form of serfdom'. Mao's largest single death-toll came in 1958–61, during an effort to make up for the failure of collectivization to boost production. The so-called Great Leap Forward involved the mass mobilization of rural labour to build dams, irrigation and other infrastructure. This meant that there were fewer people to work the fields, while more grain was taken for the towns. The result was a rural famine in which perhaps 30 million people died.

Finally, to complete the grisly arithmetic, in 1966 Mao launched the Cultural Revolution, which turned out to be ten years of deliberate chaos designed, if that is the word, to shake up all the party institutions and established officials. This period took the old idea of divide and rule to its ultimate extreme. It is thought that a million or more people died as a result of the ructions and persecutions of the Cultural Revolution, and something like 100 million were scarred by it, physically or mentally.

All these death-toll figures are estimates. China is a big place, so the figures might be expected to be large; but they should be seen in proportion. If Mao is held to have been responsible for some 33 million deaths in less than thirty years, that is equivalent to 6 per cent of the population of 545 million which China had when he took over in 1949. Mao Zedong's picture still hangs in a prominent, open-air position at the entrance to the Forbidden City in Tiananmen Square, the great martial drilling-ground in central Beijing. Yet it is no wonder that his memory is a tarnished one for all but the hardest core (and hardest hearted) of today's communists. As is said in one of the euphemisms of which the party is so fond, he made 'many mistakes'.

*

His handling of economic affairs was one of the mistakes: hence the famines and China's continued relative decline. Even so, when Deng Xiaoping took power in 1978, two years after Mao's death, China had already had more economic growth in the previous twenty-five years than for the previous century. This was because, by Chinese standards, it had had an unusual amount of peace and law and order, combined with some Stalinist technology and much Stalinist organization. But it wasn't good enough. China was getting weaker and poorer, relative to the rest of the world, and was still struggling to feed its growing population.

Deng's solution was simple: capitalism. Or, to put it another way, greed. Gradually, he implemented most of the typical economists' generalizations about how poor countries could catch up. He introduced market prices for farmers, and as they got richer they started to buy consumer goods; he established some property rights for the first time since 1949; he allowed towns and villages to build and own some light industry; he opened China to some foreign trade and investment, so that technology could be imported. It was, he said in another more splendid euphemism, 'socialism with Chinese characteristics', in which, rather more straightforwardly, 'to get rich is glorious'.

The result was dramatic, and is by now familiar. China's GDP grew at 7–13 per cent a year for almost two decades, incomes quadrupled and the economy grew more than fivefold in all; its share of world GDP (when measured by purchasing-power parity) rose from 5 per cent in 1978 to 11.8 per cent by 1998, its income per head rose six times faster than the world average. Those measures may well be misleading, both because the underlying GDP figures are distorted and because a purchasing-power parity comparison is debatable, to say the least. Nevertheless, the simple fact remains: China has been developing rapidly, for it had a huge amount of scope to do so, thanks to its historical instability and to the criminally incompetent way in which Mao's communists had managed its economy in 1949–76. The simplest consequence is also the most immediately important: over 20 per cent of the population – 270 million people – was lifted above the subsistence line in 1978–2000. Moreover, compared with the repressions, disruptions and lack of choice of the 1960s and 1970s, people suddenly enjoyed some freedom. Hundreds of millions gained the freedom to choose what to spend their money on and even, for many of them, where to live, as they were increasingly allowed to move to the cities, where the new jobs were.

Despite all this progress, despite the shining modern hotels, sky-scrapers and shopping malls of Beijing, Shanghai and other coastal cities, despite the fact that in those cities the bicycles and Mao suits have been replaced by traffic jams and a great variety of fashions, for most Chinese the country nevertheless remains both a poor and a repressive place. Western visitors (including the present author) often wonder why the ordinary Chinese put up with it. Justice is arbitrary. Treatment of dissenters and even of the physically handicapped and the mentally ill is cruel and brutal. Despite the economic success, unemployment is rising, as former state-owned companies are either restructured or closed. Inequality is soaring, both within each city or region and between the prosperous ones and the many more backward ones. According to official statistics, in 1984 the average urban income was 1.7 times its rural counterpart; by 1999 the multiple was 2.65 times. Newspapers are mere propaganda sheets. Independent movements to campaign for democracy itself or just for particular political issues are either banned outright or suppressed as soon as they gain any weight.

The answer, however, to why all this has not yet caused another revolution is straightforward. It is that the present may be flawed in many ways but it remains quite a lot better than the turbulent past. Those who lived through the Cultural Revolution do not instantly hope for more disorder, more disruption, which is what would happen if there were an effort to overthrow the communist oppressors.

The economic achievements since 1978 have been huge. But in many ways those were the easy years. Growth then consisted chiefly of allowing some of China's natural potential to be realized, as the inefficiencies of collectivized agriculture and centrally planned light industry were being eliminated. Management writers talk of the need first to 'pick the low-hanging fruit', and in many ways that was what China was doing, during the 1980s at any rate. Since the mid-1990s, however, things have become much more difficult, and they promise to become more difficult still. This is because although capitalism has taken hold and worked its magic in China's economy, it has not yet taken over altogether: state-owned industries still account for a little under half the economy. Badly run, over-manned legacies of central planning, most of these firms would be bankrupt if they were exposed to conventional accounting and were subject to the normal pressures from their bankers to pay interest on or repay their loans. But those banks, too, are state-owned and, again, would be insolvent if they were run on Western lines.

Looked at coldly, this again merely measures the size of the opportunity. Think what China could achieve if capitalism were to take over the whole economy. There is more low-hanging fruit to be plucked. And some of it is already being plucked, as new roads, railways, airports and river navigations are built to reduce transport costs to China's provinces, and as old state companies restructure and list their shares on the public equity markets in Shanghai and even Hong Kong. The successful, efficient, stable capitalism of Hong Kong has long since spread to take in a large area of southern China, especially around the Pearl River delta, both before and after the smooth handover of sovereignty over the former British colony to China in 1997.

Yet the difficulty can be measured, too: by the size of the vested interests in the state industries that oppose being restructured, by the size of the transitional unemployment caused by such change, and by the fact that in these old industries, the employers took care of all the welfare facilities for their staff, including schools, hospitals and retirement pensions. Workers in modern industries have to fend for themselves. Moreover, banks in today's China are merely distribution channels for private savings to be sent to state-owned companies and then essentially destroyed; they are not banks in the conventional sense but rather, in reality, part of the public system of taxation, expenditure and monetary creation. It will not be easy to modernize the banks, to make the move from the old system to a new one.

The task is huge. But so is the determination to carry it out, and the ambition to achieve further economic growth. That was shown, in 2000 and 2001, by the Chinese leaders' drive to gain admission to the World Trade Organization (WTO). Membership of the WTO will, over the years, open up new areas of the economy to foreign competition, and will expose China to internationally agreed rules of behaviour. It was also shown, in the spring of 2001, by China's surprisingly calm and eventually friendly response to the emergency landing on Chinese soil (Hainan Island) of an American spyplane which had been damaged in a collision with a Chinese fighter plane.

Although there was plenty of posturing after the collision, in the end the language used to attack the Americans was fairly moderate by Chinese standards, and the crew and plane were both returned to America surprisingly quickly. I visited Beijing while the plane was still on the ground at Hainan Island, and was astonished to hear officials, even at the foreign ministry and the People's Daily, the main propaganda newspaper, speak quite moderately about what had happened. I asked them what they thought of the United States, and along with a few muttered phrases about arrogance and so on they also managed to find flattering things to say about America's economic and educational achievements. I interviewed the foreign ministry's top arms-control negotiator and expected a particularly strong tongue-lashing from him, but instead he was calm and quite jolly – at least until we got on to the subject of Taiwan, at which point he made me jump by banging the table hard and declaring that he was, personally, willing to die in order to get back Taiwan.

China is well aware of its dependence on access to Western markets and know-how, and of the need for Western support for its membership of the WTO, which remained in the balance at the time of the spyplane incident. Alongside the routine attacks on America for 'hegemonism' there is in Chinese officialdom a widespread awareness that there is much to learn from the world's leading superpower, as well as a realization that America's influence in the Asia–Pacific region brings at least short-term benefits to China. It keeps the region stable, and reduces the chance that other regional rivals – Japan, Korea – will emerge to dominate the area during the period when China is concentrating on building up its economic strength.

Mere determination to carry on reforming and modernizing the economy may not necessarily be the end of the matter, however. The Communist Party's leaders believe, it seems, that they need to foster economic growth, and that there is no alternative to modernization. There is no going back. Intellectually, that is surely true. But going forward is not a great option either. Unemployment and other related changes are bound to provoke big social problems. Given growth in the labour force and the departure of more people from the countryside as rural productivity rises, China needs to create 8–9 million new jobs each year, even before catering for the millions – already about 4–7 million a year – being thrown out of work in the state-owned industries. So the communists want economic growth in order to keep themselves popular and to make the country stronger; but they also need it if they are to keep the lid on unemployment and themselves securely in power. The country has to run fast, merely to stand still.

China's next few decades will consist of a constant contest between the creation of new jobs in modern industry and the destruction of old ones in state firms. The 'gales of creative destruction' inherent in capitalism will be a dominant feature of China. The question, though, is whether China's political system is resilient enough to absorb these gales. If for any sustained period destruction outpaces creation, whether because of a sagging domestic economy or of a disappointing external one, then political pressure will build. So far, anger at repression, arbitrary justice and official corruption has been kept at bay, partly by the fact that most Chinese have felt that their lot was improving, partly by effective organization and policing. But it is worth recalling that in 1989 a demonstration by a few thousand students in Tiananmen Square in Beijing was considered to be such a threat to the regime that troops were sent in, who killed hundreds of the students. That demonstration had economic troubles at its root, as rising inflation coincided with an economic pause. Think what impact the existence of many millions of unemployed could have, if they came to expect their plight to last. Down south, in Hong Kong, they would see a richer, freer sort of China, in which legal protections are more secure and in which there is even a tentative bit of democracy. Why not, the aggrieved might say, extend Hong Kong's ways and freedoms to the whole of China?

*

That economic uncertainty is the basic threat to the country's political stability. It is a vast country, the biggest decisions concerning which are taken by about two hundred mainly elderly men – the leadership of the Communist Party – who head what is in effect a vast armed bureaucracy. You might think that an armed, bureaucratic dictatorship would be quite well equipped to absorb gales of creative destruction because it does not need to worry about elections or public opinion. Its weakness, though, is that it has no shock absorbers, no system of accountability that can deal with public criticism. In such regimes, handling succession is also difficult: there is no open system of selection and promotion. Mao's death in 1976 was followed by two years of chaos, at the end of which Deng Xiaoping, a Long Marcher who had been jailed for years as a 'capitalist roader', took the helm. When Deng died in 1997 he was succeeded by a triumvirate – Jiang Zemin, Li Peng and Zhu Rongji – which surprised observers by its durability. The length of Deng's final illness in the run-up to his demise – he fell into a coma in 1995 – may have made the transition smoother, but so did the prevailing circumstances of rapid economic growth.

Two of those three leaders, Jiang and Zhu, got rave reviews from Western businessmen in their period at the helm until 2002. Jiang was held to be a safe pair of hands, very sensible; Zhu is thought of as a real star, a brilliant technocrat, tough-minded and no political liberal but nevertheless a man with a vision for his country, a man who got things done. Important visitors are immensely flattered to be granted an audience with, or even dinner with, such leaders, and emerge convinced that the country is in excellent hands. So much better than those dubious, know-nothing politicians we have in the West.

It is a classic misconception, or perhaps a classic self-delusion: the idea that everything must be fine because the boss has said it is; the idea that a huge country, and increasingly a huge economy, can be steered by a handful of men, however brilliant or visionary they are;

the idea that their version of order, and stability, must surely be better than any alternative way of running things.

It is only necessary to look at Indonesia in the late 1990s to see how wrong this can be, and how difficult it is for a dictatorship to handle a political crisis and subsequent change. President Suharto, dictator for more than three decades, did not preside over as well-rooted a movement as the Chinese Communist Party. But he had the army on his side, and did, in Golkar, have a well-organized party under his command. Nevertheless, amid economic collapse and popular demonstrations he was forced to resign. Even his own army withdrew their support. And his departure made the economic situation even worse, because in Indonesia there was no true rule of law, no secure property rights. Old contracts made by businesses with a corrupt and arbitrary regime, and assumptions made about it, were suddenly called into question, especially those made with the Suharto family itself. An economic crisis caused by foreign debts and a collapsing currency was then amplified by a collapse of investment as confidence evaporated.

In China, too, there is no secure rule of law, and contracts have their force chiefly because of faith in the continuation in power of the officials and the regime with which they have been negotiated, or which regulates them. As in Indonesia, the danger is that an economic crisis could then become self-reinforcing, as contracts become worthless and confidence in all sorts of regulatory arrangements disappears.

The Communist Party's control has already been weakened by the dispersal of power to individuals, to companies and to the regions. Such decentralization has been both inevitable and desirable as the economy has developed. If this process were to continue, or even accelerate, the Party would surely wither away. It might remain in place as a convenient fiction, but true power would lie elsewhere, in a lot of hands rather than a few. This possibility makes it tempting to draw the opposite conclusion to the one commonly drawn by those visiting Western businessmen wined, dined and impressed by Zhu Rongji: that rather than being run by a small group, democracy might simply develop of its own accord in such circumstances, as a way gradually to balance the interests of all those different hands that now hold power. Perhaps, by the time an economic crisis occurs, a political means to handle it, or at least channel it, will have evolved.

Experience in all other countries suggests that, in time, economic freedom brings about pressure for greater political freedoms. That was the experience of the rich West, but also of South Korea, for example, and China's own 'renegade province' – that is, Taiwan. The pressure comes partly from freedom itself, partly from the need to deal with economic downturns, partly simply because the interests of non-governmental groups and individuals have expanded to the point where they demand protection and accountability. Even in Singapore, a small city-state that remains a one-party affair, the presence of legal redress and of regular elections in which the rulers can, in principle, be punished, provide a vital safety valve.

It therefore seems likely that in China, too, democracy of some sort will emerge, because it will become both necessary and desirable. Again, if a Western businessman in China is asked whether the Chinese want democracy, he will reply with a snort: 'Of course not; they want stability, and they want to get rich.' This is probably true, on both counts, but it misses the point. Recession means unemployment, which means renewed poverty and probably instability. As has already been noted, the last time the economy sagged, crowds gathered in Tiananmen Square to call for democracy, and troops were sent in. What people in such circumstances are demanding is accountability, and they tend to want it more the richer they get, for they want to protect their gains against mismanagement or confiscation.

*

The real question for the future is whether in China accountability will actually mean democracy, or at least a smooth path towards it. Two other intermediate possibilities ought also to be borne in mind, given Chinese history. One is the chance that the demand for accountability could bring protracted bloodshed in a civil war and a consequent return to the 150-year pattern of stagnation. The other is the possibility that in response to bloodshed or to mass, quasi-democratic pressures, someone might try an adapted form of dictatorship, playing on China's Confucian traditions under which individuals are supposed to support the state, rather than the other way round. Everyone needs to band together, it would be argued, to do their duty to make China great. Just don't call it communism.

Such an authoritarian approach, exploiting the 'Asian values' of collective responsibility and duty propagated in recent years in Malaysia and Singapore, would be likely merely to delay the day when the market economy finally shows that it is incompatible with centralized power. But communism itself, like the lengthy capitalist dictatorships in Indonesia and Chile, endured for a surprisingly long time. The liberal claim that a free economy leads also to a free politics applies only to the long run, and ignores a lot of bumpy short runs along the way.

Some argue that while such communitarian politics can work in a city-state like Singapore, it could not possibly do so for a billion-plus Chinese. Perhaps that is so, but with lashings of nationalism and some stirring up of anger at old humiliations it just might work. It is, after all, the way Taiwan was run for some forty years. The result would be grim for today's democratic Taiwan, and would create a very real dilemma for Asia's biggest regional power, Japan. But it might yet again win some support in the West, where many people are disturbingly willing to believe that the freedoms they value for themselves are not necessary or desirable for the poor.

The most important thing, however, for the present purpose is not to speculate about what might happen to China's political system, but rather to work out what the consequences might be while this development is being played out. A Chinese official would respond, if he admitted that any change is ever conceivable, that this would be a private Chinese matter which would not be of any concern to the rest of the world. After all, he would say, China has never in its history been a territorial aggressor. It has never sought to expand its boundaries, to attack others.

Tibetans and the Uighurs of Xinjiang province might well beg to differ. But it is true that China has not in the past been in the habit of invading Japan, for example, or even its immediate neighbour, Korea (except when the Korean War was already under way in the 1950s), or any of the South-East Asian islands and peninsular nations. This is not, however, entirely reassuring, for two reasons.

The first is that despite that professed lack of territorial ambition China nevertheless disputes plenty of the territory around the South China Sea, in particular believing that it should have the right to explore the sea-bed for minerals, oil and gas, and that it should have the chance to place naval bases on the various reefs and islands there, a few of which it has already seized. Sensibly, in terms of its own interests, it believes in keeping options open in case in the future it needs those minerals, energy or bases; indeed, like Japan in the 1920s and 1930s, China could become most dangerous at a time when there is some sort of energy shortage and when it believes it might be denied access to that and to other natural resources.

The second reason why China's lack of an expansionist history might not be reassuring is that its biggest territorial dispute is with itself: over the rich island of Taiwan, a Japanese colony from 1895 until 1945 but then home to the exiled Kuomintang from 1948–9 onwards. Officially, Taiwan is considered to be part of China, and it is assumed to be only a matter of time before the 'renegade province' is again unified with the motherland. Now that Hong Kong (1997) and Macao (1999) have returned to the fold, Taiwan must be next, say the mainlanders. Currently there is an awkward but durable status quo between the two, under which as long as Taiwan does not actually declare itself independent, the communists seem to be willing to wait and simply state their claims. Taiwan's military forces, with advanced weapon systems bought from America, could almost certainly beat the communists in a direct conflict as long as nuclear weapons are not threatened or used.

The real questions, though, surround an indirect conflict: most likely, there would a blockade, a long period of intimidation of Taiwan by Chinese forces, which would be intended to force the Taiwanese to sue for peace. In China, even political dissidents profess to feel patriotic about reunification with Taiwan; it is a hot, nationalistic issue. No Chinese leader can afford to sound soft about reunification. This also means, however, that at a time of political strain or even struggle, Taiwan is an obvious card for a faction to play, an obvious way to garner support by tugging at the nationalistic heart-strings. The bet that such Chinese nationalists would have to place if they were then to contemplate military action is a bet that the outside world, by which is chiefly meant America, would not step in to help Taiwan. American administrations have long sought to deter such action by giving the impression that they would indeed join such a war on the Taiwanese side.

A time may come, however, when that starts to look less likely, perhaps because of economic strain at home or a sense of frustration with the outside world. And, if it occurs, that moment of temptation for the Chinese military planners would be the most dangerous moment of all – quite possibly, in so far as one can tell this far in advance, the most dangerous moment of the whole of the twenty-first century. Wars are often the result of miscalculation. If there is ever a fight between the United States and China, it is likely to arise from what would be the greatest and most fateful miscalculation in the history of mankind.

4

Japanese Vulnerability

China may resent the presence of American military bases in the Pacific Ocean and even the South China Sea, an area the Chinese consider to be their own sphere of influence. But if there is one thing that China would resent more than American power in Asia it would be the revival of Japanese power in Asia. During the 1970s and 1980s, as Japan's economic strength grew and grew, it must have given many Chinese palpitations.

Not just the Chinese. At that time, virtually anyone writing a book or speech about the future line-up of the great powers of the world was sure to include Japan. Some, indeed, would have gone so far as to predict some form of Japanese supremacy, a *pax Nipponica* to succeed the *pax Americana* that has led the free world since 1945. Japan seemed to be unstoppable. It was growing far faster than either America or Western Europe, and had been doing so for more than twenty years. By the mid-1980s, it was increasing its command over the rest of the world by means of vast exports of capital. Like Britain in the nineteenth century, Japan was becoming a huge creditor nation, one to which others owed debts and obeisance but never the other way round. In its economy, and above all in its manufacturing industry, Japan was doing something mysteriously right, which the decadent folk across the Pacific or in Western Europe were unable to emulate or to compete with. And, through its booming stock and property markets, it had found a new way to finance its growth, with capital abundant and seemingly free. This great new economic power would inevitably, it was said, seek to take on political power as well, to shape the world according to its interests.

Now, virtually no one makes this argument. After Japan's stock and property markets crashed in 1990, the country endured disappointment after disappointment. Its fabled growth rate plummeted. Its banks, once feared around the globe, became laughing stocks rather than growth stocks, noted for their poor management and huge burden of bad debts. Incomes languished; unemployment rose. Public finances that in 1989 had been notable for their solvency, with a hearty budget surplus, became notable for their insolvency, with a general budget deficit nearing 10 per cent of GDP by 2002 and government debts exceeding 140 per cent of GDP.

Most of the manufacturers that had been feared as invincible during the 1980s suddenly took on more earthly dimensions. Nissan, Japan's second biggest car-maker, had to be rescued by France's Renault. None of Japan's computer firms was in the world's top rank by the end of the 1990s. In telecommunications equipment, one of the fastest-growing industries in the 1990s, Japanese firms remained active and quite successful, but chiefly as subcontractors to others. Except in very specialist niches, the only Japanese firms whose names were still on the tip of the tongue of those seeking to identify the world's pacesetters were Toyota and Sony. The close relationships between different firms, and between businessmen, bureaucrats and politicians that were once lauded as the very source of Japan's energy and clarity of purpose were now derided as rigid, selfish and corrupt, the epitome of a crony capitalism that served to explain why the country found it so difficult to change and indeed why it had lost its clarity of purpose.

Japan's lost decade of the 1990s can all too easily produce a reaction of *schadenfreude*, of pleasure at the misfortunes of others. Some people's pleasure is at the expense of Japan itself, pleasure at seeing the mighty, and by the late 1980s mightily arrogant, humbled. Others' pleasure is at the expense of all those analysts, particularly in America, who in the 1980s gave their breathless warnings about Japan's imminent supremacy, and who claimed that the West must either start to copy Japan's ways or start to confront it. Such *schadenfreude* is not very constructive. But, once viewed with the perspective of a few decades hence, such a reaction will not appear terribly pertinent or intelligent either.

One reason why it will not is that such thinking is essentially ephemeral in nature – just as ephemeral as the claims of Japan's imminent supremacy turned out to be. It is the error of using short-term evidence to prove a case about long-term trends. Like Japan in 1990, the United States suffered a devastating stockmarket crash in 1929 following a decade of apparently immense industrial achievement, and then 'lost' the decade of the 1930s to the Great Depression. Yet to have written America off at that time because its banks had just collapsed and because its workers were queuing outside soup kitchens would have been a truly historic error. It may have been one of the errors that tempted Adolf Hitler into his expansionary boldness in Europe. By 1945, this apparently failed nation held a military and economic lead over the rest of the world which has never been matched before, and will probably never be matched again. It does not of course follow from America's example that Japan, too, is bound to follow a terrible decade by jumping into a position of world leadership. But the parallel does give warning that one needs to lift one's eyes from short-term phenomena and try to identify underlying strengths and trends.

A second reason is related to the first. It is that the over-estimation of Japan's potential and importance in the 1980s and the (almost certainly) under-estimation of it in the 1990s and early 2000s both imply that popular (and even much academic) analysis tends to fasten itself on to the wrong indicators of power, of potential leadership and – most important for the present purpose – of geopolitical significance.

Most likely, this is because power itself is a slippery concept, dependent on context and relativities rather than capable of being measured in absolute ways. Another explanation is that statistical indicators of power tend to have a self-amplifying character, thanks to currency movements: towards its cyclical zenith, a country appears to be even further ahead of others on whatever indicators are chosen because its currency tends to appreciate in value at the same time. The rising yen from 1985 until 1990 (and, off and on, until 1995) pushed Japan to the top or near the top of many leagues – of income per head, aid donations, public resources, even military spending – just as the strong dollar in 1995–2001 then expanded America's apparent lead on many measures.

But it is also because the sequence of analysis used to evaluate power and potential is generally upside-down. A perception arises that a country is now powerful, or might be in the fairly near future, and then pundits and scholars search for indicators that might explain or give substance to that perception. Attention therefore alights as much on correlations as on causations. So, during the 1980s, the perception of Japan's rise was dominated by three things: its exports of manufactured goods, particularly cars and electronic equipment, giving rise to a big trade surplus; its exports of capital; and the value of the Tokyo stockmarket. Laments at American and European weakness tended to focus, correspondingly, on the decline of manufacturing, on trade deficits, on imports of capital (which showed how control of Western economies was falling into Japanese hands) and on local stockmarket volatility, notably during and after a crash on Wall Street in 1987.

But move to the late 1990s and things begin to turn round. Perceptions of America's economic strength, indeed its supremacy, became dominated by different things: imports of high-tech equipment and its use in the service sector, especially via the Internet and modern telecommunications; imports of capital, which now supposedly signified how America's economy offered more attractive returns than anywhere else; and, the only measure it had in common with Japan, the value of the American stockmarket. Deficits had become signs of strength, not weakness; manufacturing prowess was no longer an end in itself but rather just one aspect of the adoption of high technology and of the effort to raise productivity throughout the economy. Computer software and use of the Internet were believed to matter the most. And Japan's continued trade and capital surpluses? These were now just signs that Japan's domestic demand was anaemic, and that its savings could not find profitable opportunities for investment at home. Not strengths at all.

*

Where does this leave Japan and its future? Clearly, popular diagnoses in the past have been wrong or misleading, but what might a better diagnosis look like? The first step towards such a thing is to jettison the notion, common in the 1980s, that Japan might somehow soon become 'number one' or, in other words, assume a position of world leadership. This idea needs to be jettisoned not because it is *ipso facto* implausible but rather because the chief determinant of whether or not it could ever occur does not reside in Japan. It resides in the future course of the United States of America.

Leadership is America's to lose, rather than Japan's (or anyone else's) to win. The reason lies in the countries' relative size and conditions. One is a nation of 280 million people with what is now far and away the world's largest economy. The other is a country whose population is less than half as big (126 million), and whose economy too is only half as big. Currency movements may alter that gap in either direction. But they do not alter the basic situation. Over the medium and long term, it could not be 'success' of any plausible magnitude in Japan that would fundamentally alter the relationship between these two countries. It would essentially have to be failure in the United States itself – economic and probably social dislocation that condemned America, not just to a cyclical downturn for a year or two but rather to slow or stagnant growth for a sustained period, probably a generation or more, and, perhaps related to it, a sustained decision in America to cease its engagement in world affairs. Such an outcome is certainly possible, even though an earlier chapter in this book argued that it is not probable.

The world has in the past seen periods when a modestly populated island nation – Britain – could boss others around, including far bigger countries. Indeed, the Japanese name for Britain, *Eikoku*, can be translated literally as 'number one country', having been adopted during the late nineteenth century when England was thought of as just that. (The Japanese word for America, incidentally, is *Beikoku*, or 'rice country'.) But the path from today's world back to such a situation would have to cross so many tortuous junctions and requires so many speculations that it would not be worth spending much time on. Nevertheless, if such a period of sustained American failure or withdrawal from world affairs were truly to occur, then unless there had been an extraordinary number of other political and economic earthquakes, Japan would in reality surely be just one of several powerful nations rather than supreme in its own right. This would not be a world where being 'number one' meant very much to a nation of Japan's size and heft.

Having jettisoned that time-wasting issue, two much more productive topics need to be examined. One is the state of Japan's economy, and its relationship to the country's social structure. In recent years, things do seem to have gone badly wrong, so anyone interested in Japan's future contribution to geopolitical stability or instability needs to form a view about whether that change signifies fundamental weaknesses and problems, or whether it might simply be a temporary phenomenon. Japan's economic course will, for good or ill, affect both the country's interests and its behaviour.

The second topic is the security climate surrounding Japan, in East Asia: does Japan have reason to worry about what could happen in its region, and might those worries – justified or unjustified – alter the country's stance and behaviour? Regardless of whether its economy continues to stagnate or roars forward, Japan could become geopolitically significant because of its reactions to developments elsewhere, most obviously, as things stand at present, in the Korean peninsula and in China. In anything like its current economic size, Japan has both the means and the strategic importance to make a big difference, both in its region and in the world – if it chooses to try to.

*

Of these two topics, the economy demands to be analysed first, for it is closely identified in most people's minds with Japan itself. What was once Japan's pride and joy – such that President Charles de Gaulle of France famously derided the country as a nation of 'transistor salesmen' – has in recent years looked more like an embarrassment. As the twenty-first century began, the country was burdened by a financial system piled high with worthless assets; by households which were laden with savings but which lacked the confidence to spend their money; and by companies hemmed in by regulations and by a widespread resistance to change. Everyone seemed to know what needed to be done – clean up the financial system, deregulate, stimulate demand through monetary expansion – but without knowing how to go about it. Vested interests stood in the way. Change seemed to be essential, but also impossible.

The degree of this resistance to change, of paralysis in the face of adversity, has been surprising. Those analysts, including the present author in a 1989 book *The Sun Also Sets*, who foresaw the turnaround in Japan's economic fortunes in 1990 nevertheless generally expected that it would take only a few years at most for Japanese officials and businesses to work out a way to deal with it. One cliché is that the cohesive, consensual nature of Japanese society means that although it may take some time to agree upon what needs to be done, the implementation of a decision, once made, is fast and thorough. The Japanese supposedly run together like a herd, so once it has become clear that the herd must change direction, it will surely do so, in unison, to impressive effect. Another, perhaps more cynical assumption after the stockmarket crash of 1990 was that in Japanese politics nothing talks louder than money – indeed, arguably, virtually nothing else gets a word in at all. So once the pain of stagnation started to hurt the providers of money to the main political parties, particularly the Liberal Democratic Party which ruled Japan almost uninterrupted after 1955, these donors and stringpullers would surely insist on changes.

Neither of these assumptions proved to be correct. The herd did not change direction. And the political donors did not enforce a change either. What might well have been a five-year problem more than doubled in length and became much deeper than it need have been. One reason for the delay may have been that it was a long time before any real sense of crisis took hold: living standards stayed high, unemployment rose but was still fairly low. Life was not as good as it might have been, but it wasn't too bad, either. So the urge to change, to endure the difficulties that change always involves, was blunted. A second reason was that the main policy remedy deployed during the 1990s to try to revive the economy, huge amounts of public borrowing to finance public works, proved extremely convenient for one of the biggest groups of corporate donors to the Liberal Democrats, the construction industry, as well as for other firms dependent on their activities. So the idea of beneficial, self-interested pressure from the corporate stringpullers, all pushing in the direction of deregulation and reform, proved to be naïve.

But there was a third reason, of a deeper nature. It lies in the fact that the refusal to change did not date back simply to the aftermath of the stockmarket crash of the 1990s, to the end of what the Japanese now call their 'bubble' period of the late 1980s. It dated back to well before the bubble itself, at least to the early 1980s and perhaps even earlier. Indeed, that refusal helps to explain why the financial bubble became inflated in the first place.

By the end of the 1970s, Japan was testing the limits of what had been a phenomenally successful period of economic growth since the 1950s. Indeed, those twenty years capped a phenomenally successful century in economic terms, a century which saw Japan rise from being a rather undeveloped pupil of the West to becoming its equal. It was a century of huge economic and social change, in which Japan was transformed from an essentially rural country into a highly urban one, especially during the 1950s. It was a century in which Japan had essentially industrialized twice, for example overtaking Britain to become the world's largest shipbuilder during the 1930s, and then overtaking it in overall industrial output in the 1960s, having picked itself up from wartime defeat.

Rapid economic growth in the 1960s, led by export industries such as shipbuilding, motor vehicles and electronics, took an abrupt knock in 1971 when President Richard Nixon abruptly devalued the dollar against the yen and other currencies, and then another in 1973–4 when oil prices suddenly rose tenfold amid an Arab oil embargo. Such an event should have been – and was – especially painful for a country that imports almost all its energy. Yet it recovered rapidly from a short recession and bout of inflation, becoming the industrial world's most efficient user of energy under pressure from those high prices and with some steering by government. A rising government budget deficit also helped to boost domestic demand.

By then Japan was a country that, in essence, had two economies. One, the advanced export industries and their supplier networks, was open to international trade and competition, was free to innovate and create new markets, and was a match for rival firms anywhere in the world. This large sector was led by companies that had been founded by entrepreneurs in the 1950s, such as Honda and Sony, plus some whose origins could be traced back before the Second World War but which had not been part of the industrial establishment. Toyota and Matsushita Electric (maker of the Panasonic brand of consumer electronics, among others) were notable examples. Such firms had their own networks of suppliers and customers, but were not beholden to any large group of other companies. Many firms that were part of such industrial groups, or *keiretsu*, looser successors to the old pre-war conglomerates, or *zaibatsu* (which had been broken up by the American occupiers in the 1940s) also took part in the export effort, but were not in the vanguard. Mitsubishi Electric, Hitachi and Fujitsu are examples. Here prices were low and productivity high.

The other economy, however, consisted of relatively backward and protected domestic markets: examples include agriculture, distribution, telecommunications, airlines, many consumer goods, construction, retailing, land and all financial services, most notably banking. Here, prices were high, competition was restricted, productivity was low. Some of this second, inefficient economy can be explained by social policy: a desire, especially strong during the 1950s when people were flooding from the countryside into the towns, to preserve the jobs and livelihoods of vulnerable groups. But not much can be explained in this way. Social policy might explain early farm support, and some later concern for small shopkeepers, but not the state of the banks, telecommunications or airlines, or many other sectors. These were protected and restricted for reasons familiar in other countries: because a product or service was considered to be a national utility, best run and controlled by the state (such as telecoms and civil aviation); because a product or service was considered too risky to be allowed to operate freely (such as banking); because a group of industrialists or workers successfully lobbied politicians and bureaucrats to grant them privileged support or insulation against competition (such as construction, most retailing, distribution and many consumer goods).

Ideally, what should have happened is that as the advanced, internationally competitive industries matured and began to grow more slowly, so other sectors of the economy should have been opened up through deregulation, stimulating new competition, investment and innovation. Then, the base of growth would have been widened and new sources of vitality could have been tapped. To some degree, of course, this did happen. Even banking had a fair amount of deregulation in the early 1980s. Other deregulation occurred under pressure from trading partners, notably America. But it met considerable resistance, not surprisingly, from companies and employees who stood to lose their protection. Whenever government controls are strong and the future of those controls is under debate, the sensible, rational reaction is to devote your resources to lobbying, persuading and bribing the relevant political and governmental powerholders to keep rules that benefit you or to bend any changes in your direction.

Such a response is not unique to Japan. But it was made easier as well as more potent by the monopolizing of government by one party, the LDP – the Liberal Democratic Party. Parliamentarians in that party formed themselves into groups, known as *zoku* or tribes, dedicated to controlling the legislative process for particular sectors, and, more to the point, to controlling the flow of donations from firms in those sectors. The essence of successful raising of campaign finance, in other words, became the successful organizing of resistance to deregulation. Opposition parties, which in Japan in the 1970s and 1980s mainly meant the Socialist Party but also a Buddhist-backed group called Komeito, or the 'clean government party', also played their part in this process, either by participating in it or by not obstructing it. They were rewarded with a share of the proceeds.

In the late 1970s the impetus of export growth, and with it the expansion of related industries, was starting to weaken. The dollar had declined ever since Nixon's devaluation, reaching its lowest point in 1978. Japanese exports were getting costlier. The government's budget deficit was getting larger, and might soon have become unaffordable. The pressure for change, for efforts to stimulate domestic demand in new ways in order to generate more growth, began to increase. But the moment passed. Ronald Reagan was elected as American president in 1980, and implemented policies that made the dollar soar in value for the next five years. The yen became cheap again, and so did Japanese exports. Economic growth could proceed again in Japan, without too much pain from deregulation. That task could be handled slowly, or simply not at all.

The country's second-tier economy thus gained five years more grace. The trade surplus continued to grow, and with it came a surplus of capital which began to be exported, first in the form of investments in foreign securities, but later as more visible purchases of foreign property, factories and companies. Overall economic growth was not spectacular in the first half of the 1980s, but at annual rates ranging between 2 per cent and 5 per cent it was pretty good, especially in comparison with a United States that in the early 1980s was struggling out of a recession. Pressure grew from American industrial competitors who felt unable to fight off cheap and high-quality Japanese goods in their own markets but also felt they could not gain comparable access to Japan's market because of official and unofficial barriers. Meanwhile, however, the profitability of Japanese companies was weak. It is often argued that this arose from a preference for market share at the expense of profits. There may be some truth in this, but it was also the case that Japanese firms, as a rule, were not very efficient and proved poor at allocating their capital.

After 1985, the external economic situation changed dramatically. Thanks to America's large trade deficit and thanks to a deliberate effort, co-ordinated with other central banks, to make the dollar less attractive to investors and to make other countries' currencies more attractive, the dollar's value collapsed. It halved in value against the yen in just two years. And then in October 1987 a stockmarket crash raised fears about the American economy and with it those of other rich countries. This gave rise to a new effort to co-ordinate monetary policy between central banks, all aimed at cutting interest rates and making more money available. To stop the dollar falling further, Japan's part was to cut its interest rates even more. And thus began the financial bubble of 1987–90.

Money was pumped vigorously into the economy. The yen rose in value. But the painful effects of that rise were more than compensated for by the benefits of cheap money, reinforced by soaring share and property prices. A virtuous circle emerged. People – banks, households, companies, institutional investors – took out loans on the security of their rising real estate assets and used them to invest in shares. Rising share prices then made capital appear costless to companies, which could obtain it through bond issues convertible into shares at a later date. Confidence that the conversion would be highly profitable thanks to capital gains led investors to agree to earn no interest on the bonds or even, in some cases, in effect to pay the borrower. Companies could therefore splash out on all sorts of investments and acquisitions, both inside Japan and outside. Consumer spending boomed, as households felt richer than ever before. Remarkably, annual economic growth accelerated, ranging between 4 per cent and 7 per cent each year. But there was no inflation to worry about, as imports were getting cheaper thanks to the strong yen and energy prices were falling, at the time. So the Bank of Japan could keep interest rates low.

The sense of power, and of new opportunities arising almost effort-lessly, was heady. But two groups benefited particularly greatly from the stockmarket bubble. One consisted of the politicians, who found a new source of campaign finance. Helped by big securities firms (who wanted favours, of course), they could make quick profits by trading on insider information, as well as longer-term profits from other investments. The other group was broader: private companies whose profits were otherwise being squeezed were able to make money on the stock and property markets. This was particularly welcome to exporters struggling to deal with the yen's rapid rise in value against the dollar. They could use what became known as *zaiteku*, or financial engineering, to make up for losses in their main, manufacturing businesses. For example, in the year to March 1988 securities profits accounted for 58.8 per cent of the pre-tax profits of Matsushita Electric, 65.3 per cent of those at Nissan, 93 per cent of those at Matsushita's subsidiary, JVC, and 73 per cent at Sharp.

Capital seemed to be free, profits could be made in new ways, and the world was Japan's increasingly cheap oyster. The stock and property bubbles again put off the painful day when deregulation and reform might be necessary to broaden the base of economic growth. Things were going along fine without it. And all Japan's foreign admirers were saying during the 1980s that it had discovered a new and brilliant way to run its economy. So why change? Why indeed. The bubble was convenient to those who might have had to endure the pain of change. It was beneficial to those, including politicians, companies and ordinary investors, who thought it was making them rich. And the fact that the economy was humming along without causing inflation, and that its masters in the finance ministry and in the LDP approved of it, meant that the Bank of Japan did not feel inclined to bring the party to a halt early.

The bubble burst when the Bank did, finally, make money costlier by raising its interest rates, and, as always happens eventually with bubbles, when confidence in ever-rising prices dissipated. It left behind it a mess, as bubbles always do. Companies had over-extended them-selves, borrowing and investing because they thought they were rich and that money was free. Households had over-borrowed too, on the security of their suddenly valuable houses and shares. Banks had lent the money to finance this binge, and found themselves with a larger and larger pile of debts which the borrowers could neither service nor repay. More and more property developers and conventional firms alike began to go bankrupt. Companies that had been making their money from *zaiteku* rather than their normal activities found their weaknesses exposed. Households started to worry not only that their breadwinners might lose their jobs, but also that their nest-eggs, in life insurance policies, bank deposits, mutual funds and direct shareholdings, might be worth a lot less than they had thought, or possibly nothing at all. So they began to save more out of their normal incomes and spend less, in order to make up for the losses and the uncertainty.

The stockmarket crash began on 2 January 1990. Eventually, share prices fell by two-thirds, and so did property prices. After such a financial shock, a slowdown or a recession was inevitable. What was needed was for the resulting sickness in the financial system to be cured; for demand to be stimulated in order to keep activity going; for the confidence of households in the value of their savings to be restored; and for previously untapped energies in the economy to be released, in order to set off a new cycle of investing and spending. Only the second of these occurred: a series of huge budgetary packages designed to prop up demand. But neither the financial cure nor the releasing of energies took place, and so households' confidence continued to seep away.

The reason why neither of these things occurred is the same reason why deregulation and modernizing reforms were so muted in the 1970s and 1980s: resistance to change. This resistance was not, as the myth-makers would have it, some mysterious national characteristic, founded deep in a conformist, consensual culture. It was rather a resistance by particular groups within Japan, made successful by their ability to capture, or just to blockade, the legislative process. Each of these groups may within itself be characterized by conformism and herd behaviour. But that is not true of the country as a whole: there is no homogenized Japanese polity, resisting change. Indeed, at many elections during the 1990s, the vote for change and against the status quo was considerable. It just failed, for too long, to muster a workable majority and to dominate parliament. If only there had been a homogenized Japanese polity, change might have been possible.

That, in the 1990s, emerged as Japan's most important political, and therefore economic, weakness: the ability of numerous interest groups, representing bankers, life insurers, farmers, the telecommunications industry, wholesale distributors, the postal savings system, the construction industry and others, to block or severely delay regulatory reform and, in some cases, penalization for past misdemeanours. It turned an economy that had once seemed impressively vigorous and willing to adopt new ideas into one that was sclerotic.

*

Solving that problem is essentially a political task. It will never be achieved in its entirety: in all countries, interest groups succeed some of the time in preventing change. It was the task that Junichiro Koizumi, a maverick, reformist member of the LDP, pledged to carry out when he rose to the prime ministership in April 2001. He achieved extraordinary levels of personal popularity on the basis of it, which then faded when he appeared to be failing to achieve very much. Whether or not Mr Koizumi turns out to be a successful reformer is merely a short-term issue, however. Two different questions matter for the longer-term purpose of this book. First, if the task was indeed carried out to a reasonable extent, how strong could the Japanese economy then become? Second, if it is not carried out or is not successful, what might the consequences be?

Although a great deal of reform needs to be done, the fundamental characteristics of the Japanese economy are highly favourable to continued economic growth. The labour force is well educated, with scores on reading, scientific and mathematical literacy well above those in the United States, according to OECD surveys. High-school education ranks with the world's best, and is completed by a higher proportion of Japanese children than is the case in America or Western Europe. Japanese universities are below the level of the world's best, but there are enclaves of top quality, especially in the sciences.

One factor that will in future alter the way the economy performs is the rapid ageing of Japan's population structure. Thanks to a huge post-war baby boom, until the late 1980s Japan had a younger population, and thus a younger labour force, than was the case in America or Western Europe. This helped to restrain its wage, pension and health costs. Since then, the ageing of that post-war cohort has meant that

Japan's labour force is now older than America's (which is kept young by immigration and a rising fertility rate) though similar to those in several European countries. In 1990, just 12 per cent of Japan's population was over 65 years old; by 2000 the figure had risen to more than 16 per cent, and it is forecast to reach a peak of 23.5 per cent in 2020. It will then have the highest proportion of its population over 65 of any of the big industrialized countries.

That age-structure is bound to hold the economy back to some degree: wage costs are rising, as are pension and health costs for the care of the elderly. In time, Japan's fabled high personal savings rate will decline, perhaps sharply, as more people are spending their savings and fewer are putting money away for the future. But although that may reduce the economy's potential growth rate a tad, there is no reason why its growth rate in such conditions should not be healthy. Further into the future, late in the twenty-first century, Japan's population could be in decline if present trends persist, for its birth rate is below the level necessary to replace those who are dying, and immigration is virtually nil. But much can change over such time periods: fertility rates might revive, immigration might be countenanced.

In the shorter term, on any measure, Japan's economy is well placed to understand and deploy information technology in a wide range of industries. The same is true of other waves of technological change that are currently under way, including biotechnology and the fuel cell. Technical expertise is high, and broadly based. Industrial relations have been peaceful ever since the 1950s. An inability, so far, to prosper in software businesses might be thought to pose a big disadvantage in the supposed IT age, but a country does not have to be good at everything in order to be able to grow. It has to be able to stimulate investment and spending, and to keep increasing productivity across a wide range of industries, year after year. In the short to medium term, Japan should, in fact, have a fine opportunity to boost productivity since it has a decade of poor performance to catch up with, a decade that has left many of its industries well behind in the use of computer hardware and software. Indeed, one measure of Japan's future potential is the very existence within it of what was described earlier as its second-tier economy: all those sectors that have remained protected, or over-regulated, or only partially deregulated. If they were to be genuinely opened up to new competition, then the opportunities for new firms and for outside competitors would be mouth-watering. There is plenty of low-hanging fruit to be plucked.

One issue, perhaps, concerns Japan's ability to produce, and finance, new entrepreneurs. It does not have a Silicon Valley tradition of venture capital and enterprise. But neither do most other countries; America is the sparkling exception in that regard, not the rule. Japan's record in encouraging entrepreneurship is about as good – or as bad – as that in continental Europe. It could and should do more: its bankruptcy law, for example, is excessively penal for failed entrepreneurs, and should be changed. Even in the arid conditions of the 1990s and early 2000s, an array of small firms have sprouted up, and new stockmarkets have emerged to channel finance to them. If the banks were cleaned up and if demand in the economy began to revive again, many more would be likely to follow their example. One thing that is certain is that there is no shortage of capital available domestically to finance their investment: Japan has a large savings surplus, and has no need, for the time being, to import capital.

The prospects for a reformed, deregulated Japan are good. A great deal of energy is waiting to be released. But there is a second question for the future: what if economic reforms are not carried out, if deregulation causes more problems than it solves?

The answer is political, not economic. If there is a further failure of political will, a further failure to assemble or maintain a majority in parliament in favour of change and of breaking the interest-group gridlock, the result would be political despair. The economic outcome would be further stagnation and probable economic contraction, falling incomes, rising unemployment, bankruptcies and more – all with a government whose ability to borrow more money to finance itself was becoming severely limited by the level of its debts. Japan is not an international credit risk, because the government's debts are owed to domestic not foreign lenders. But their willingness to carry on lending is not limitless.

In that situation, the likeliest outcome would be the rise of extremist parties and politicians. The conventional solutions would already have been tried, or at least conventional attempts to implement conventional solutions would have been tried. The way would be open for new ideas to be offered, or at least new rallying points. The likeliest of those is some form of Japanese nationalism.

Since 1945, nationalism has been a hard word to use in connection with Japan, wartime memories and taboos being so strong. There is a strong current of pacifism, because of past militarism and because of the atom bombs that were dropped on Hiroshima and Nagasaki. But, naturally enough, there has always been national pride. During the 1980s and 1990s this began to manifest itself at an intellectual and political level, as study groups sought to define Japan's own interests and special ways of doing things, and to seek ways to promote them. During trade spats with the United States, some politicians achieved popularity by attacking the Americans, most notoriously a maverick LDP member called Shintaro Ishihara, who produced a book called *The Japan That Can Say No*, written jointly with Akio Morita, the boss of Sony (as mentioned in Chapter 2). Mr Ishihara left mainstream politics for a while, but returned in 1999 to run as an independent for the governorship of Tokyo, which he won. He proceeded to use that position as a platform from which to prepare for a return to national politics, if an opportunity were to arise, and to proselytize his nationalist views, chiefly now at the expense of China rather than America.

Mr Ishihara is one obvious candidate to emerge to exploit an atmosphere of despair, but there could certainly be others. A nationalist, flag-waving programme would not be much of a substitute for economic change, but it might divert people's minds for a time. It might even be the way to assemble the majority needed if reforms are ever to be forced through. Its successful adoption as a political campaign might reflect a feeling that the outside world – America through its own troubles or its disdain for Japan, China through its aggressive export competition, China and South Korea through their sniping about Japan's past – was now more hostile than friendly. But it would carry dangers, too. A campaign to overturn entirely the provision in Japan's post-war constitution that forbids military action overseas would be highly divisive. (It was bent during the Afghan War in 2001, but only to enable Japanese ships to support somebody else's war, not to make war on their own.) Social unrest would be a risk, possibly exacerbating the already disruptive consequences of economic failure.

A sharp increase in defence spending might help revive the economy for a time, but that, too, would spark controversy, both within Japan and outside.

*

A move to a more nationalist political stance, probably also a more internally divisive, provocative politics, would be the likeliest outcome of continued economic failure. It is also, however, the likeliest outcome of the economic and political changes that are under way in the Asian region that surrounds Japan – a more assertive Japan, one that stands up for its own interests; or a more anxious Japan, worried about how things are changing in the world around it and worried that it is no longer enough for it to depend on its fifty-year military alliance with the United States – if that alliance endures at all. Either way, the result is likely, over time, to be some sort of reassertion or revival of nationalism in Japan. And that development could well be the change in Japan in the coming years that has the most geopolitical significance. Its economic ups and downs mainly affect its own people. Such a political or security change would affect many others.

Since 1945, Japan has largely subcontracted its foreign policy to the United States. Deprived (by defeat, its own pacifist lobbies and its post-war constitution) of the option of using military spending or deployment to exert influence abroad, it has sheltered under a security treaty with the United States, signed in 1951 and revised and extended in 1960. This gave America several military bases on Japanese territory. In addition, despite its own bar against nuclear weapons, successive governments turned a blind eye to the use by the American navy of its Japanese bases as refuelling and maintenance ports for nuclear-armed ships patrolling the Pacific. Japan did develop its own friendships with other nations, using not only diplomacy but also its increasingly large budget for overseas aid, and defended its own interests in multilateral trade negotiations. And while depending on America for most of its armaments it did seek to maintain some indigenous capability in military technologies by subcontracting the manufacture of some fighter planes, for instance. But as long as the main security threat to Japan was the Soviet Union, and as long as any subsidiary threats from, for example, North Korea could also be monitored and dealt with chiefly through American intelligence intercepts and military deterrence, there was neither a need nor a motivation for Japan to move beyond the alliance with the United States.

That has been changing, roughly for the past twenty years. China's military means, and the extent of its navy's and air force's activities, have been growing. Tensions between China and Taiwan have also been growing; whereas Koreans have remained hostile to their former colonial masters in Japan, the Taiwanese have been friendlier, and have built close relationships with many Japanese politicians. Taiwan's position also matters for the sea lanes surrounding it that carry much of Japan's merchandise trade. North Korea, even as its economic situation has declined, has been trying to build a capability to deploy weapons of mass destruction of various sorts, making up for its weakness on every other measure.

Indeed, taken as a whole, Asia has become a more menacing place. Many of the region's countries, particularly in East Asia, are now richer and so can afford bigger armies, navies and air forces. But the biggest change has been caused by the spread of nuclear weapons and of long-range missile technology. As Professor Paul Bracken of Yale University points out in his excellent and provocative book *Fire in the East: The Rise of Asian Military Power and the Second Nuclear Age*, the countries that now have nuclear or chemical arsenals and are developing ballistic missiles run all the way from Israel to North Korea, taking in Syria, Iraq, Iran, Pakistan, India and China.

The worst trouble-spots are somewhat distant from Japan: India and Pakistan, and the ring of venom that takes in Israel, Syria, Iran and Iraq, and could in future embroil others such as Saudi Arabia. But two of them are, relatively speaking, right in Japan's backyard: China and Taiwan; and North Korea. During the 1990s, that point was brought firmly home to the Japanese by two events. The first arose when China held a series of aggressive missile tests in the Taiwan Straits in 1995 and 1996, prompted by an apparent increase in Taiwanese political debate about the island's independence. The response from the United States was reassuring, both to the Taiwanese and to Japan: it sent two carrier task forces to patrol in the area, as a signal of its concern and its support for Taiwan (or, formally, to its opposition to the use of military means to solve the dispute between China and Taiwan). But the point had been made, and underlined: military conflict between Taiwan and China had become a real possibility, and, particularly if America chose to back Taiwan, Japan might well be drawn in too.

The second event took place in the sky. It was the firing by North Korea of a long-range missile, which flew over Japan and landed in the Pacific Ocean. It showed not only that Japan could be a target for such missiles but also that, in the fairly near future, so could the west coast of the United States. Given that North Korea was also thought to be trying to develop biological and chemical weapons, both of which could be delivered on such a missile, this was quite a scare for the Japanese.

Not long afterwards, North Korea appeared to enter a phase of détente with its old enemies in the South, and its leader, Kim Jong-Il, entertained his Southern counterpart, Kim Dae-Jung, at an unprecedented summit meeting in the Northern capital of Pyongyang. So perhaps things would become more peaceful, and perhaps in due course the Korean peninsula would become a single, unified, democratic country once more. Perhaps. But such possibilities are not what military and strategic planners have chiefly to watch for. They have to watch for the growth of potentially threatening military capabilities. And they have to watch for possible periods of change that might affect the motivation of countries to use such capabilities. Korean unification, or the threat of it, could be one such period.

Thoughts about Korean unification raise two other, related, questions: what would happen to the existing American military bases in South Korea after unification, and what stance might China take towards unification? As such questions move further into the future, there are more uncertainties about what might be the prevailing political conditions at the time in either China or the United States. As Chapter 3 argued, China might by then be itself in a state of political instability. As things stand, however, the likelihood would be that communist China would not support unification unless there was a plan for America to withdraw its troops from the new Korea – and China's support for unification, or at least acquiescence in it, would surely be necessary, given that it shares a border with North Korea and has long been the North's sole remaining ally. America's presence in the region would thus be weakened. And, as has often been the case in history, China would be likely to seek to make the new, unified Korea something of a client, or at least a somewhat dependent state in order to keep its north-eastern border and coast secure. Given that unification would be very costly for Korea, one can easily imagine a contest among outsiders, chiefly Japan, China and America, to offer help in return for future friendliness.

If Korea does unify, and if American troops then withdraw, Japan would be left as the sole remaining base for the American military in the region. The bases on Japanese soil are in any case becoming controversial, particularly, but not only, the southernmost base, on Okinawa Island. There, disputes over land and noise have combined with controversy over the rape of local Okinawan girls by American servicemen. The result has been a strong local campaign against the base. The base brings money to an otherwise fairly poor island, so it has also had its backers. But its position there is far from secure. If there is a further rape, the base's days could well be numbered.

*

The result of all this change is that Japan is likely to feel increasingly vulnerable. In the longer term, Japan's economy might well feel considerably stronger than it does today, though it could take a crisis of some sort to bring about the political and policy reforms necessary to rebuild that strength. Let us hope it does feel stronger in future, for that would at least steel Japanese nerves against a regional security balance that is likely to look more and more wobbly.

Missiles, territorial tensions and nuclear proliferation are making North-east Asia feel less secure. The presence and influence of Japan's old regional rival, China, is growing. Although the presence and influence of the United States in the region remains strong, and indeed valued by governments of almost all the countries of the area, there are good reasons to question whether or not in future Japan will always be able to rely upon the American alliance for the bulk of its security. America's planned national missile defence system, which is said to envisage protective shields for American bases abroad and thus potentially for Japan itself, might, for example, take a long time to develop and might still not be reliable enough for Japan to feel able to depend on it altogether. It would take truly cataclysmic events for it actually to break away from its alliance with the United States. But it may well become in the interest both of Japan and of the United States for the former to start to move beyond the alliance.

Such a move would gain further fuel if nationalism does gather strength in Japan in the wake of an economic crisis. By the same token, growing worries about regional security, especially about threats from China or North Korea, would add fuel to the rise of nationalism itself. Such actions might well have a self-fulfilling character. Signs that what is by far Asia's largest economic power, and the Asian country that has most recently a history of conquering others, was rearming and becoming more assertive would be likely to make others accelerate their military programmes as well. The circle would be a potentially vicious one, giving a sharp kick forward to one of the most worrying movements in geopolitics. But, from the Japanese point of view, that outcome may well look unavoidable.

Japan feels vulnerable now with its weak economy, and it is likely that it will feel even more vulnerable in future even if the economy eventually revives. Japan already boasts the world's third largest defence budget and has a navy larger than that of Britain. But, hemmed in by constitutional restrictions and by its own anti-nuclear principles, this is not enough to make the country feel secure. It is also not enough to make America entirely happy about its ally: if Japan were to become able to pull more weight in promoting regional security America would be likely to welcome it, albeit with some reluctance. A more nationalist government, a more powerful navy and air force, a more visible military presence in the region, even, in the end, a publicly acknowl-edged programme of nuclear research and development – all these must be considered likelihoods for Japan during the first few decades of the twenty-first century.

5

European Envy

There is currently only one place in the world that matches the United States of America in terms of economic strength, on almost any statistical measure: sheer output, trading clout, output-per-head, savings, tax revenues, population, even the size and value of financial markets. That is the European Union (EU), the treaty-based organization that (as of 2002) pulled together fifteen great nations of Western and Central Europe, and is poised by 2005 or so to be adding more: perhaps, within a decade from now, as many as fifteen more. Nimble America may always be thought of as outpacing sluggish old Europe, but this is not so: over the past twenty years, the fifteen countries of today's EU have outpaced the United States in terms of economic growth. Only recently, in the late 1990s, did the United States start to leave the Europeans behind, and that growth was partly fuelled by the high-tech stockmarket bubble and associated over-investment in America. Once you eliminate those steroids from the race for economic growth between Europe and America, it starts to look remarkably well balanced over a long period, with bursts of speed and periods of sloth on both sides of the Atlantic.

It is natural to be sceptical about the EU. Anything with a name and set of institutions as boring as the European Union is going to find it hard to be taken seriously. In principle, it is a name no more mundane than 'the United States of America', but its problem is that it still feels abstract, unreal. Germany, France, Great Britain, Italy: those are names that can set the pulse racing, countries with long, eventful histories. None of these countries has recently been setting the world alight in political or economic terms (though Germany's unification was a historic moment), but they remain forces to be reckoned with –

particularly if you consider them as a unit, or as a team, rather than separately.

Moreover, sharing the same land mass there is another force that had to be reckoned with virtually throughout the twentieth century: Russia. It certainly still has to be reckoned with, for it remains not only a nuclear power but also a sometimes truculent one, it has allies in awkward places (for example, Iran, Serbia, Tajikistan) and has borders not just with the rest of Europe but also (across its vast expanse) the Caucasus (Georgia and Azerbaijan), Central Asia (Kazakhstan), Mongolia and China.

Despite being part of Europe and with a history of great contributions to Europe's culture and civilization – to its royal families, as well as to music, literature and the other arts – Russia is generally considered separately from Europe. The reason, in essence, is that it has often recently been fighting wars with the countries to its west, especially with Germany. But what if it were to be considered as part of Europe? After all, Western Europe has found a way to put its old, warring ways behind it, so why shouldn't the same apply to its relationship with Russia?

Russia may be too large, too unwieldy, too independent-minded for it to consider becoming a full member of the European Union during any easily foreseeable period in the fairly near future. But, now that it has shed the separate destiny offered to it by communism, it is surely likely to see much of its future destiny in a closer relationship with the rich countries to its west, for that is what will increase its own wealth, living standards and overall strength.

Arguably the biggest development in world-wide political affairs after the 11 September attacks of 2001 was the rapprochement between Russia and the United States, as the two former foes increasingly found common cause, both over terrorism and instability in Central Asia and over the need to control the spread of weapons of mass destruction. That rapprochement, and the evident friendship between President Vladimir Putin and President George W. Bush, made it seem as if a Russian–American alliance might become a way to bypass or even do down the West Europeans. In the immediate wartime atmosphere, that feeling probably contained some truth. But President Putin's main motive for rallying to America's cause is economic: he thinks Russia is a sick country which needs the economic medicine that only Western trade and investment can bring. Some of that medicine will doubtless come from American multinational companies and from American support for eventual Russian membership of the World Trade Organization. Geography, however, with all its economic implications, demands that the main source of that trade and investment will be on Russia's own continent – that is, Europe. In time, and if its fledgling democracy and market economy achieve any kind of stability, then both Russia and its European neighbours are likely to seek some sort of deepened political and economic association, to cover both trade and security. Russia will have a seat at the European table. On some international issues, Russia and Europe may even seek to act in concert, for many of their interests are likely to be shared.

Looked at in those ways, the future weight of Europe – broadly defined – in the world begins to look formidable, certainly in economic terms. Those writers and historians who share the Marxist frame of mind are apt to conclude from this economic strength that Europe must inevitably, at some point, start to match America in terms of political muscle-power. Economic strength, after all, determines the political sort, in the long term. For the moment, to be sure, on the weightiest matters the great nations of Europe do not speak and act as one, either in foreign policy or when considering the deployment of military power. They are nation-states which co-operate with one another when convenient, but which mostly act and think separately. But, to this line of thinking, some or most of them will eventually wish to form some sort of a political union, well beyond their current arrangements, because the benefits of doing so in terms of power on the world stage will seem overwhelming. And when they do, the world will not have one superpower but will again have two.

Back in 1992, Professor Lester Thurow of the Sloan School of Management at the Massachusetts Institute of Technology, a popular scholar who often makes predictions of future trends, concluded in a book called *Head to Head: The Coming Economic Battle among Japan, Europe and America* that Europe was bound to win the battle he was envisaging. His argument was partly negative. Japan had had a stockmarket crash in 1990, but its main problem was that its economy was too inflexible, too slanted towards the interests of producers.

As for America, he wrote: 'What we do know for certain is that the American system as it is now formulated is not working. That is what falling real wages, stagnant productivity growth, and a growing high-wage trade deficit mean . . .'

It is likely that Professor Thurow now wishes he had not written those sentences, particularly the word 'certain', given the nine-year economic expansion, featuring rapid productivity growth and rising real wages, that began in America almost at the moment he was completing his manuscript. His forecast about America was firmly embedded in the conventional wisdom of the time, which now looks woefully incorrect. But Professor Thurow also had a more positive, longer-term argument about Europe, one that might eventually stand the test of time: this was that as the Europeans steadily integrated their economies, bringing inside their single market the former communist countries of Central and Eastern Europe, perhaps even Russia, so they would not only build the most dynamic economy in the world but their Union would also eventually become so important in world trade that it would be able to bend world trading rules towards its own interests. 'Future historians', wrote Professor Thurow, 'will record that the twenty-first century belonged to the House of Europe.'

Now, in 2002, that prediction looks outlandish. The European Union is far from united, and still looks more a collection of nation-states than a political union, even an embryonic one. It is talking about a new constitution for the EU, but that is because the Union's existing constitutional arrangements, based on treaties, are considered an off-putting muddle. The EU's economies have achieved only dis-appointing growth in recent years, with Germany's in particular show-ing a worrying inclination to return to stagnation or recession almost immediately after emerging from it. Unemployment has remained high almost everywhere outside Britain and the Netherlands. Monetary union, with Europe's much-vaunted new single currency, the euro, was launched successfully in 1999, but since then it has gone on with more of a whimper than a bang, and has not yet fulfilled its backers' hopes that it would serve to accelerate the process of integration and of liberalizing the EU's economies. In foreign and defence policy, too, the Europeans talk a lot about co-operation but still essentially act separately, with their plans for a collective defence force fairly meaningless as long as none of the big countries is willing to spend more on defence.

European governments spend a lot of time sniping at America over missile defence, the war against terrorism, global warming or any number of trade disputes, and many of them seem determined to define themselves (and sometimes their foreign policies) by their distinction from America rather than by any positive characteristics. That tendency is particularly pronounced among the French, in a modern tradition which dates back to the presidency of General Charles de Gaulle (1959–69), but it is shared, to a greater or lesser degree, by others among its European neighbours. Yet this still amounts in practice to little more than posturing, for when push comes to shove Europe's interests and America's seem mostly to coincide, and there is little genuine will to challenge American leadership, or to head in a truly different direction. During the past five years, in particular, the Europeans have often sounded like a bunch of adolescent teenagers, insisting that they must be consulted and listened to, and losing no opportunity of finding small ways in which to rebel. But in the end they are happy that the real adults, the Americans, are there to sort things out, to provide a secure home and to pay the bills.

All that, however, could be a short-term phenomenon. This book is concerned with greater sweeps of history, both back into the twentieth-century past and forward into the future. On such a sweep, it is not at all impossible that Professor Thurow could be proved correct, at least in some form or another. If you leave aside his grandiose claim that the twenty-first century could 'belong' to Europe, whatever that might mean, his broader argument could still carry force. The European land mass is home in all to 800 million people. Of those, close to 400 million already live in the European Union, and another 70 million or so in countries likely to join the EU within the next three or four years. Russia, Ukraine and Turkey, with their 260 million people, are not likely soon to form part of the EU, but they may well find their lives increasingly intertwined with it. The great wealth of the existing EU was built in 1950–90 on the liberalization and integration of just half of the continent, one that was divided by the ideological and military barrier of the Iron Curtain. Now that the curtain has gone and communism has collapsed, the potential for new growth, new trade, new investment between the two halves of the continent is huge, both for those who do join the EU and for those who merely find a peaceful, trading rapprochement with it.

This Europe, wealthy, economically powerful, would certainly be a force to be reckoned with in trade negotiations. The EU already speaks as one on trading matters and already carries great weight in global negotiations, but its further expansion across the continent would make that weight even greater. It would also have formidable interests to defend in other global negotiations – over climate change, for example, or other environmental issues. But would it ever speak as one political entity, with a single army, a single foreign policy, a single commander-in-chief-cum-president, able to look the American president squarely in the eye? Today, that looks unlikely, impossible even. But so, in the 1840s or 1850s, to a sceptical European it may have looked unlikely that the new-born United States of America would ever be led by a strong central government, wishing or willing to exert influence around the globe and to send American troops to fight in far-away wars. By the end of the 1860s there was even a terrible civil war between the northern and southern states of that apparently fissiparous nation. Before a hundred years were out, however, a united and strong America had made decisive interventions in two world wars, and had essentially designed the international institutions that shaped the world after the second one.

*

Could Europe get from here to there? It could, if it wanted to. It could be America's equal, even if to become its clear superior would in truth require American decline as much as European emergence. But there's the crucial question: does it want to? Today, the answer is clear: it (if by 'it' is meant the apparent view of the peoples of the fifteen current members of the European Union) does not want to. It does not seem to want to be unified as a single state or as another entity capable of speaking with a single voice. There are plenty of symbols of European identity to be seen throughout the Union, from flags to coins, but most people's primary sense of identity – and certainly their primary source of political engagement – remains national. But might that change in future? Leaving Russia and Eastern Europe aside, for the moment, and concentrating on the rich countries of Western Europe, the current

EU, the rhetoric of the EU's founding fathers, with their talk of 'ever closer union' (a phrase that still resides in the EU's treaties) would suggest that the Union will indeed want to become a single voice in future, and that it is heading inexorably in that direction. The historical record, however, suggests otherwise.

The record shows that ever since its foundation in 1957 the European Union has had a split personality. It is split, moreover, in several different ways. It is in part a supranational entity, in part an organ of inter-governmental co-operation. It is part liberal, part conservative, part nationalist. It is also in part an economic club and in part a political one. It is formed of some countries – notably Belgium and the Netherlands – that do seem to want to become part of a greater political whole, to echo America's slogan *e pluribus unum*, 'out of the many, one', and even to use that unity as a counterweight to America itself. But it is also formed of some other countries – notably Britain, Denmark and Sweden – that most definitely do not, that want to have the benefit of collective strength in a few areas of activity but which want to remain as independent as possible in other ways. Even the big countries, Germany and France, which have been the Union's driving force throughout its existence, appear confused or at odds: they seem to favour some form of unity but are divided among themselves over what form that unity should take, and each retains a powerful sense of national identity and interest. They seem driven most of all by the desire to increase their own clout in the world by supplementing it with that of their neighbours, not to make a greater Europe, but to use Europe to make a greater France or a greater Germany.

To some extent, this split personality arises simply out of the effort to design and build an entity under the guidance of first six, then nine, then ten, then twelve, and now fifteen governments. It should remind us of the cliché that a camel is really a horse designed by a committee. But there is more to it than that. This split personality can be understood only in the context of Europe's history during the twentieth century. Most people think of that history in just one dimension, but in fact there are three aspects that need to be borne in mind.

The first is the obvious one: Europe's main powers spent much of the first half of the twentieth century at war with one another. Indeed, between 1870 and 1945, France and Germany fought three wars and altered their territorial boundaries each time. Britain took part in two of the wars; Belgium and the Netherlands were invaded in the same two; Italy fought on one side in the 1914–18 war and another in that of 1939–45. The borders of many of the continent's other countries – Finland, Poland, the Czech Republic, Austria, Greece, all of the Balkans, Lithuania, Latvia and Estonia, and many more – changed on several occasions during the century. The habits of nationalism, of interference, and of being defensive about national interests, are deeply ingrained. Europe's twentieth century is thus justifiably and conventionally seen as a story of the perils of nationalism and of its ugly sister, racism; and the European Union, under all its post-war guises of Coal and Steel Community (1951), European Economic Community (1957), European Community (1987) and now EU (1993), is justifiably seen as having the prevention of war as one of its principal goals. Prevention: we should note, therefore, that the EU was born on the basis of a negative.

Yet the twentieth century, and within it the origins of the EU, also offers a different sort of tale about nationalism and then about prevention. This tale is of the dismal consequences of beggar-my-neighbour, or stop-the-world-I-want-to-get-off economic nationalism. That is the second dimension of the EU's history that needs to be borne in mind. Stalin's 'socialism in one country' was a disaster. But so was the capitalism in one country that was attempted throughout Western Europe between 1914 and 1950.

Before 1914 European countries were already quite protectionist, with high tariffs on imports in France and Germany; even Britain, once the high priest of free trade, committed apostasy in 1915. But in the 1920s and 1930s economic nationalism intensified. One immediate cause after 1918 was the creation of new countries – three from the break-up of the Austro-Hungarian empire, five from Russia's borderlands – which gave themselves new tariffs, import quotas and subsidies to protect them both against outsiders and against the formerly integrated markets they had just left. Another was the creation of the Soviet Union, which raised an ideological barrier to trade. But France, Germany and Britain all raised their own barriers, too.

Intra-European enmities loomed large in motivating these measures, along with the financial instability that came with the post-1918 debts and reparations. So did the notion, arising from the First World War, that self-sufficiency, particularly in the possession and processing of basic resources such as iron ore and food, was needed for survival as well as to win wars. But the outside world also played its part. America raised its tariffs in 1921 and 1922, making it harder for the Europeans to export goods in order to repay their war and reconstruction debts to the United States. In 1924 Congress shut off immigration from Eastern and Southern Europe and from Asia, taking away what had for decades been Europe's safety valve. Concern in Europe was growing, as it often does, about the rise of new, low-wage rivals in Latin America, Canada, Japan and Australia. And then, in the biggest blow of all, America raised its average tariff to 59 per cent in 1930, with the Smoot–Hawley tariff act. The result was a devastating drop in world trade and the intensification of the Great Depression.

In response, the Europeans retreated into various forms of isolation. Britain, France and the Netherlands hunkered down with their empires, raising tariffs to give preference to imperial trade and defaulting on their war debts both to each other and to the United States. Fascist Italy went for corporatism, favouring national firms in alliance with government. Nazi Germany, hit hardest by the depression of the 1930s, went for arms manufacture and barter trade.

The result of that history of economic nationalism, stretching from 1914 until the 1940s, was that, by the time the Treaty of Rome to set up the Common Market was signed in 1957 by France, Germany, Italy, Belgium, the Netherlands and Luxembourg, the economic map of Europe was a strange one – not the sort of map that nature would have drawn. Normally, a country's neighbours are among its largest trading partners, certainly on a continent such as Europe with close historical and cultural links. Transport costs favour the neighbours, and it is generally likelier that firms relatively near to one another will establish the trust and depth of mutual knowledge that favour business transactions. Yet in 1957 Germany's biggest trading partner was not France, Italy or Britain but America. During the 1930s, France's third biggest trading partner was its own, impoverished colony of Algeria. Britain's trading patterns were also biased towards the colonies that it was shedding in the 1940s and 1950s. The natural patterns of trade and personal interchange were heavily distorted by two wars and fifty years of economic nationalism. And this is even before mentioning Central and Eastern Europe, whose distorted or stunted trading patterns in the 1930s were further distorted by the Iron Curtain, from the 1940s until 1990.

The European Economic Community, or Common Market, can thus be seen as an attempt to recreate those natural patterns by liberalizing trade and investment flows, albeit at a time when another political divide – the Iron Curtain – was cutting the continent in half. Admittedly, the effort to avoid a repeat of economic nationalism was already being pursued at a global level by GATT, and through the establishment of the IMF and the World Bank in order to help safeguard financial stability. Yet West Europeans wanted to go further than looked likely to be possible at a global level, and they were encouraged to do so by a United States of America that did not want ever to have to bail them out again.

In line with this explanation of the Common Market's launch, it would seem natural to think of the essence of the European idea, and indeed of the Treaty of Rome itself, as being economically liberal, in the classic nineteenth-century sense: it required signatories to renounce nationalist economic policies which had seemed individually desirable but which were collectively disastrous; it and later treaties helped to make the renunciation binding and credible; and it transferred sovereign powers away from meddling national politicians. The free movement of people, goods, capital and services: what could be more liberal than that?

Many of the principal achievements of the EU have indeed been liberal ones. They include: the abolition of internal tariffs (completed between the original six countries in 1968) and the transfer of external trade policy to the EU executive, the European Commission; the outlawing of state subsidies to companies, a process begun in 1983 but not yet completed; the establishment of anti-trust policy at a European level, begun in 1990 (though anti-cartel measures had begun earlier); the outlawing of non-tariff barriers to internal trade, begun by a ruling at the European Court of Justice in 1979 (the *Cassis de Dijon* case) but not properly undertaken until the single-market project of 1985–92; and the adoption on 1 January 1999 by eleven countries of a single currency, transferring power over monetary policy to an independent European Central Bank, in a process that culminated in the adoption by those countries (plus Greece, a later joiner) of euro notes and coins as legal tender, replacing national currencies from 1 January 2002.

Yet all those dates, coming long after 1957, carry a powerful clue. It has taken more than forty years to establish anything like an integrated, 'common' market. Only in 1999 did an integrated financial market begin to develop, thanks to the euro. In many areas – transport, telecommunications and energy, to name but three – the common market is only just beginning to be created. Far from moving too rapidly towards integration, towards a genuinely liberal, single market, as the EU's British detractors often claim, the opposite is the case: it has moved far too slowly.

Why? This is where the third dimension of the EU's foundation and of its history in the twentieth century comes in, as at least a preliminary explanation. It is that the moment when this peacemaking, economically liberal entity came to be created was also a moment when a different, illiberal set of economic ideas had become fashionable: central planning. They were fashionable, as Chapter 7 will argue, because of the experience of the Second World War in which organization and planning, led from the top, had been of paramount importance; and because of the perception that the newly powerful Soviet Union was doing something mysteriously right, and that that something (shared with Hitler's Germany in the 1930s and 1940s) must be its use of central planning.

It was an idea of the moment and, because of post-war reconstruction, it was perceived to be a necessity of the moment. Even for those whose belief in central planning was lukewarm, what better way could there be to bring together the former combatants of two world wars than to oblige their governments to sit regularly around tables, drawing up plans? That was certainly the belief of the Frenchman who was the single most important architect of the Coal and Steel Community of 1951 and the Common Market of 1957, and who is even now venerated almost as a god by Euro-enthusiasts in Brussels: Jean Monnet. His background and expertise was as a planner.

He was not a planner in the style of the Soviet Gosplan, nor did the birth of the Common Market seek fully to match the efforts of the men in Moscow. But alongside the notion that the six founding members were creating a larger 'space' for free, private activity, ran also the idea that in certain sectors nothing could beat a good plan, put together by good planners, setting targets, allocating quotas, co-ordinating national activities. And following that example, there was a further founding fact of the Treaty of Rome: that French farmers successfully insisted on agriculture being given special protection and care within the new Common Market, and that the protection should be led at European rather than national level, an aim given its full form when the common agricultural policy (CAP) was established in 1964. The cliché that the EEC was founded on a trade-off between subsidies for French farmers and access to French markets for German industrialists is an over-simplification, given that it took seven years before this arrangement was consummated in the CAP, but it is one that nevertheless contains a great deal of truth.

Once established, and especially once laid down in a treaty, European policies are hard to alter in any material way, and extremely hard to reverse or abolish. It is hard to get a whole swathe of countries to agree on a policy, and harder still to change the policy once some of them have been reaping the benefits. That is why the CAP, nearly four decades after its foundation, remains the EU's biggest collective spending policy by far, consuming half the EU annual budget. It is a planner's delight – or nightmare – under which bureaucrats in Brussels, accountable to national politicians only through Europe's Council of Ministers, seek to direct the type and quantity of foodstuffs produced by farmers all around the EU, fine-tuning the subsidies and quotas for products as wide-ranging as linseed, or sheepmeat (the strange EU name for lamb), or olive oil, and, increasingly in the 1980s and 1990s, paying farmers to stop farming some parts of their land. There is certainly nothing liberal about it.

Despite being planned at a supranational level, the CAP has become a nationalist feeding trough. It is a case study of how a system of subsidies is almost impossible to dismantle once it has been created, for farmers in every country lobby their politicians to maintain subsidies, quotas and rules that favour them. It is also highly protectionist and throttles poor countries' farm exports. A study published in 2001 by Patrick Messerlin, a French economist, for the Institute for International Economics in Washington, DC, estimated that the total cost to EU consumers of its external protectionism – including that on manufactured goods as well as on food – could be as high as 93 billion euros ($84 billion, at 2001 exchange rates) a year. As Mr Messerlin put it in his study (*Measuring the Costs of Protection in Europe*), European trade policy has

a very distinctive flavour: it has a high proportion of political content, because the EC has no other way (foreign policy or army) to express its political views; it can be sticky and chaotic, because it is based on cast-iron, sometimes inconsistent, often poorly drafted (with regard to external relations) Treaties; and it relies on an institutional process that tends to be intrinsically biased toward old-fashioned ways of economic government.

The common agricultural policy is the biggest contradiction to any idea that the EU's purpose is one of freedom, liberalism or even integration. But it is not alone, either at a European or at a national level. Indeed, even among the original six members, the liberal ideas of unity and free movement have been widely subverted by national policies. Subsidies, non-tariff barriers, closed financial systems, national champions: all these have been used by EU members to keep their economies apart ever since 1957. The EU has been fighting a constant battle against the divisive, competing tendencies of national governments. Meanwhile, however, countries have sought to divert European Union powers and resources to their own national benefit, and to establish at a supranational level the protectionism and government intrusion that liberals hate.

Regional and structural funds, which have been designed to improve the infrastructure and industrial development of poorer regions within Europe by using collective resources, provide another feeding trough. The coal and steel treaty, set up in 1951, was used in the 1970s and 1980s to delay the restructuring of those old industries and to establish a *de facto* cartel. Countries vie to turn external trade negotiations to the benefit of their local pressure groups. Social rules – the so-called 'social chapter' – have in practice protected existing labour legislation in France and Germany against competition from smaller, poorer countries such as Ireland, Spain and Portugal.

A few European members still believe in co-ordinating industrial planning, research, protection or subsidies at a European level. Others believe collective action, in an economic space much larger than a single country, is the way to keep change (that is, Americanization in the 1970s and 1990s, or Japanese competition in the 1980s) at bay. What is now thought of as the European social model, with extensive protection of jobs and generous social insurance (a model essentially created in the 1960s and 1970s, and then extended thereafter), is deemed to be itself in need of the protection that comes both from collective European clout, from a willingness not to undermine each other's welfare states, and from the reassuring existence of a large European market for local firms.

This centralizing, or interventionist, strain is not at all the monopoly, or dominant idea among Europeans, even among the European zealots. Some think the use of European rules is the only way to make their national politicians act as economic liberals. In that they echo the view of Friedrich von Hayek, who in his seminal book warning of the spread of central planning, *The Road to Serfdom* (1944), argued that a federal Europe would be a good way to allow the rule of law to govern economic and social activities rather than the rule of national bureaucrats or politicians. Other European enthusiasts see all this economic and trade stuff as just a price to be paid for the establishment of a unit large enough to bargain on equal terms with the United States and Japan, and to carry foreign-policy clout.

Nevertheless, the resulting picture is muddled and often contradictory. It is a picture of an entity which has achieved a great deal, which has succeeded in burying its region's destructive past, but which has done so in a manner destined to make it hobble rather than sprint into the future, so heavy are its burdens and contradictions. Recently, with stronger competition enforcement, the single currency and the single-market programme, the liberal tendency has gained some ground. As the Union becomes larger it is becoming harder to operate an activist supranational government, harder to pursue the old interventionist, planning tendency, which has in any case gone somewhat out of fashion. It is widely assumed that enlargement of the Union will 'inevitably' mean that the infamous CAP will have to be reformed, possibly drastically. And liberal optimists think the euro will eventually force national governments to free up their own labour and goods markets because competition across borders will be intensified by the ability to compare prices, and because more highly regulated and costly countries will then lose out and suffer higher unemployment. This transformational ambition for the euro has not come to pass in its first few years of existence, but that is not long in the broad sweep of history, nor in the life of currencies.

The current drift is a more liberal one. Moreover, work is under way on a new constitution for Europe, a new settlement or treaty to govern a new relationship between the institutions and nations of an enlarged European Union. An inter-governmental conference is due to discuss ideas for such a thing in 2003 and 2004, advised by a constitutional convention that began its deliberations in 2002. Within a decade, the European Union could, in theory, have both enlarged greatly and have established a more stable and enduring constitutional framework – and it could be doing so in a more liberal, free-trading manner. At that point the suspicions that now obstruct collaboration between the various factions among the nation-states could disappear, and thus the way could be open for broader, political integration, under the restraint of a new constitution, but capable of forming a genuine European consensus behind common foreign and defence policies.

That, however, looks too optimistic a forecast. The drift towards liberalism is not at all immutable. It will be challenged by recessions, in which the pressure of producers and of trade unions for greater protection and for government intervention will intensify, as it always does. It is already being challenged by fears in many countries of large-scale immigration, and these have helped to strengthen the support of extreme right-wing parties in several countries, including Austria, France, Germany and the Netherlands, that are also hostile to the European Union. Hopes of reforming the CAP will be challenged both by the conservatism of those who currently benefit from the CAP and by a widespread desire among environmentalists to replace the CAP with a new network of subsidies, rules and quotas to encourage organic farming and conservation.

The drift towards liberal unity will also be challenged by pressure from the single currency itself, under which one monetary policy is supposed to fit all currency members (twelve, as of 2002), and even national fiscal policies are subject to collectively imposed constraints. The currency is a unifying force, of course, for it will induce more companies to think of Western Europe as a more-or-less single market, will encourage consumers to do more shopping (or, at least, comparison-shopping) across borders, and will make it harder for governments to maintain national tax and regulatory policies that make their countries' prices higher for easily tradable goods. Politically, though, this unity also has the potential of bringing about explosive disunity. During deep recessions, the single, one-size-fits-all monetary policy could pit national politicians against the European Central Bank, as a feeling grows of national impotence in the face of rising unemployment. It is not at all improbable that one or more member countries might withdraw from the euro and reintroduce their national currencies at some stage during the currency's first decade.

There could be a moment, in other words, in the depths of a recession, in which one government is under pressure to take action against unemployment at home, but meanwhile the European Central Bank refuses to cut interest rates or other countries refuse to allow that government to expand its public spending. Opposition parties would then have a field day, stirring up anti-European emotions. The result would be a country's withdrawal from the euro and its reintroduction of a national currency. It would be a drastic step, taken only *in extremis*. But it is not at all inconceivable. Countries have introduced new currencies before: recent examples include the Czech Republic and Slovakia which had to replace their joint currencies when Czechoslovakia was dissolved in 1993; and Argentina, which introduced new currencies repeatedly during the 1980s in its hyperinflationary period, and which also did so in 2002.

*

Compared with pesky single countries such as the United States, China and Japan, the European Union does offer an advantage for the writer seeking to jump beyond the short term and to identify the things that will matter decades ahead, during the twenty-first century. Countries tend to hop around in response to events and to electoral changes. That is also true of the fifteen individual members of the EU, of course. But in their collective endeavours, the countries in the Union actually tend to set their course some way ahead. Some of the most important aspects of their destiny are set in train years earlier and find their full effect many years afterwards. Like the common agricultural policy, such collective agreements are hard to change, once they have been painfully or ponderously agreed to by the Union's members.

One such project was the adoption of the single currency: first formally proposed in 1971, with a framework set up in the Treaty of Maastricht of 1992, a formal launch in 1999 and full use of notes and coins in 2002. Another, just as important, is the enlargement of the European Union to take in countries of Central and Eastern Europe, among others. This was proposed by several West European leaders in 1989–91, as the Berlin Wall came down, as communism collapsed along with the Iron Curtain, and as the Soviet Union was dissolved. The first group of new members are likely to join in a 'big bang' in 2005, bringing in Poland, Hungary, the Czech Republic, Slovakia, Slovenia, Latvia, Lithuania and Estonia. Many others will follow during the next decade. The borders of the European Union will soon extend far to the east, to Russia, Ukraine and Belarus. Each phase of expansion may encounter its own obstacles. But the push towards further expansion is likely to endure. Once the EU sets a direction and starts to move, its momentum tends to be relentless.

Two things will follow from enlargement. One is that much, probably most, of the energies of the European Union in the next two decades will be devoted to the task of adjusting to the arrival of all these new members, and of helping those new members adjust to their own arrival. What that means is that there will be little time for, and even less prospect of, a formal political union being created. One might have been possible had the EU remained a consistent size. Enlargement to the east means that the terms and conditions of any such political union will keep on changing, in such a way as to keep it elusive for its advocates, irrelevant for its opponents.

The other reality for Europe's next quarter-century or more is that, one way or another, the European Union's nature, behaviour and policies will be shaped by its emerging relationship with the other countries of Eastern Europe, most notably with the giant among them, Russia, as well by the EU's relationship with the most important country to its south-east, Turkey. Both are decidedly awkward neighbours. During the past two centuries both built empires to rival those of the West Europeans and, as their empires collapsed, left marks, enmities, friendships and traditions in the countries from which they withdrew. Both have sought in their recent histories to define themselves by their differences with Western Europe, not their similarities; by their separate destinies, not their close relationship. In both cases, however, today's logic implies a reversal of that twentieth-century strategy in the twenty-first. Turkey, by repeatedly seeking to join the European Union, has already acknowledged that logic. Russia, which is by far the more important of the two, has not accepted that logic and applied to join, at least not formally. But the likelihood must be that it will do both.

Russia has long been proud of its separateness, of its distinctive nature, of its Slavic spirit. It fought the bloodiest battles of the Second World War trying to protect itself from Germany. For forty-five years it was one of the world's two superpowers, and it still possesses one of the two largest nuclear arsenals. It sent the first man into space and was a close contender to put the first men on to the moon. It is a country rich in oil, gas and other natural resources. It has a population which, at nearly 150 million, is 80 per cent larger than Europe's second largest country (Germany, at 82 million). All these factors argue against the prospect of a Russia seeking close congress with its western co-Europeans. Other factors, however, push strongly in the other direction. Chief among them is the fact that Russia at the turn of the twenty-first century is poor and weak, with a shrinking population and a declining life expectancy. And it no longer has the ideological motivation (communism) which made it pretend it could be rich and strong.

Plenty of Russian politicians and pundits think their country should follow an independent path back to greatness, and many will doubtless continue to argue for this in future. But the strategic question is what in the absence of communism such independence might mean? The re-adoption of capitalism and the gradual move towards full participation in international trade – now that China has joined the World Trade Organization and begun to adhere to its rules, Russia is bound to follow – mean that in economics Russia will in future follow a path of inter-dependence. That is the only means by which it will be able to regain its former strength. As it emerged from communism, in 1992, the first year after the fall of the Soviet Union, Russia's wealth, measured by GDP per head of population, was a mere $4,600 a year. That placed it slightly poorer than Poland and Hungary, less than half as rich as Greece or South Korea, for example, and barely a quarter as rich as the West European average. Since then, Russia has fallen even further behind. Only capitalism, stimulated by trade and foreign direct investment in Russia, will enable it to become wealthier. And that has already, despite a very rough first decade back in the market economy, pushed it closer to the West Europeans.

In 1913, when trade within most of Europe was rather freer than it became between the world wars, 45 per cent of Russia's trade was with Germany. In 2000, a mere 9 per cent of Russia's trade was with that country, and 31 per cent with the European Union as a whole. Given its currently unsophisticated range of products, the nearest countries to Russia are initially likely to be its main trading partners as long as they have some money with which to trade (a point which reduces Ukraine's importance). That means the countries of Central Europe, including Poland, Hungary, the Czech Republic and the Baltic States as well as Germany. By 2005, most of those main trading partners will be in the European Union, however. Taken as a whole, the EU will be far and away Russia's most important trading interlocutor. The chances are that it will also provide most of whatever foreign investment goes into Russia, just as it has been the main source of such investment into the Central European countries. Politically, summit meetings with the American president will remain flattering and important, for as long as Russia remains a big nuclear power. In reality, meetings with the German chancellor and with the EU's trade commissioner will be the encounters that matter most.

Economic links are not everything. And it takes two to trade, so this economic interdependence with Europe need not mean dependence, unless Russia falls substantially into Europe's debt. Given its geography, Russia will always have its special interests that mark it apart from Europe, in the Caucasus and in Central Asia in particular. It is even an Asian power, with a Pacific coast and with natural concerns about the stability of the Koreas and of Japan, let alone of China. Even as its democracy stabilizes and matures, Russia may remain determined to use brutal methods to suppress what it sees as troublesome domestic minorities, as it has done in Chechnya since 1995. If so, that too will set it apart from the EU, just as the brutal suppression of its Kurdish minority has set Turkey apart.

In considering the world stage, however, rather than very local interests, a question must be asked about what Russia could achieve standing entirely on its own. If it were not for its nuclear weapons, which it cannot really afford, it would be a Euro-Asian Brazil, big in land area and in population, important to its neighbours, but, thanks to its continued poverty, not a power that matters a great deal in world affairs. Given economic development, it could matter more than it does now. But it would require a quite extraordinary turnaround, sustained over many decades, for it again to be one of the world's leading powers – it would have to 'do a Japan'. And even Japan has essentially built its international position around its alliance with the United States rather than setting its own course.

Perhaps the option of emulating wealthy Japan, but as a nuclear power, might lie half a century ahead. There is plenty of potential for economic growth in Russia, if the country can ever establish a proper rule of law, stable institutions and property rights. In the meantime, though, the strategy of France, Russia's old European friend (setting aside Napoleon's attempted invasion), will surely gradually increase in its allure. France's belief ever since it co-founded the EU has been that it is better able to achieve a world-wide influence through an alliance with its European neighbours, particularly Germany, than on its own. Russia is in the same position. The legacy of the communist period has, in recent years, led many to foresee an emerging alliance between Russia and China. In future, though, Russia is going to have more interests in common with its biggest trading partner, the EU. On most topics the rich, developed EU will also be a more powerful and attractive ally. Russia's interests, like France's, will best be served by working together with Europe.

A similar logic is likely to prevail in security matters. NATO – the North Atlantic Treaty Organization – was originally set up in the post-war years to oppose the Soviet Union's own 'Warsaw Pact'. Its expansion during the 1990s to include countries in Central and Eastern Europe still reflected that history; the new members were keen to join in order to buttress their security against pressure from their big eastern neighbour. In time, however, that motivation is likely to fade away as trading and other economic links build up between the former foes. Just as it is now hard to imagine why Germany could ever again think it advantageous to invade France (or indeed Poland or the Czech Republic), it is becoming hard to imagine why Russia should ever in future think of bullying or invading the Baltic States or Poland. For unstable, impoverished Georgia or Kazakhstan the same cannot be said: it is still easy to imagine Russia marching in during a future time of trouble. But that is not likely to apply to Poland, or other new members of the European Union.

There is another way of looking at this. In the past few years, the main way in which Russian nationalists have made their country a continued force in world affairs has been by being a small-time troublemaker: by offering sympathy and support (for a time) to Serbia's dictator, Slobodan Milosevic, and Iraq's Saddam Hussein; or by selling military technology to countries that are out of favour with America, such as Iran. These tactics have achieved little. How much more could be achieved by becoming part of a European alliance? Russia would then be one of Europe's three nuclear powers (France and Britain are the others) and would give Europe three votes in the UN Security Council. Like the EU, for much of the time Russia would want to align its policies with those of the United States. But like the EU, on occasion it will want to oppose the United States. An alliance ranging from the Atlantic to beyond the Urals, loose and informal as it would almost certainly be, would nevertheless be a formidable sight – even from Washington, DC.

*

Let us return, now, to the question posed at the start of this chapter. Can Europe become a single 'it'? The current trend does not suggest the imminent or even likely formation of a tightly knit European solidarity, a genuine political, and politically effective, superpower to rival the United States, or at least to throw its weight around in the world. Feelings are too contradictory. Politics, and political movements, remain too national, as do people's primary sense of identity. Europeans feel accustomed to their governments collaborating rather than fighting, and to visiting each other's countries for peaceful reasons rather than hostile ones, but they do not feel patriotically European. They feel more differences with one another than similarities. In principle, that could be no different from Americans feeling, for example, Texan first and American second, but although European identities are similarly split (but even more: Catalan first, Spanish second, European third), the dominance of regional and national over their European feelings is much greater. One or two small countries may exist where the sense of national identity is so weak as to make citizens feel that they are chiefly Europeans; Belgium springs to mind. But that is not true, or becoming true, of France, Germany, Britain, Spain or Italy, and it will not be true of the new members in an enlarged EU, for Poles and Hungarians and Czechs feel proudly Polish, Hungarian and Czech. Russians certainly feel emphatically Russian.

Could anything make things turn out differently? What could occur to make Europeans decide they need to become Europeans? The only plausible answer is an international crisis, or series of crises, in which Europe's politically fragmented nature becomes a serious threat to the survival of its people and of its freedoms – in other words, fear. Ambition on the part of European enthusiasts is unlikely to be enough. Nor are the purely theoretical benefits of unity, of integration, of forming a superpower, likely to cut enough ice with electorates. Such things appeal chiefly to élites, to political leaders themselves, not to voters.

It is hard, now, in the peaceable age of early twenty-first-century Europe, to imagine what such a crisis could be. Compared with the countries of Asia, the big European powers feel fairly safe. It is true that they live not far from some trouble-zones, in which countries are seeking to develop long-range missiles and weapons of mass destruction: Iran, Iraq, Syria, perhaps eventually other countries in the Middle East and around the Persian Gulf. But this threat does not seem to stir the blood of Europeans. They certainly no longer fear each other. The only big question before them is whether they might in future discover new reasons to fear Russia. For the reasons explored extensively above, this looks unlikely. Even if that view proves to be wrong, Europe already has NATO to look after its security.

In the late 1990s the Europeans made their first real efforts to build a genuinely European defence capability, agreeing to a British and

French initiative to develop a European 'rapid reaction force', to be co-ordinated with NATO but able to operate separately from it. What they had in mind for this force was deployment in a trouble-spot such as the Balkans or North Africa. This new force nevertheless caused some concern in Washington, where the Clinton and Bush administrations feared that the force, by duplicating resources and planning, might end up undermining NATO. But the biggest reason to be sceptical about it is not the possibility of duplication but the probability that, at present, it will be ineffective. The reason is that the European countries spend too little on defence to be able to put together a viable force, and what they do spend is devoted too heavily to maintaining conscript armies and too little to equipping them for modern warfare.

No large European country comes close to matching the more than 4 per cent of annual GDP that the United States spends on defence. France at 2.7 per cent and Britain at 2.6 per cent came the closest in 2000, but the other big countries spend much less: Germany (1.6 per cent), Spain (1.3 per cent), Italy (2 per cent) and the Netherlands (1.8 per cent) reveal the pattern. If Europe is ever to build a defence force and capability of its own, its governments will have to spend a lot more. With other pressures on their finances, including the rules of the European single currency itself, they are unlikely to be persuaded to do so by idealism or the intellectual appeal of unity.

To force that to change, Europe's post-1945 alliance with, and even military dependence on, the United States would have to have been shattered. America would have to have withdrawn its bases from Europe, and to have shown that it would no longer – or could no longer – meet its NATO commitment to consider any attack on one member country as an attack on all. That would require a truly drastic change both in America itself and in its global circumstances. It would also require, most probably, a sense that America had become actively hostile to Europe, perhaps not in any military sense but in terms of policy and interests.

Can that be likely? Certainly, America and Europe have been drifting gently apart for a long time. The closely bound alliance of the cold war years is no longer necessary; in future it will surely become much looser. Co-operation in multilateral institutions and processes is becoming more difficult. But hostility or contemptuous neglect? Given the mutual interests the countries on either side of the Atlantic have built up and developed, and given the depth and breadth of corporate and personal links that criss-cross the ocean, this is extremely hard to envisage. Spats, yes; sulks, certainly. The disagreements after the 11 September attacks over how far to widen the war on terrorism, and over how much support to give to Israel, offered a fine example. But to produce the sort of hostility that would make Europeans feel they needed to unify for their own future security and survival requires something rather more than such niggles or disagreements. It would probably require the complicating actions of a third party, such as Russia or China, causing mischief and, most crucially, causing Americans and Europeans to think their interests had diverged. Or it would require a considerable and, from a global point of view, catastrophic, decline in America's strength and leadership.

None of this looks worthy of being predicted. Professor Thurow's vision of a European economic and political superpower looks no more than a theoretical possibility. It is more likely that although the European countries will indeed prosper economically as they develop and integrate with one another, their collective endeavour will be characterized more by muddling through, a process hampered by their contradictory policies and goals. That muddling through will, on occasion, be given a stiffer character and purpose amid a temporary difference of opinion with the United States; it may even, as predicted in this chapter, involve a loose and informal alliance with Russia. But it will still be a muddle.

The European Union is a success, measured by the continued desire of countries to join it, and by the failure of any member so far to leave. But it is a muddle, chronically lacking a clear direction, for reasons that are likely to endure. Its muddles are not of a sort to pitch nation against nation, to threaten dissolution or break-up; but, short of a mind-concentrating crisis, they are likely to keep the EU as an envious, but fragmented force. Western Europe is a collection of rich and stable countries that will remain so, and will be further invigorated by the maturing of democracy and capitalism in Central and Eastern Europe. Shared envy of the United States and a mutual interest in trade and investment will bring Russia to Europe's side. Muddling through, finding a way to accommodate each country's concerns among an ever-widening group of countries, is the most maddening aspect of the European Union and the main reason not to expect it to play a dominant role in the world. But it is also its greatest talent for survival.

6

Turbulence and Terror

The human world is not, by its nature, a peaceful and stable place. It has certainly never been so at any time in its history. For Thomas Hobbes in seventeenth-century Britain, life was 'nasty, brutish and short'; now, given improvements in life expectancy, for many people living in the world's more turbulent regions life has simply become brutish and long, with niceness or nastiness a bit of a lottery. During the past hundred years, wars have been fought between great powers and between small powers, between colonial empires and their oppressed peoples, between the regions or tribes of individual countries, over ideas and over land, over resources and over peoples, over identity and over personalities.

The bloodiest wars involving Europeans and Americans took place in the first half of the twentieth century, making war now seem a fairly distant thought to many people on both sides of the Atlantic. But this is not the case for those living in Congo, Angola, Ethiopia, Afghanistan, Chechnya, Georgia, Rwanda, Azerbaijan, Israel, Sri Lanka, Kashmir, Yugoslavia, Colombia, Somalia, Yemen or Sierra Leone – to name but a few of the places in which armed conflicts have taken place during the past twenty years. Then there are the victims of terrorism or just terror-inducing slaughters, sometimes associated with those war-zones and sometimes not, who will also think violence is something painfully close to home: 8,000 or so Afghans in Mazar-i-Sharif in 1998; many thousands of Bosnians in Srebrenica in 1995; 3,000 people in Northern Ireland over thirty years of 'troubles'; 800,000 Tutsis in Rwanda in 1994; 3,000 residents of New York and Washington in 2001; and many more, all over the world.

Immediately after 11 September 2001, it seemed unlikely that that final example would ever be included in a general list of this sort. The flying on a beautiful September morning of two hijacked commercial airliners into New York's World Trade Center, of a third into the Pentagon in Washington, DC, and of a fourth into the ground in Pennsylvania (in what for its hijackers was a failed mission) felt like an event in a category all of its own. And in some respects it was. This was an event using wholly new techniques of mass murder, the first successful large-scale assault on American soil since Pearl Harbor in 1941, the first on the American mainland since the British set fire to Washington in 1814. The perpetrators had committed suicide in order to bring the attack about, and appeared to consider their martyrdom glorious. It was not the first attempt at such an assault – terrorists with the same background as those in 2001 had tried to blow up one of the World Trade Center towers in 1993, and then Los Angeles airport in 2000 – but success is far more shocking and attention-grabbing than failure. It was far and away the deadliest attack on the world's leading power since the Vietnam War in the 1960s. And it was an attack not only on that superpower, not only one designed to spread fear and terror, intended to draw attention to the 'cause' of the perpetrators, but also one aimed at the symbols of modern, urban capitalism, the tallest skyscrapers in the very home of skyscrapers and of Western capitalism, New York City.

The idea that it was an event in a category of its own gained further force from the rhetoric of the man ultimately behind the attacks, Osama bin Laden. Following the attacks he became the most notorious and well-known man on the planet, but it is worth recapping that he is (or was?) a Muslim born in Saudi Arabia to a family originally from Yemen, who had established terrorist training camps first in Sudan and then, once he was expelled from there, in Afghanistan. He had inherited some wealth from his family, which runs a successful Saudi construction business, and had received his first military training and arms in Afghanistan during the 1980s as a *Mujahideen* fighter against the Soviet Union. With his attacks in the 1990s and in 2001 bin Laden claimed that he was launching a *jihad* against America, an Arabic word capable of wide interpretation (ranging between effort, struggle and war), but taken in his case to mean a holy war. He and his followers were calling on Muslims everywhere to rise up against the infidel, to drive the infidel from Islam's holy lands and, in the end, to bring about its collapse.

The attacks were thus seen by some as the first example of 'the clash of civilizations', a phrase given currency by a Harvard professor, Samuel Huntington, first in an article in *Foreign Affairs* in 1993 and then in the title of his book expanding the idea in 1996. He had forecast that the post-cold-war world would be shaped by conflicts, physical or otherwise, between the world's seven or eight main cultural groups. Here were two of them – Islam and the Judaeo-Christian West – already in confrontation.

But was it really such a clash, was this really an event of a unique, or at least new, character? The question matters chiefly for our view of the future. For if the 11 September attacks were a new sort of event, then that might herald big changes in life and in geopolitics in the next few decades. We should expect not just a 'new world disorder' of the sort with which we had become wearily familiar during the 1990s, but a deeper, more alarming challenge to the very basis of Western civilization, one that would be visible not just on our television screens but on the streets of our own cities.

*

The first answer to the question is that history does not support the idea that bin Laden and his al-Qaeda terror network have formed a wholly new category of challenge. Their challenge is large and worrying. Technology could in some respects make it more deadly than previous ones. But it is not new.

To see why, it is as well to separate the main elements of al-Qaeda's approach and apparent philosophy: the use of suicide, in a death-cult or cult of martyrdom; the notion that the West's values are depraved, degenerate and offensive to a true human soul; the idea of a holy war; the belief that salvation lies in being able to live according to one's true identity and traditions; the belief that Arab, or Muslim, peoples are particularly oppressed; the use of small 'cells' of fighters or activists to conduct a war supposedly in the interest of hundreds of millions of people. Once these have been eliminated as possible sources of novelty or specialness, there may well, nevertheless, be some other elements that could have a notable effect on the future. Those elements are likely, however, to be shared with the other potential sources of turbulence and terror.

Martyrdom, in suicide attacks, is an especially frightening thought. It is hard to take precautions against those seeking to use it. By the time someone has been identified as intending to carry out such an attack, it is generally too late and that person has in any case decided to die, taking many others with him, so he is hard to deter. (These suicide attackers are almost always men, but not invariably; there have frequently been female suicide bombers in Sri Lanka in recent years, for example, and the first Palestinian female suicide attack took place in January 2002.) To the modern Western mind martyrdom is also frighteningly irrational, implying either a way of thinking that must be inhuman or one that is the result of brainwashing. But while martyrdom is fortunately not common, it has nevertheless occurred many times in the past century. And, taken most simply, the feeling that a noble death may give meaning to a life of anguish, disappointment or despair has not been at all uncommon.

For example, Yukio Mishima, a Japanese novelist, used his suicide in 1970 both as a noble, celebratory act (he had written of such acts in his novels) and as a way of drawing attention to his belief that the Japanese spirit was being eroded and degraded by modernization. He even recruited his own private army, and led them into Japan's defence agency headquarters in Tokyo, where he took his own life. In the end it was a rather pathetic gesture, but it had been intended to be a grand one. In an article in the *New York Review of Books* in January 2002 about 'Occidentalism', or hostility to the West, Ian Buruma and Avishai Margalit (an Anglo-Dutch writer and an Israeli professor, respectively) cited also a cult that surrounded 145,000 German soldiers who died in 1914 in a sequence of futile attacks at the Battle of Langemarck. The First World War was full of such futility, but these deaths were celebrated as heroic sacrifices as part of the propaganda effort inside Germany concerning the war. The words of Theodor Koerner, a writer in the early nineteenth century, were quoted in remembrance of the martyrs: 'Happiness lies only in sacrificial death.'

Cults of heroism, of the nobility not only of risking your death in a just cause but simply of risking your death, have been common features of martial cultures. The Japanese *kamikaze* pilots of the Second World War were, of course, the most famous suicide attackers; what is striking, or perhaps alarming, about them is how numerous they were. But in many ways the same spirit lay at the heart of the appeal of Nazism in Germany and fascism in Italy, the idea that greatness could be achieved if only people could join together in a heroic mass movement, putting aside their selfish individual interests – which could ultimately include their own lives.

Young people, who feel for some reason frustrated, disappointed, rejected or angry, have given up their lives in violence and war before, and will do so again, horrible though the thought is to someone who feels differently. There is also a long tradition among rebel groups of using opposition to the West as a rallying point, of arguing that modern, Western ways are destroying something more genuine, more real, more valuable, more traditional. That was one of Mishima's cries, too, about Japan. Such opposition has often had a religious flavour, for one central characteristic of modern Western societies is that they are secular; many citizens within them may be religious, but the laws by which the society is run are secular, as is the state. This secular character is taken as a threat or as a useful opponent by those in other countries who think that their own religion dictates laws from a god that ought to have primacy over laws from mere men. Such beliefs bring powerful political implications, for they give a self-selected group of interpreters of God's laws enormous sway with their adherents, as long as they can maintain their credibility with those adherents. Extreme appeals to absolutism and purity, combined with the useful identification of a Western threat to those values, have often been effective ways of obtaining that credibility.

That was what happened in a previous Islamic revolution, one that successfully pitched the revolutionaries against the United States as well as against their previous government: the revolution in Iran in 1979. A notable feature of the overthrow of Iran's ruler, the Shah, was also the fact that the overthrow was supported by many pro-Western liberals in that country, who felt the pro-Western Shah was a despot, and did not think (wrongly, as it turned out) that Ayatollah Khomeini could be worse. In revolutionary Iran, although the new 1979 constitution included some democratic elements, the religious clerics were given dominance; among the clerics, power was concentrated in the hands of the Supreme Leader, Khomeini, and a handful of senior clerics known as 'Objects of Emulation'.

The appeal to pure, genuine, spiritual values was also a feature of Japan's military campaign in Asia in the 1930s and 1940s, which was said to be an effort to cleanse Asia by removing the imperialism of Britain, the Netherlands and France and thus purging Asia of Western ideas. The true Asian identity could then shine forth, as part of a 'Greater East Asia Co-prosperity Sphere'. In this case the divinity in whose name it was all being done was the Japanese Emperor, supposedly a descendant through an unbroken line from Amaterasu, the sun goddess.

Moreover, the desire among Arab nations to regain a lost pride and a lost independence of thought and action is a long-running one. All are keenly aware that, like the Chinese, the Islamic nations were more advanced than the Europeans until early modern times. Throughout history, Arabs and other Middle Easterners were mainly ruled and suppressed by fellow-Muslims, by the Mongols who converted to Islam, and later in Turkey's Ottoman empire from the fifteenth to the nineteenth century. That pattern had already been rudely interrupted by Russian victory in non-Arab Persia (now Iran) in 1828. A century later, however, Ottoman rule collapsed and was replaced by varieties of colonial domination, chiefly by Britain and France, but also intermittently by other European powers.

Turkey's own Kemal Atatürk brought about a modernizing revolution in his country from 1919 onwards. In the 1950s Egypt's Gamal Abdel Nasser threw off both his country's monarchy and the remnants of colonial domination of the Suez Canal. Algeria fought for its independence from France in the 1950s. Colonel Qadaffi took power in Libya in a coup in 1969, and proclaimed himself as a beacon of pan-Arabism. In 1973, following the third war against Israel since that country was established in their midst in 1948, the oil-producing Arab states, led by Saudi Arabia, announced that they planned to restrict oil supplies to Europe, Japan and North America in a bid to exert their collective but independent power against the West. That time, known to most as the first oil shock, was actually the high point so far of pan-Arab co-operation. It was a period of extensive Arab terrorism, chiefly (but not only) perpetrated by the Palestine Liberation Organization and Yasser Arafat's terrorist group within it, Al Fatah – most notably at the 1972 Munich Olympics where terrorists held hostage and then murdered eleven members of the Israeli team. But it did not get the Arabs very far (although it made some oil producers a lot richer).

Many *jihads* have been declared against the West, by various political and religious leaders over the years. In numerous countries, governments have chosen, or been forced, to adopt more 'Islamic' laws and practices, including not just the Arab nations but also Pakistan, Bangladesh, Indonesia, Nigeria and Afghanistan. Meanwhile, despite oil, the economic record has been relatively poor. Of the Muslim nations only Malaysia has achieved consistent rises in standards of living; Indonesia did for a time but then collapsed after 1997. Even Saudi Arabia, despite sitting on the world's biggest oil reserves, has only managed to reach a GDP per head that is a third less than that of the poorest European Union country (Portugal). It is also a highly unequal society, with gold bath-taps aplenty among the royal family but poverty abundant among ordinary people.

The final characteristic of the al-Qaeda terrorists is their pursuit of messianic goals on behalf of a mass movement, by using small cells of fighters. The most successful user of such tactics was Vladimir Ilyich Lenin, whose Bolshevik terrorists were *jihadi*s in the cause of international socialism. As long as Lenin was merely a terrorist, or what is known today to scholars and the more pompous pundits as 'a non-state actor', all he could do was issue propaganda and cause occasional bouts of trouble. The Bolsheviks and others suffered a setback in 1905, when a revolt was suppressed in Russia. But in 1917 they grabbed the opportunity provided by Russia's failure in the First World War to seize power there, and hence to gain the resources of one of the world's biggest states. That is why that Marxist *jihadi* became one of the shapers of the twentieth century: because he took control of a powerful state. For Osama bin Laden to become one of the shapers of the twenty-first century, which is surely his goal, he needs to emulate Lenin and to capture a state, perhaps Saudi Arabia, Egypt or even Pakistan.

All this historical background is by way of elimination. It tells us what is old, what in the al-Qaeda brand of terrorism merely continues old traditions of disorder and dissent. The old world of the twentieth century and the new one of the twenty-first are both worlds of suicidal fanatics, haters of the West, holy warriors, seekers of identity through tradition, pan-Arab dreams, Islamic fundamentalist retrenchment, terrorists who seek new sources of power. The sources of such rebellion and terrorism are too eternal, too multifarious, to expect them either to be eliminated by modern development or suddenly to spring into action in wholly new forms. Osama bin Laden produced a big shock, but he was in a long tradition. What was new, though, was the magnitude and location of the attacks he unleashed: in the heart of the West itself, and with deadly force.

*

It is that, and only that, which distinguishes the al-Qaeda-led terrorist *jihad* from other sources of turbulence and terror, in the past and in the present. This is no small distinguishing feature, however, no small challenge. The home of al-Qaeda – Central Asia, ranging north into the Caucasus and south and east into Pakistan – has long been a turbulent place, in which warlords wield violence and money (often from drugs and gems) and clerics wield religious evangelism, all in the effort to gain power over places and groups of people. Similar stories can be told of large parts of Africa. But such places are not a direct threat to global security now, any more than they have been at any time in the past. The threat they pose arises from the fact that lawless places make it possible for law-breaking terrorists to live, train and move around with impunity; and from the fact that their terrorist acts may trigger off wider conflicts between states and further instability elsewhere, with consequences that could in the end threaten the security of the whole world.

Before returning to the specific threat posed by the *jihadi*s of al-Qaeda and similar groups, let us look at this wider context of turbulence and disorder within which they have been able to dwell. There are three things that can be said that connect the elements of disorder: one is the effect of the end of the cold war, the second is the amplification of a 200-year trend, and the third is the potentially alarming contribution of new technology.

The effect of the end of the cold war is in reality also an effect of the demise of empire during the whole of the twentieth century. Empires bring many bad things and cause many conflicts. But they help suppress other conflicts and disorder, by force of arms or other deterrents and incentives. As well as the straightforward wars between states during the first half of the twentieth century, then and in the immediate decades after 1945 many of the conflicts that occurred were liberation struggles of one sort or another. The cold war did not create a formal American empire, and even the Soviet empire was limited to the contiguous zones around Russia's borders. But both superpowers extended their military presence around the globe, directly through bases and interventions and, more commonly, indirectly by persuading – that is, bribing – governments to act on their behalf. The result was that local wars and civil wars were suppressed or else took on a flavour of superpower versus superpower.

With the end of the cold war came the end of that suppression and the proxy wars. The normal pattern, in effect, reasserted itself – but was also reinforced by the armaments left behind by the cold war. There were now no imperial rulers present and willing to stamp out conflicts. In a few cases – former Yugoslavia, Somalia, Sierra Leone – what has come to be given the grossly misleading name of 'the international community' has intervened, generally after several years of conflict and always with mixed results. There is no 'community' willing and able to exert itself sufficiently to deal with this disorder, but rather just a disjointed set of outsiders, some with interests in the conflicts, others with consciences tugged by the killings.

Along with the armaments left behind by the cold war, an unpleasant aspect of modern capitalist life has also appeared to exacerbate things: the fact that the trade in arms, small and large, has become a worldwide affair, in which economies of scale along with new manufacturing technology mean that the prices of automatic rifles, bullets, grenade launchers and all the other paraphernalia of disorder have fallen. Western companies take part in this trade and their governments often glory in the jobs it creates, hiding behind a pretence that the arms are being sold or sent only to other governments and only for 'defensive purposes'. Yet governments use their arms for all sorts of purposes, and arms are often then sold to others by their underpaid armies. In large numbers of countries, the route to power comes, as Mao Zedong memorably put it, from the barrel of a gun. So warlords have proliferated, using their weapons and private armies to control swathes of their countries, extracting taxes and tolls from whatever trade passes through their areas, especially illegal drugs.

Modern Afghanistan is the prime example, a perfect case of the elements of post-cold-war disorder. The scene of proxy wars between the superpowers during the cold war, it has armaments lying throughout the country, left behind by the Soviet withdrawal in 1989 and brought in cheaply since. It has warlords and it has the trade in illegal drugs. It has had fundamentalist religion brought in by one set of warlords, the Taliban, as a tool to extend their rule over a larger area of the country, with help from a neighbouring power concerned about Afghan disorder, namely Pakistan. Into its midst, with money, more weapons, fundamentalist beliefs and an anti-Western crusading agenda came Osama bin Laden and his al-Qaeda terrorists. The particular cocktail may vary, but the basic situation is not greatly different in Somalia, Sudan, Sierra Leone and an awkward number of other places.

The 200-year phenomenon applies more clearly, however, to places that do have entities that could be recognized as governments. This is nationalism, an idea that really began to prevail only in the nineteenth century as cheaper transport and communications made people able commonly to think of 'their' area as larger than just a village or county, and 'their' people as meeting a much wider definition than before. Thanks to empire and the slow spread of that technology and of the associated affluence, however, there were by 1914 only sixty-two separate states formally in existence and recognized by each other as legitimate. By 1946 there were still only seventy-four. By the turn of the century, in a process which took a great leap forward after the end of the cold war and the dissolution of the Soviet empire, there were nearly two hundred. During that cold war, nationalist movements had often been suppressed. But many were overlooked, because the battle of ideas and territory between the superpowers was more than enough to provide an organizing principle for the thinking of commentators and other political analysts. In truth, nationalism was simply bubbling up underneath, or alongside that battle.

A very large number of the two hundred or so states today play host to one or more separatist movements of admittedly varying degrees of seriousness, which claim for their own defined groups a right to nationhood. Some of those separatist groups use violence to further their aims; this is less likely where the existing state is a democracy with freedoms of speech and association, but, as Britain and Spain can bear witness, not at all impossible. Two of the most deadly separatist wars of the past two decades have taken place in democratically run developing countries: Sri Lanka, where the Tamil minority is fighting for separation; and India, where the conflict in Kashmir is partly a separatist movement and partly a battle with an alternative occupier, namely Pakistan.

Zealots for globalization or for supranational bodies of government, such as the European Union, are fond of describing nationalism as an outmoded idea and the nation-state as an outmoded form of government. In so far as they are making a prediction of a world several decades hence they cannot be proved definitively wrong. But there is little evidence that the basic emotional pull of nationalism is getting any weaker today. It is still, as John Roberts described it in his book *Twentieth Century*, 'the greatest of myth-makers, a mover of men and women, shaking up history and imagined history with their hopes, resentments and fears in potent cocktails of destructive excitement, the greatest single conscious force in the politics of history's most revolutionary century'. Nor are modern communications, through satellite television and the Internet, noticeably eroding the ties of local culture and nationalisms; they are adding some extra ingredients of foreign cultures, high and (mainly) low, but are also enabling national or ethnic groups to interact with each other more easily. They provide more outlets for cultural and national expression rather than fewer, and help groups organize themselves more easily.

What may be happening in the developed world is that, as trade, investment flows and the interchange of people become easier, the incentives among a majority in a country to resist statehood for a minority are fading. If, in due course, Scotland becomes a nation independent of what is now known as the United Kingdom, many English and Welsh may wave it a tearful farewell but its loss would not in truth make a lot of difference to them. It would provoke an awkward haggle over tax revenues and public spending, as well as over the ownership of a building or two, perhaps, but nothing that reasonable people could not agree upon in a negotiation. Life would then go on, essentially unchanged.

Only in cases when this is not true, or when a minority of the secessionist minority fear for their lives or rights in an independent state, does separation pose big problems. Those cases are, however, common enough to cause terrorism and disorder. Northern Ireland is one example, where the Protestants are a majority in the province but fear the consequences of being a minority in a united Ireland. Former Yugoslavia provides several more examples, where each time a province broke free (or contemplated doing so) during the 1990s minority ethnic groups expressed their fears with violence. And in the developing world, where ownership of a more limited range of assets often looms larger in the economy, and where fears among stranded minorities are even more common, they look likely to remain the rule rather than the exception. Indonesia, for example, is an odd compilation of territories and ethnic groups assembled by Dutch colonists over several centuries of conquest, in which separatist groups in Aceh, the Molucca Islands and other areas are how battling, not just for independence but also for control of mineral resources.

Nationalism retains its allure and thus its usefulness to anyone seeking to amplify an existing control over money and weapons into an even more powerful force. The allure is far from unique to poor countries, but it may well offer a special pull for the five-sixths of the world's population that live in them. Some optimists have argued that in the modern world no two democracies will ever go to war with one another and nor will two countries that are both homes to that symbol of globalized modernity, a chain of McDonald's restaurants. War between Serbia and the NATO countries over Kosovo in 1999 put paid to the second of those delusions. The first has more force, for democracies tend to have to stop and think before acting militarily, a pause during which cooler heads might be hoped to prevail. But it cannot be relied on. Democracy is a broad term, which takes in countries with a wide variety of constitutional set-ups and built-in restraints even before the obvious fakes are excluded from the definition, such as Zimbabwe. And it should be remembered that nationalism is a popular force, not an idea dreamt up by the élites: it is not too difficult to imagine a pumped-up sense of national outrage emerging in democracy A about the fact that democracy B has done this or said that.

So nationalism is likely to stay, alongside or reinforcing other forces for group identity such as religion or a local tribe, helping a sense of resentment, outrage or hope to coalesce, stimulating wars between nations as well as within them, stimulating conventional conflicts as well as terrorist campaigns. It is less a source of new world disorder than a continuation of an old source of disorder, but it is there and powerful nevertheless, and is likely to remain so. Which brings in the third of the things that can be said about turbulence and terror in the future, the potentially alarming contribution of new technology.

One thing that was notable about al-Qaeda's terrorist attacks on 11 September 2001 was that they used simple technology: gangs of men, armed only with knives, hijacking commercial airliners and turning them, in effect, into massive firebombs. They had, however, done their planning using advanced technology: laptops, e-mail, mobile phones. What soon also became obvious, however, is that the terrorists had been trying to obtain more sophisticated weapons and would have used them had they succeeded. Those possible weapons could range from poisons to bacteria to the most frightening sort of all, radioactive or nuclear weapons. Collectively known as 'weapons of mass destruction', these chemical, biological or nuclear tools would cause just that, mass destruction. Not just 3,000 but perhaps tens or hundreds of thousands, or even millions, of people might die in an attack.

In some senses, there is nothing new about this fear. At least since the early 1960s, when the number of countries possessing nuclear weapons expanded to five and then beyond, there has been a danger of such weapons falling into what those countries would call 'the wrong hands'. Both South Africa and Israel showed that they could develop a nuclear capability. What is new is that with the fall of the Soviet Union in 1991 the availability of knowledgeable scientists and of nuclear material increased hugely. On this chilling topic, it may be best to read the words of a specialist. Writing in *The Economist* in November 2001, Graham Allison, an expert both on Russia and on nuclear proliferation, at Harvard University's Kennedy School of Government, argued:

The past decade has seen scores of incidents in which individuals and groups successfully stole weapons material from sites in Russia and sought to export it – but were caught. Boris Yeltsin's assistant for national security affairs, Alexander Lebed, reported that 40 of 100 special KGB suitcase nuclear weapons were not accounted for in Russia. Under pressure from Russian colleagues, he later retreated to the official Russian line according to which all nuclear weapons and materials are secure and accounted for – but the fabric of the denials left more questions than answers. Over 1,000 pounds of highly enriched uranium – material sufficient to allow terrorists to build more than 20 nuclear weapons – sat unprotected in Kazakhstan in the mid-1990s. Recognizing the danger, the American government purchased the material and removed it to Oak Ridge, Tennessee . . .

. . . The same dynamics that tore down the old prison walls also liberated individuals and undermined systems that previously controlled some 30,000 nuclear weapons and 70,000 nuclear weapon-equivalents in highly enriched uranium and plutonium at more than 100 sites across Russia . . . Thanks to extraordinary professionalism on the part of the Russian military and security guards who have protected this arsenal, and significant efforts to assist them by the far sighted Nunn-Lugar Co-operative Threat Reduction Programs, which have amounted to almost $1 billion per year, many attempts to steal weapons have been thwarted.

Those words were written in the context of the effort to track down and contain al-Qaeda terrorists. But before returning to the question of how to deal with such terrorists, it is worth reflecting on the possible contribution of nuclear proliferation to the broader state of disorder and nationalism in many parts of the globe. The difficulty of handling nuclear, chemical or biological weapons makes it unlikely that local warlords or criminal gangs will seek to obtain or use them to shore up their power. Conventional weapons provide them with plenty of potency. But the turbulence of the world does increase the pressure on governments to get hold of them, to use them either as a deterrent, or for potential retaliation, or for sale to others.

In the Middle East and Central Asia, for example, Iran has long found itself in an especially turbulent spot. It had Iraq seeking such weapons to its south-west, Pakistan possessing them to its east, Israel possessing them further to the south-west and Russia holding them to its north. It is not surprising that the Iranians feel a desire to get hold of such weapons themselves. In East Asia, Taiwan and South Korea both find themselves close to countries – China and North Korea, respectively – that either have such weapons or would like to, as well as being near a Japan that could probably develop them quickly if it thought it worthwhile. In Africa, there is too little technological sophistication to make a nuclear programme easily viable for any country bar South Africa, or possibly Nigeria. But it is not at all inconceivable that a country could seek or develop chemical or biological weapons, for use against other countries or even against its own people. Sudan and Libya are both thought to have had research programmes for such weaponry.

And then there is the confrontation, seemingly ever-present, between India and Pakistan, both declared nuclear powers. They have fought three wars since independence from Britain, one in 1947, one in 1965 and one in 1971, as well as smaller skirmishes, the latest of which was in the Kargil region of Kashmir in 1999. At the turn of 2001–2, the old rivals again came to the brink of war, when a Pakistani terrorist group mounted an attack on India's parliament in Delhi and came close to killing many members of the government. Most likely, such a war would be strictly conventional, and probably confined to the disputed region of Kashmir. But in 2002, as in 1971, Indian divisions also lined up further along the border with Pakistan, preparing to invade the flatter lands of the Punjab as well as mountainous Kashmir. If that were to happen, victorious Indian forces might well quickly overrun large parts of Pakistan, which could in turn lead some parts of the Pakistani establishment to argue for the use of nuclear weapons in order to defend the very survival of the country. Perhaps sanity, and fear of retaliation, would always have prevailed. But war brings about its own dynamic, one in which it is not at all impossible that nuclear weapons might be used.

*

What can be done to prevent such disorder gaining a new power of destructiveness? It sounds a pretty ghastly and terrifying prospect. It is, in some respects. But what must be kept in mind is that such disorder is, in truth, a description of the present and the past as well as of the future. It is something we have learned to live with, in different ways and at different times. Experience suggests that it is too much to hope that disorder can be eliminated, or even greatly reduced, in the foreseeable future. But it can be contained, to some extent.

One way to contain it would be to recreate an imperial policeman, to obtain in a non-colonial world one of the benefits of colonialism. There are two obvious candidates for the role: the United States of America; and collective action of some sort through the United Nations. A third candidate might, just might, be collective action at a regional level: Europeans in Europe, Africans in Africa and so on. The trouble with this third possibility, however, is that it is almost always hampered by the fact that one or more of the countries supposed to be involved in the regional police force will also have an interest in whatever fracas needs to be sorted out. The other countries do not want to bully those with an interest. A regional force may, alas, prove uninterested, but it can rarely be disinterested.

Before assessing the chances of the two main candidates, another point needs to be made which applies to both. This is that many conflicts, whether civil wars or wars between states, cannot readily be 'solved' by an outside police force. Intervention may well make things worse, or just delay things, or end up being exploited by one side in the conflict. William Shawcross, in his book *Deliver Us From Evil: Warlords and Peacekeepers in a World of Endless Conflict*, puts the point well when he asks what might have happened if European powers had tried to intervene to stop America's Civil War in the 1860s. Terrible as the war undoubtedly was, the outcome, with the nation united and slavery abolished, had its merits compared with what might have been accomplished through some sort of mediated compromise. Sad to say, wars are a part of life as well as death, and squashing them does not necessarily solve the disputes that give rise to them. This does not apply in all cases. But the task of choosing which are the solvable cases and which not could well be one for a deity, not an international committee or a task force at the Pentagon.

Could America play a bigger role as an imperial policeman, having a go at making those choices? It could, but it is unlikely to do so on a really large and sustained scale, a scale that would last through much of the twenty-first century – even now that its foreign policy is dedicated to combating threats to global security. The reason is twofold: most disorder does not pose a direct threat to global security, and the risks and costs of entanglements abroad where there is no such clear threat are too high. The attacks on 11 September 2001 made America newly determined to be active abroad, following a decade of hesitancy. Nevertheless, even for as long as that determination lasts, which could well be as much as a decade, America is likely to focus its efforts on cases where direct threats to global security do clearly exist. For the moment, such threats are defined by international terrorism and by 'rogue' states such as Iraq that possess or wish to possess weapons of mass destruction. As this book went to press, it looked likely that America would soon lead a war against Iraq to enforce United Nations resolutions concerning Saddam Hussein's weapons programmes – and would do so with international support, or at least acquiescence.

Such a war is intended not only to deal with a specific global threat, but also to deter other potential 'rogue' states. Moreover, in future America will probably also respond to non-global threats by using selective interventions to deter trouble-makers. That is what it did during the 1990s, in Somalia, Bosnia and Kosovo, but intermittently and with arguably too many promises and too little action. President Theodore Roosevelt said in the early twentieth century that America should 'speak softly, and carry a big stick'. Much of America's louder noises will be directed at terrorists and the global threats of weapons of mass destruction. But it can and probably will intervene sporadically elsewhere, as during the 1990s.

Nevertheless, the threat of a big stick could have a salutary effect on governments pondering flexing their muscles. Given the new aware-ness of the danger of weapons of mass destruction being used by terrorists and others on America itself or on Europe, public and politi-cal support will generally be sufficiently forthcoming for America to be able to make credible threats of punitive military action against the most dangerous proliferators or would-be users of such weapons. It will not always be necessary or desirable to wait for a transgression to occur, given the power of these weapons; pre-emptive military action may well take place, rather as Israel bombed an Iraqi nuclear power station in 1981, when it suspected Iraq was also developing a nuclear weapon. Proliferators and would-be users will now take such threats more seriously than was the case during the 1990s. The potential punishment for being found to have tried to develop a nuclear capability has therefore risen, quite sharply. At the same time, the potential rewards for giving up such efforts have also risen: freer access to trade, the removal of sanctions, flows of aid and other benefits. The onward march of technology is making it steadily more likely that satellite surveillance will be able to detect such efforts. It is not foolproof at present, but it could well become so, quite soon.

That combination of big sticks and juicy carrots ought to be able to reduce the danger posed by nuclear and other terrifying weapons in the hands of governments. It is unlikely to eliminate it altogether, for technology of all kinds can cross borders too easily; and it will be less effective as a deterrent against biological and chemical weapons programmes, since such programmes are much easier to hide. Nor will it, on its own, deal with the threat posed by such weapons in the hands of terrorists. To increase the chances of containing these threats, collective action will be needed, to supplement the efforts of the United States.

Such collective action is unlikely very often to mean the United Nations acting as a policeman. The UN finds it too hard to move rapidly and decisively, given the number of countries involved both in approval and in action. It is much easier for it to mount peacekeeping operations, where soldiers are not expected to be doing much shooting. The UN is also vulnerable to conflicts of interest, as with regional collective action, because of the veto-holding powers in the Security Council. Finally, it runs up against just the same problems as would individual American action: the difficulty of imposing settlements and peace where none exists. Sometimes it can be done. But often it cannot.

There are, however, two ways in which collective action might help in the future. One is in the development of a system of international law and justice, through the International War Crimes Tribunal and the International Criminal Court. Both suffer from the weakness Stalin identified in the pope: 'How many divisions does he have?' No war criminal or mere criminal is going to fear these courts if he does not also fear being captured by an international or American military force, or being handed over to the court by his own country's government. The whole difficulty with such warlords is that they live in a culture of impunity; in general, the only people who can punish them are other warlords with more men, weapons and money. That is likely to remain true, but the international courts can have an effect on the margin, by demonstrating that crimes committed in wars do have consequences and that punishment can be meted out in cases when an international force does capture a criminal or when a successor government hands one over.

Many Americans – and a clear majority in Congress and in both the Clinton and Bush administrations – oppose the idea of the International Criminal Court. They fear it could be used against American soldiers and statesmen, even when they are trying to act for the common good by being global policemen. The American opposition is unfortunate and misguided: the new court is an experiment and, as such, America would have been wiser to let the experiment proceed for a while before pronouncing its verdict, since it could always withdraw from the court later. But its opposition will not prevent the court from being established. Support for both these international courts is strong and is likely to remain so: seeing justice handed down and seeing other countries co-operate with the courts, more countries are likely to do so over time.

One should, however, be sober about the potential power of such international justice. Even over several decades, it is hard to imagine such courts having a substantial deterrent effect. Power comes from the barrel of a gun. When you are holding the gun, it is tempting to use the power. And when in a conflict life expectancy feels short in any case, the idea of a future prison sentence is unlikely to make a lot of difference.

The second way collective action may help is in the effort to control nuclear proliferation, as well as access to other weapons of mass destruction. Admittedly, the biggest immediate task, in the 1990s as now, is a bilateral one: the two originators of the largest stocks of weapons and weapon materials, America and Russia, need to step up their collaboration to control the management, protection and disposal of their stocks. But the technology is much more widely known and held than that, with seven acknowledged nuclear powers in the world already (the United States, Russia, France, Britain, China, India and Pakistan), and probably Israel too, with others – Iran, Iraq, North Korea – known to have made a lot of progress towards becoming one. The know-how for the development and use of other weapons of mass destruction is spread far wider still. And nuclear material is being produced and stored in dozens of countries around the globe that have nuclear power stations. Their material is not weapons-grade, but it could be made to form part of a hybrid device designed to spread radioactive fallout over a large area.

Treaties to curb proliferation and nuclear testing abound. There is little need to invent more. What is in shorter supply is the willingness and the capability to enforce the treaties. The rapid development of surveillance technologies will help. But perseverance and pressure from diplomats, intelligence agents and others in a whole range of countries, in effect ganging up upon suspected proliferators and weapons programmes, ought to play a big role, if countries are willing to try. Often, they are not: during the 1990s, when UN weapons inspectors were trying to fulfil the Gulf War ceasefire resolution and ensure that Saddam Hussein was not developing or stockpiling weapons of mass destruction, several countries aided and abetted Saddam's efforts to thwart the inspectors' task: the most culpable were France, Russia and China. Given such thwarting of what had begun as an admirably multilateral initiative, the only method remaining to stop Saddam becoming a destructive threat to the world was unilateral military action by the United States, which explains why the Bush administration became so keen on it.

The sad truth is that, short of unilateral efforts by America, the process of controlling weapons proliferation by collective endeavour is best promoted by fear, a fear so strong that it can outweigh other national interests, such as commercial ambitions. The hope must be that the first piece of clear proof that nuclear terror is a real danger will be a failed attempt: that a nuclear 'suitcase bomb' or some other device will be intercepted, somewhere in the world. Then, with that evidence of a clear and present danger, it ought to be easy to gird developed and developing countries alike into collective action on detection, control and enforcement. However, the first such attempt at nuclear terrorism may, alas, be successful. But let us hope it is not.

*

Which returns us to al-Qaeda and other terrorists. American leadership, combined with collective action, will stand a chance of containing the international effect both of local turbulence and of governments' desire to obtain and use weapons of mass destruction. The fact that the chance of such containment is now at least fair, where once it was poor, can be ascribed to al-Qaeda. They have provided America with its single prism for foreign policy, and, despite many qualms about such a prism, have made Europeans and other allies more determined to quell the turbulence and the weapons proliferation. But what of al-Qaeda itself?

The distinguishing feature of the 11 September attacks was, we should remember, not the origins of the hostility or the nature of the terrorists' philosophy but rather the size and location of their attacks. This carries discouraging aspects as well as encouraging ones. The most discouraging aspect is that the attacks may have set a benchmark for future martyrs. Would-be suicide bombers will have noted that the greatest glory and the greatest amount of attention can be obtained by bringing off a huge and daring atrocity, in the heart of the West. Although it seems that some of the nineteen hijackers did not know that they were on a suicide mission, for those planning a future suicide mission the threshold for achieving an impact has now been set chillingly high. Given America's ready victory in dislodging the Taliban from Afghanistan and knocking al-Qaeda's local fighters over like skittles, it is hard to see what the point of a future attack would be.

But that is the second discouraging aspect of the attacks: that terrorism of this kind may not need a coherent point. Hitting at the West, but particularly America, may be a point in itself, just as Yukio Mishima made control over his own death an objective of its own. That urge may fade once several attacks have been seen to have no effect on America's power, its role in the world, its status and its will to deploy its power. The thought of that as a learning process is also chilling.

Another, also discouraging, feature of the al-Qaeda group should be borne in mind, however: hurting America is not really the ultimate aim. That aim, if you take seriously bin Laden's various propaganda videos and other statements, is to build a new pan-Islamic state from which the infidels have been expelled and which includes various important holy or historical sites – Mecca and Medina in Saudi Arabia, and the old seat of the Caliphate in Baghdad. In other words, what bin Laden or his followers really want to do is not to be terrorists but to become a government of a country and, through that, several other countries. The best analogy from history is one cited earlier: Lenin, and his long and ultimately successful struggle to gain power in Russia. That analogy should be a sobering one for anyone inclined to believe that the war in Afghanistan in 2001 might have finished al-Qaeda as an effective organization.

The war against such a group, in which it is not even clear whether Osama bin Laden is the ultimate equivalent of Lenin or Trotsky or whether someone else might emerge to take those roles, will be long and hard. The most important thing will be to avoid declaring victory prematurely, and to avoid complacency. That, however, is also an encouraging point, in a perverse sort of way. For the terrorists' weakness is that any future attacks, either on the United States or on others, will strengthen America's will, not weaken it. They will also, each and every time, assemble supporters to America's side. That would be true even of a nuclear, biological or chemical attack, terrifying though it would be; no country, and no government, could afford to respond to an attack of that magnitude by curling itself up into its own shell rather than fighting back.

The strength of terrorism – that it is dispersed, and capable of striking anywhere, at any time – is also its weakness, in the longer term, for this characteristic is liable to bring unity to all countries that feel vulnerable to it. And the more countries that feel vulnerable to it, the more that will participate in the effort to detect and imprison the terrorists. The risks of being a terrorist rose sharply after 11 September, even as the apparent psychological rewards of being one also climbed. Terrorism can be contained, even if it cannot be entirely quelled.

*

That is a chilling note on which to end the chapters of this book devoted to geopolitics and the challenges to peace. But the essentially optimistic outlook remains unchanged. There is indeed a great deal of disorder and violence in the world, but it is not of a new sort. Nor can it be said, after a century involving two world wars and several genocides, that the world is becoming appreciably more violent as the twenty-first century gathers its years. It is not. But violence and disorder are certainly not going away, and they cannot be expected to disappear any time soon. Future disorder looks truly nastier only in one respect, namely the possibility that it will involve weapons of mass destruction. It may well do so. But, to put it brutally, the real difference then will chiefly be the impact, on psychology and on death-tolls, of single acts, rather than a step-change in the level of brutality itself. Hitler, after all, was able to kill six million Jews. He just did it slowly.

PART TWO

CAPITALISM QUESTIONED

7

Unpopular

The thought of disorder is chilling. But also, to someone (such as the present author) who was born in comfortable, peaceable, democratic Britain in the second half of the twentieth century, it is hard now to imagine either that fascism and communism could have appealed to billions of people, or that the regimes founded on those ideas, now widely scorned as idiotic as well as barbaric, could have endured for so long. Yet twenty years ago it would have been natural to describe the century as a war amongst 'isms', one in which fascism had been defeated but in which the real, most profound battle, that between capitalism and communism, was still under way. Capitalism, with its supposed political associate, liberal democracy, was under attack for being unstable, unjust, unpopular and plain ineffective. This was a battle of ideas.

Or at least it was seen as one. Marxism and its adaptations, Leninism and Maoism, were said to be up against liberal, democratic capitalism in its various forms. An egalitarian ideology, rejecting private property and the profit motive, and enforced by totalitarian methods, confronted an ideology of inequality made acceptable by freedom, democracy and private property. Central direction by experts or ideologues stood in stark contrast to free markets, tolerance, the rule of law and chaotic change. It was Karl Marx versus Adam Smith, or Vladimir Ilyich Lenin versus Friedrich von Hayek. In 1989, when the Berlin Wall came down and the Soviet Union began its collapse, the battle was over. Smith and Hayek had won. Marx and Lenin had lost. Capitalism was secure.

But was it, really? The idea that it was depends on the view that the twentieth century was, in essence, a period in which the alternative to capitalism that had been dreamt up in the nineteenth century was tested, and found wanting. It certainly was found wanting. Some communists, however, continue to believe that the alternative was never really tested. That is one possibility. Another, however, is that to focus on the alternative and its weaknesses is to look in the wrong direction. The right place to look is at capitalism itself, and to ask a different question: Why did anyone want to dream up an alternative? And, the important rider to that question for the twenty-first century: might the same impulse appear again?

Admittedly, the century's turbulent history can be reinterpreted without looking quite so critically at liberal capitalism. It is a fair bet that many historians, writing in 2050 or 3000 with the detachment that such a vantage point will offer, will wonder whether this was really a fight about the ideas of Karl Marx and his descendants and about the evils of capitalism, or whether instead it might just have been a tussle between different forms of another idea, nationalism. The best evidence for this view is the fact that Marx's basic theoretical propositions had already been proved wrong by 1917, when Lenin's Bolsheviks seized power in Russia. At the moment of its first and probably greatest triumph, the ideology of communism already looked empty – or, at least, it does in hindsight.

Marx predicted in *The Communist Manifesto* in 1848 and *Capital* (1867) that the industrial working class would get poorer, more miserable and more alienated from the ruling and bourgeois classes, an inevitable economic process that would lead to a social and political revolution. But this did not happen. The industrial working class did grow in Europe and America as people flooded to cities from the countryside or from abroad, but by the turn of the century they had become considerably better off, in both relative and absolute terms, in most countries. The grievances and interests of that new urban working class had, as Marx expected, become the focal point of politics, but revolt was advocated only by a tiny minority, even in Russia. According to Marx, industrialization would create two classes, the bourgeois capitalists and the proletariat, who would become increasingly alienated from one another. But in fact the situation became muddled by the emergence of a middle class, which shared some of the interests of their poorer compatriots but also the aspirations of the richer ones. Far from showing international class solidarity in the face of an imperialist, bourgeois, capitalist conflict, workers opted for nationalism and fought in the trenches of the First World War, with surprisingly few mutinies. The automatic economic laws which, at least to its adherents, had given Marxism its pretensions to be a science proved not to be automatic after all.

But perhaps it didn't matter, for neither of the two big countries in which communist revolutions took place, Russia in 1917 and China in 1949, remotely resembled the industrial, capitalist societies in which Marx had said that revolts would inevitably take place. Nor did they, or Fidel Castro's Cuba or Kim Il Sung's North Korea or Ho Chi Minh's Vietnam, implement anything he would have recognized as communism, at least not after the first few years. Which is why these detached historians of the future will be tempted towards pragmatic, circumstantial explanations.

The Russian Revolution can thus be seen as merely a daring putsch by a small sect, exploiting the chaos and misery of the First World War, one in which timing and personal opportunism mattered more than the supposedly inevitable forces of history. After all, Lenin and Stalin then copied the ideas of capitalism: they exploited the modern, mass-production techniques of Henry Ford, arch-capitalist, to industrialize Soviet Russia, and used the new technologies of mass communication to establish a totalitarian grip. They turned Marxism-Leninism into a religious faith to engineer support and mask their barbarities, using that mixture of terror and belief to force change. It was fortunate for the Russian communists that the 1930s brought Adolf Hitler's fascism and his territorial ambitions in Eastern Europe, for these served to galvanize Russian nationalism and to provide some international sympathy for the Soviet cause. Moreover, the endurance of the colonial empires of Britain, France, the Netherlands and Belgium meant that in the various countries they occupied, liberation movements looked fondly to Soviet Russia merely because it was different from the Western oppressors and might provide support.

Similar circumstantial stories are already conventional wisdom about Hitler and Mussolini, fascism's tamer inventor, and their emulators in Spain and Portugal, Franco and Salazar. These dictators were creations of the First World War, which destroyed the social and political order in Germany and Italy; the Treaty of Versailles punished and humiliated Germany; and the raising of national barriers to trade in the 1920s and 1930s yielded (or perpetuated) economic failure. The capitalist democracies thus created their own enemies.

The fascist creed was an emptier one than communism, clearer about what it was against than what it was for, but Hitler and Mussolini mustered support by offering organization as a substitute for chaos (Hitler also admired Henry Ford); by amplifying the nationalism of the First World War into a spiritual creed, complete with enemies without and within; and by offering an undefined 'leadership', which was really a call for faith in what Peter Drucker in *The End of Economic Man*, the book that in 1939 made that émigré Austrian's reputation, called their 'sorcerer-like' abilities. Just as Stalin benefited by being an anti-fascist, Hitler exploited Soviet Russia's association with the idea of world revolution, painting Jews and Bolsheviks alike as internationalist threats.

And then there is China. For many years it was popular, even for those outsiders who were convinced that communism in the Soviet Union and its satellites was evil, to argue that the mass peasant poverty of China might actually mean that this was one of the few countries in the world in which communism was genuinely appropriate. But the reality of Mao Zedong's seizure of power in 1949 was more prosaic, being yet another reflection of circumstances, opportunism and dictatorship.

After decades of civil war, chaos and brutal Japanese occupation, the withdrawal of the Japanese from China at the end of the Second World War left a vacuum. It could have been filled by Chiang Kai-shek's Kuomintang (KMT), but Chiang was already discredited and weakened by his failures in government in the 1930s, by his regime's repressive brutality and by the KMT's own divisions. The KMT's American allies withdrew their support in 1947–8, and Chiang, losing more ground to the now well-armed communists, withdrew to Taiwan at the end of 1948. The communists were thus in effect merely the last men standing at the end of a long conflict, though they were also quite popular as symbols of change and liberation from the Japanese, from Chinese feudal traditions and from anarchy. In time, they turned out to be among the most nationalist communists of all, more or less shutting the borders of their country from the early 1950s onwards, and even breaking with the Soviet Union in 1959.

The apparent battle of ideas can all be seen, then, as the result of particular historical circumstances. That is what many future historians will undoubtedly conclude, though doubtless others will disagree. The ideologies of communism and capitalism did not themselves drive events, the circumstantialists will argue; they were mere tools, exploited by the great men (for it was almost entirely men) of history as they sought to respond to the political, military and economic situations in which they found themselves. Such explanations are convenient and even heartwarming for all the countries in which communism or fascism took hold, for they suggest that as long as these extreme circumstances are not repeated such regimes will not recur. ('Lesson: avoid world wars, brutal anarchy and great depressions' is not a hard idea to grasp.) Even so, this still leads to a sober view of human nature, because fascism's magic solutions and communism's utopian ones commanded initial support, or at least acquiescence, from Italians, Germans and Russians who had previously been thought too civilized and rational for such things.

Moreover, to add to the sobriety, it should be noted that some of the threads that ran through both sorts of regime could also be found in democratic countries in Europe and North America in the 1930s: an interest in eugenics and the sterilization of groups such as the mentally ill; celebration of physical fitness; social engineering; concern about shortages of population (to fight) and resources (to eat and manufacture with). And, as Mark Mazower, a British historian, points out in his book, *Dark Continent: Europe's Twentieth Century*, the fighters for freedom and against fascism and racism in 1939–45 such as Britain and France were actually rank hypocrites, since they were themselves running dictatorial empires in which racial superiority and authoritarian government were strong themes. America wasn't much better, with a democracy and no empire, but with racial segregation, unequal rights and discrimination not just in its southern states but also in its armed forces. No wonder that Mahatma Gandhi, when asked in the 1930s what he thought of Western civilization, replied that it would be a good idea.

*

Many residents of communist states shared the view that ideas were not the real issue. 'Capitalism is the exploitation of man by man,' ran an old joke. 'Under communism it is the exact opposite.' 'Socialism', ran another joke after the fall of the Soviet Union in 1989–91, 'is the historically inevitable path between capitalism and capitalism.'

These cynical or circumstantial explanations of the rise of communism and fascism are convincing in many respects, especially about fascism. But not entirely. They leave behind them a crucial doubt. This doubt needs to be addressed by anyone writing a history of the twentieth century. It is even more important for anyone thinking about the twenty-first.

The doubt begins with the fact that the communist system garnered surprisingly widespread support in some countries in the West, among ordinary voters as well as intellectuals, despite its manifest failings. This support lasted well into the 1980s, even after the mass murders, gulags and famines of Russia and China became evident, even after the economic despair of the 1930s had been left far behind, and even after it had become clear that communism was proving an economic failure. And although support for communism declined in the 1990s, it has not gone away altogether.

Why was support in the West so widespread and so enduring? Again, circumstances may provide part of the answer. Once the alternative system was established in the Soviet Union, it was a long time before the basic contest between centrally planned communism and market-based capitalism was resolved. Only by 1990 did it become absolutely clear which system had produced the best results. Even the choice of the right measure of 'best' was muddy. Was it economic, measured through data that both sides claimed was dubious? Or was it about security and stability? Or freedom, itself a slippery concept? Or something else? The two systems were, in essence, alternative means towards several ends: military strength, the economic and social welfare of the population, and, through those, to political survival, both of the regime and of the country as a whole.

In the end, communism – at least all the versions of it so far attempted – failed to meet these ends. Contrary to Marxist faith, changing the ownership of factories or farms from private to public did not make workers more motivated or direct the factory's use to better things. At best it was neutral, but over time it had the opposite effect. Even more important, central planning proved distinctly undynamic. Even the most brilliant bureaucrat could not consistently work out what product to make next, nor how many to make, nor dream up a better new way in which to make it. The point of the market is that, for all its imperfections, it is the only way yet found to conduct experiments about these things and to discover people's changing preferences. Command economies had no experiments and worked by ignoring preferences.

Command economies nevertheless took a surprisingly long time to fail. The Second World War prolonged their life, by delaying the onset of corruption in Soviet Russia, by preserving the idea of sacrifice as a national duty, by making respectable the idea of centrally directed production. That method of organizing industrial modernization seemed to work passably well as long as a country's industrial structure was fairly primitive, with a limited range of inputs and of products, and thus a limited set of tasks to plan and co-ordinate. This point proved true in other, non-communist countries which used a fair degree of governmental direction for their industrialization: Japan in the 1950s, for example, or South Korea in the 1970s. But once the economy has become mature, and the range of activities, products and services becomes complex, central direction becomes far less effective – and in the end counter-productive. Such ideas of central direction can work well in wartime, too, for there is then a clear motivation for designers, workers and managers, and a strong competitive discipline. And, of course, dictatorship suppressed the signals of dissent that would otherwise have become evident in the 1960s and beyond.

There is, however, a bigger and more important explanation for the enduring appeal of communism. It was that capitalism was a pretty dismal failure, too, for several decades from 1914 until 1945, and took a long time to offer a compellingly secure alternative. Even when the 1950s and 1960s brought greater prosperity and stability to the big capitalist economies, the memory of those decades of failure remained strong; times might be better, people thought, but they could easily become bad again. And, with that in mind, the fight for a 'fairer' system, whatever that might mean, gained new strength both in politics and in the workplace, for it was abundantly clear which classes had suffered most during the bad times.

So, while communists may or may not have been sure they were doing the right thing, plenty of troubled Westerners told them that they were. This was true both of the words of writers and the actions of governments. Central planning and public ownership became popular all over Europe. Western support and emulation arose in part also because of a delusion, especially in the 1930s, that dictatorial methods were working. Hitler's strength and popularity seemed to bear this out: he gave people jobs, raised output, built military strength. The idea that Hitler (or, more strictly, Mussolini) made the trains run on time may now seem like a slightly sinister cliché. At the time it, and similar clichés, were statements of praise.

Hitler's defeat in 1945 brought faith in fascism virtually to an end everywhere except in Spain and Portugal, but those countries were more like straightforward dictatorships than ideological states. Faith in the effectiveness of Stalin's essentially similar methods lived far longer thanks to the Soviet Union's large share in the Allied victory in 1945, a belief which faked statistics and the sputnik spacecraft later helped to maintain. The 1930s and 1940s were a period of despair and disillusion about the stability and capability of capitalist economies; the first period for many decades in which the condition of the working classes in many Western countries really began to resemble, albeit in a more modern context, the sort of things Marx and Engels had written about in the 1840s. The workers themselves responded by marching or migrating; the intellectuals by writing socialist novels and visiting Moscow, to become what Stalin called 'useful idiots' who helped the communists with their propaganda, inadvertently or not. More idiocy was displayed in the 1950s when intellectuals revelled in dreamy views of egalitarian Chinese peasant communes.

But there were other reasons, too, for the Western support. One was simply protest and alienation, a constant force in better times as well as worse ones: even in the 1980s, 10–20 per cent of the electorates of France and Italy, for example, were voting for communist parties, though few of the voters were actually party members. By then, the voters' (mainly manual workers') condition was far better than in the 1930s, but they still suffered from a sense of powerlessness and of being outcasts, and took pain or pleasure in voting for parties which, on paper at least, opposed the whole of the established political and economic system. It did not matter much whether the alternative was viable: to be able to cast a vote against the status quo was reward enough. The existence of fairly large blocks of communist votes also helped to encourage governments of right or left to make legal and financial concessions to trade union and other labour interests, in order to keep the communists at bay. So maintaining a robust communist party was a good way to shore up your own bargaining power for a trade unionist or just an ordinary worker. Another reason for Western support was romanticism about unity and comradeship: until 2000, Britain's Labour Party always ended its annual conference with the singing of 'The Red Flag', a socialist anthem. That seems merely a relic, yet even in the first round of France's 2002 presidential election three of the candidates were acknowledged Trotskyites and one (the socialist prime minister, Lionel Jospin) a former Trotskyite.

A further reason lies in the quasi-religious quality of Marxist theories as a call towards utopia, the effect of which quickly wore off inside communist states but endured outside. The idea of a utopia is always going to appeal at times of dystopia; as an ideal, a dream, it could survive the awkward fact that actual communist states did not live up to it, since perhaps perfection should not be expected at the first (or second, or third) attempt. This durability was also assured by one brilliant, debate-crushing ingredient: the claim in Marxism (known as 'historical materialism') that all freedom is an illusion, because everyone is trapped by their historical and material circumstances. No one is truly free, even if they think they are. If you disagree, you are a victim of false consciousness, inculcated in you by your circumstances. Only once mankind is emancipated, in the promised land, will people act according to their true, co-operative nature. It therefore takes a dictatorship to force them to become free.

Now, even this mind-bending defence of dictatorship fails to trap many people. But just as important as the appeal of communism was a revulsion against capitalism, against its successes as well as its failures. As François Furet, a French historian, put it in his book *The Passing of an Illusion*, for decades many apparently intelligent people in France, Britain and even America felt that 'the regime founded in October 1917 was good in spite of the disasters following its birth, whereas capitalism was bad in spite of the riches it engendered'.

Just false consciousness, in reverse? That is what it is convenient to assume, today. But it is as well to keep in mind another possibility. Capitalism is still widely considered, at least by some intellectuals, to be immoral: too devoted to a vulgar worship of money, too dependent on self-interest and greed, too deeply founded on adversarial individualism. It probably always will be. Experience may have shown that the twentieth century's favourite alternative, central planning by bureaucrats or dictators, was a failure in all but wartime. But next time capitalism stumbles, and even falls and breaks a limb or two, we can be sure of one thing that was shown all too graphically by the twentieth century: that plenty of people would love to believe that there might be a better, cosier, more comradely alternative.

*

Capitalism, it should be remembered, depends upon employment, which can be thought of as exploitation. Worse, it is not even consistently successful exploitation, being vulnerable to booms and busts, to periods in which the expectations of those it exploits are driven onwards and upwards, at the end of which those expectations are cruelly disappointed. And in that cycle of the creation and destruction of expectations lies the germ not only of alienation but of revolution. That, at least, is the sort of sweeping, even stirring statement that a revolutionary activist might make. But is it really so, especially given that, after more than seventy years of terrible, life-destroying experiments came to a close with the Soviet Union's fall in 1991, expectations of a viable alternative to capitalism have been thoroughly dashed?

It is a far from black and white issue. To see why, we should look at capitalism in another way. The twentieth-century dream of left-wing, progressive and utopian thinkers, particularly in Europe, has been of finding a way to encourage people to collaborate. To such intellectuals, working as a group, as a community, has exemplified all that is good. Acting as an individual, as a mere atom, has been seen as bad. One institution, essentially invented during the twentieth century, has been supremely successful at exactly that, at gathering together thousands, even tens of thousands of people in a voluntary, collaborative effort, to share their skills, knowledge and effort for a common purpose. This successful collective is called the private, capitalist company. It alone has found a way to blend direct financial incentives (aka exploitation) with the natural hierarchical instincts of the human tribe, and to ally both of those with the desire to work with other people and to derive self-esteem and confidence from the resultant sense of belonging.

Yet the paradox is that, despite those apparent economic, psychological and anthropological virtues, the private company seems always to have been viewed with suspicion, often bordering on hostility. Sometimes, the critical view of businesses is that of the lowly man, bemused at the incompetence of his superiors: this can be seen in Scott Adams's 'Dilbert' cartoons, the 1990s successors to a long line of lampoons. Sometimes, it has arisen from the alienating sense that the members of the group, the workers, are merely small, replaceable cogs in a vast impersonal machine, as in Charlie Chaplin's film *Modern Times* in the 1930s, in William Whyte's 1956 book on the modern American corporation, *Organization Man*, and in the many Japanese *manga* comics in the 1990s that lamented the sad fate of the 'salaryman', the ordinary white-collar worker. Sometimes, it has arisen from the sense that capitalism is a manipulative force, preying on emotions and instincts in order to distort our behaviour and make addicts of us all: that was the line of attack in Vance Packard's 1957 warning about advertising, *The Hidden Persuaders*, as well as Naomi Klein's lament at the dangers of a brand-dominated world, in her 2000 book called *No Logo*.

This suspicion has endured through a long evolution of capitalism's organizational forms. To be suspicious of the rapacious greed of capitalists would not have been at all surprising at the turn of the twentieth century, when the modern company was being invented. Until then, as Karl Marx had observed, businesses had been run by their owners and for their owners, a breed of raw capitalists that became known in America as 'robber barons': Andrew Carnegie, Cornelius Vanderbilt, John D. Rockefeller and others. Such people were buccaneering, often unscrupulous types in every country, yet especially so in a fairly new country such as the United States, in which new frontiers were forever being explored and the rules forever being reinvented. In such enterprises, workers were merely hired hands, able to be taken on or dispensed with at a whim.

By the early 1900s, however, things were already beginning to change. In America and in Europe alike technological change was making it both desirable and possible for these entrepreneurial businesses to grow much bigger, which in turn challenged the ability of the entrepreneurs to manage their firms as personal fiefs. Electrification made mechanization and mass production feasible; the telephone and radio made it easier and cheaper to communicate quickly across long distances and to co-ordinate administration; freight costs had dropped sharply thanks to steamships and railways. In America, this brought on the country's biggest ever merger boom, as J. Pierpont Morgan, with his bulbous nose and his bulging bank, acted as marriage broker, putting eleven companies together to form US Steel, for example, and creating General Electric. In Europe firms merged too, or built alliances through cartels. By either method, monopolies were created. In Europe they lasted and in some cases were expanded right through until the 1950s, with the collusion of governments keen on identifying industrial gigantism as a source of national strength. In America, however, a popular outcry against monopolistic abuses gave rise to anti-trust legislation, from the 1890s onward but especially in the 1910s. Even in the world's greatest capitalist frontier, suspicion of capitalism was rife, and was forcing the government (and the courts) to regulate the hitherto fairly free market.

Several decades on there came two more great evolutionary changes, which you might expect to have moderated or even almost eliminated hostility to the company. The first of these changes was that salaried managers took over the running of these now larger companies from owners, with shareholders becoming more fragmented and distant. From the shareholders' point of view, analysts began to worry as early as the 1930s that this might be liable to make companies less efficient as generators of profit, and thus of capital gains and dividend payments, because the interest of the managers was tending to diverge from that of the shareholders. The managers wanted to increase their own pay, power and control, pursuing their own pet projects and, some thought, exercising slacker control over their workers' productivity and pay.

The seminal description of this problem came in a book published in America in 1932 by Adolf Berle and Gardiner Means, *The Modern*

Corporation and Private Property. This recommended new legislation to assign stricter duties to managers to make them act in the interests of the shareholders. From the point of view of opponents of capitalism, however, this trend towards salaried managers ought surely to have been favourable. If the portrayal by critics such as Berle and Means of this 'agency problem' (as academics call it) was accurate, it meant that the profit motive was being blunted and that employees (the agents) were gaining more control over the resources and operations of their companies. The old conflict between capital and labour was tilting in labour's favour.

Not all of labour, perhaps: a new divide was opening up between the salaried managers, especially the senior ones, and the junior workers. But, at least to a degree and particularly in America, the pain caused by this divide was soothed by the fact that the ranks of management looked more and more like a meritocracy, in which all had some hope of advancing to the more privileged and well-remunerated rankings. This was reinforced by the second great evolutionary change, which was the development, most rapidly from 1920 until 1960, of mass education in all the main developed, capitalist countries. This gave workers the sense that there was, or would soon be, something like a genuine equality of opportunity.

The divide between managers and workers thus looked unbridgeable only to those who felt that a climb up the ranks was impossible because of a lack of education or because of racial or other discrimination. The subset of workers who felt dispossessed or permanently alienated was getting smaller or narrower – at least, narrower than in any Marxist analysis of it. Meanwhile, the disadvantages of the agency problem to shareholders became clearer and clearer during the 1970s and 1980s, as productivity and profit growth stagnated. This posed a threat to prosperity and living standards, but it would have taken a particularly topsy-turvy, or perhaps deviously inventive, mind to turn this agency problem into a general criticism of capitalism. A critic would have to argue that the incentive structure of modern corporations was holding back corporate and thus economic growth, in such a way as to produce misery for the proletariat.

Such an idea would have been implausible, to say the least, unless what you wanted was more profitable, more ruthless capitalism. By

1946, in his book *The Concept of the Corporation* (written chiefly about General Motors, but drawing broad conclusions from the example of America's leading manufacturer), Peter Drucker rightly observed that the company had replaced the Church as the representative institution of society – the one in which most people spend much of their lives, to which they devote most of their energies and from which they gain much of their sense of status and worth. The company was becoming the closest thing society had to a meritocracy, and it was no longer the creature of one hugely wealthy individual or family. Then along came a third great change, chiefly in Britain, America and the Netherlands, though also to a lesser extent in Japan: the company pension fund. In its modern form, as a fund that sought to provide for workers' retirement through broad, diversified investments in equities and bonds, based on financial contributions both from employers and from the employees themselves, it was popularized in 1950 by Charles Wilson, boss of General Motors, Mr Drucker's emblematic firm, who later became President Eisenhower's secretary of defence. Within a year, 8,000 other such plans had been set up in America.

These pension plans gave employees a direct interest in corporate profits and in broad economic growth, as well as some long-term security for their retirement. They were now, in the term that became popular during the 1990s, fully fledged 'stakeholders', with their interests no longer confined simply to the terms and security of their employment but also to these wider economic concerns. In time, ownership of corporate America and corporate Britain was essentially transferred to the pension funds and their institutional sisters, life-insurance companies; in other words, indirectly, to ordinary employees themselves. In another of his trend-spotting books, *The Unseen Revolution*, published in 1976, Mr Drucker called this phenomenon 'pension-fund socialism', the only successful form of socialism ever invented. Today, the principal owners of corporate America and corporate Britain are ordinary people, through their pension funds and life-insurance investments. The same is true, directly or indirectly, of many other big industrialized economies.

*

All this money, all this ownership, has not, however, bought popularity for the poor old private company. Even in capitalist, ambitious, greed-loving America, where free enterprise in general is welcomed, big business still draws suspicion. In June 1999 – in the eighth year of an economic expansion, amid an extraordinary stockmarket boom and at a time when it was newly popular to work in or even launch new technology or Internet firms – the Gallup opinion-research firm asked American people whether they had confidence in big business. Only 30 per cent said they had a lot (fewer even than for newspapers), 44 per cent grudgingly said they had 'some' and 25 per cent said they had very little or none. In Britain, polls by Market and Opinion Research International (MORI) have, since 1969, found increasing dislike of corporate profits. In 1969, two-thirds of respondents thought profits at big companies were good for everyone. By 1999, two-thirds of people thought they weren't. Four-fifths thought that 'as they grow bigger, companies usually get cold and impersonal in their relations with people'.

This is curious. People seem to want the jobs and status that companies provide, they buy their products and services with gusto, and their retirements are increasingly financed by corporate earnings. And yet they are suspicious of business. Simple dislike of the profit motive may help explain it, but that is not enough: few people reject the role that selfishness plays in their own lives or those of their friends and family, so why do so when evaluating business?

At the risk of drifting into pop psychology, one reason is that people are more hostile to groups than utopians or anthropologists suppose. Groups demand conformity and impose uncomfortable mutual obligations. Unlike a tribe, ethnic group or nationality, to join a company requires a voluntary act, rather than simply an accident of nature and then nurture. There may be a good reason to join it, and benefits from doing so that cannot be found elsewhere, but it is perhaps as well to keep your distance. Companies, after all, demand a lot of commitment, but all too often show little commitment in return.

Then there is a simple if banal fact. People may be employed by one company and thus share interests and perhaps allegiance with that business, but they are in something like an adversarial relationship with the many other businesses with which they have contact. When they buy a firm's products or services their interests differ from those of the firm: they would prefer the price to be lower, the quantity to be larger, the quality higher. Similarly, if they live near a factory they suffer from its noise and dirt without, for many, even the compensating advantage of being paid wages for working there.

The evolution of companies away from personal or family owner-ship has made big corporations more alienating rather than less, even though they are now run by managers rather than a domineering owner. With that change from proprietor capitalism, which was already evident by the 1930s, the company took on a life of its own, a permanence beyond its founders, a chance for each generation of individual employees to take possession of the firm for a time. As stewards of an enduring entity, each generation of employees has the chance to influence the firm's nature and development. Yet, combined with size, this also means that those at the top are likely to have no personal contact with those in the middle or at the bottom. The company loses its personality, its soul. It is, as the MORI poll answer said, cold and impersonal.

In fiction, this sense of firms as sinister, soulless groups of people, in which individuals bury their personalities, was strikingly reflected in *The Stepford Wives*, a 1975 film about a company town in which women are turned into robots. It pops up in a whole series of other Hollywood movies, from the more recent mega-corporation villains in James Bond films to the polluting company against which the heroine carries out her crusade in *Erin Brockovich*, a story based on real life. Having lost the Soviet Union as a source for his novels about spies and betrayal, John le Carré turned, in *The Constant Gardener*, to the pharmaceutical industry for a story about evil-doing in Africa.

Is this fair? As a generality, no. But at the extreme, a company can certainly lose a sense of its wider social and (especially) legal responsibility, or it can seem to. Large groups of individuals, who gain their direction, their self-esteem, their status and their ideas essentially from each other, can risk losing sight of wider values. It may sound like an unfair comparison, but the Japanese Imperial army in the 1930s was an exaggerated example of this tendency. Let loose into China and other parts of Asia, with no effective political oversight of its actions, its soldiers behaved abominably. Their only reference point or sense of accountability was to each other, and then in a more abstract way to the idea of the emperor back in Tokyo. No firm, one hopes, has ever behaved in quite the same way as did the Japanese Imperial army. But it is through the same syndrome of an entirely internal network of accountability that cover-ups, evasions or the desire to ignore safety risks in products or processes can occur in what seem to be the most respectable of companies. In big companies, when this occurs it occurs on a big scale, as it did at the Enron energy-trading firm in 2001, aided and abetted by its accountants, Andersen.

Once such malpractice has been discovered, it is disastrous for the company, for its reputation will be in tatters and it may well become the target of criminal investigations or massive civil lawsuits. For that reason, doing the right thing is also the self-interested thing to do. There is no need to invoke a special sense of corporate social responsibility – except in circumstances when employees may come to think their crimes may never be detected. Nevertheless, when such cases as Enron do come to light it is bad for the reputation of all companies, as many people will assume that the rarity of the case is not the malpractice but the fact that it has been exposed.

*

So businesses can appear soulless, distant, selfish, rapacious. But so can people, as can lots of other sorts of organization. The chief difference about the private company is its sheer size. Of other organizations, only the state itself, or in the past the Roman Catholic Church, has offered such a vision of gigantic, overwhelming power, extended far from home. Indeed, in the roughly thirty or forty years since freer trade and capital markets, and new telecommunications technology, during which companies have been allowed to organize themselves on an international or even global scale, the story of multinational firms has become more and more like that of the Catholic Church in the history of Europe and of Asia.

Multinational companies are not only gigantic and overwhelming, they are often forces controlled from abroad. In fair weather, such forces are welcome, for they bring money and new ideas. In foul weather, however, they can come to be considered as alien creatures, controlled from abroad in the interests of foreigners, and who are liable to crush all who dare to get in their way. In fair weather or foul, they tend, as the Catholic Church did, to divide those societies in which they operate into two: those people and groups who choose to throw in their lot with the outsiders, becoming dependent on their fortunes; and those who do not, and who may even build a self-interest in the failure of the outsiders.

Companies do seem to be getting bigger, as they merge and invest across borders. The late 1990s provided one of the greatest booms in mergers and acquisitions that has ever been seen. This occurred chiefly in the United States, though the boom there included a large number of acquisitions of American companies by foreign ones, and the boom did spread overseas, too, especially to Britain and, to a lesser extent, to continental Europe. Many of the mergers have failed, because it is hard to meld organizations with different histories, national cultures and ambitions, and because the larger a firm gets the harder it is to manage it successfully. Even so, not all mergers fail, and whether or not they ultimately fail they still grab a great deal of attention when the deals are initially struck, which itself acts as a spur to other budding deal-makers.

Hence, one of the great new fears: that a few multinationals might soon dominate the world. There is certainly such a trend in a few industries. Aircraft engines is one: General Electric, Pratt & Whitney and Rolls-Royce dominate, at least in the market for the largest engines. For civil airliners themselves, Boeing and Airbus share the market, with competition for smaller regional planes principally between Embraer of Brazil and Bombardier of Canada. Oil is another. Software, at least the part of it for desktop personal computers, is a fourth, in which Microsoft holds the high ground. Media feels as if it might become a fifth, with a small number of giants emerging that are capable of making and distributing visual, audio and written content across a wide range of channels, world-wide: AOL Time Warner, Disney, Bertelsmann, Vivendi Universal, Sony and News Corporation simply tower above all the rest.

The standard way in which worries about this are expressed is the observation that many of the world's biggest companies are now larger than many countries' gross domestic product (GDP). For this reason, it is argued (for example by Noreena Hertz, a British academic, in her book *The Silent Takeover*), companies now hold far more power than sovereign governments. They have taken over the world, or may be about to. Yet this is wrong, badly wrong, in two ways.

The first is that the comparison of companies' size to countries' GDP is wholly misleading, not to say economically illiterate. These comparisons always use either a company's stockmarket value or its level of sales turnover. One is a measure of asset value rather than cash flow or output; the other is a gross measure of transactions which has no reference to the value added by the firm and hence extracted as profits. GDP, by contrast, is a measure of value added: it does not estimate the total number of transactions in an economy but rather eliminates intermediate transactions in order to aggregate the value only of final goods and services. In other words, if a loaf of bread is made by a factory and sold to a wholesaler, who in turn sells it to a retailer, who in turn sells it to a consumer, the additional GDP measured represents the final price paid, not the sum of all the prices paid by everyone involved. The correct way of comparing companies and national economies would be by comparing value added in both cases, which for simplicity's sake could simply be the company's post-tax profits compared with GDPs. That, though, would make even the biggest companies look puny compared with all but the tiniest economies.

The second way in which the claim of corporate hegemony is wrong is that states retain not only a predominance of size but also of powers. They – even the smaller countries – retain all the traditional capabilities of states to control and punish groups within their borders: laws, judicial systems, enforcement by police and armies. Many of those powers do not even require riches to be effective; although money is needed to establish proper policing and armies, states can use laws to expel companies or even to seize their assets. The only respect in which the size of companies ought to be a legitimate concern arises from their potential ability to use their wealth to subvert political systems by direct bribery or simply by buying influence. That is not, in truth, a new concern: the danger of excessive influence by the rich and powerful has been ever-present in long-standing democracies such as America and Britain, and a constant feature of dictatorships. In the Indonesia run by President Suharto as a dictatorship for thirty years up to his fall in 1998, for example, the best way to make yourself rich was to become a favourite of the Suharto family; companies won favours through their bribes and political assistance, and in return were given contracts and protection. But the fact that this danger is not new does not make it any less a danger.

There are, however, some mitigating characteristics in today's turn-of-the-century globalizing world. The very things that are driving many of the mergers and acquisitions are also factors that limit the danger of excessive corporate concentration. Massive, cross-border mergers are made possible only by the opening up of national markets. That very opening up, though, increases the amount of competition by allowing in new firms to fight for the markets; as long as the barriers to such new entrants are kept low, the danger of monopolization will also be kept low.

An example of how this has worked over several decades is the car industry. It still has a large number of high-volume producers, despite mergers and purchases in recent years: DaimlerChrysler, Volkswagen and BMW in Germany; Renault and Peugeot-Citroën in France; Fiat in Italy; GM and Ford in the United States; Toyota and Honda in Japan. Before Japan's economy entered its stagnation in the 1990s, there were nine car-makers in that country alone: the two aforementioned, plus Nissan, Mitsubishi Motors, Subaru (Fuji Heavy Industries), Mazda, Suzuki and Daihatsu. Mazda and Suzuki both had foreign shareholders (Ford and GM, respectively) but were essentially independent. Now the number of truly Japanese car-makers is down by four, as Ford and GM have taken closer control of Mazda and Suzuki, and Renault and DaimlerChrysler have both bought large, more or less controlling, stakes in Nissan and Mitsubishi Motors, respectively.

Today's ten big global car-makers, many of whom have in recent years been gobbling up smaller, specialist firms, could consolidate further in future. That is what an extrapolation of the trend of the past decade might imply. Yet past experience, over a longer period, offers a different prediction. It is that there is unlikely to be a settled trend towards domination of this business by fewer and fewer companies. The biggest reason for this prediction is the fact that new competitors keep on arriving, typically from newly industrializing countries. Japan was the biggest source of these in the second half of the twentieth century, providing in the car industry what were, in effect (though some had been founded in preceding decades), nine new firms competing on world markets. General Motors' senior managers famously concluded in the early 1970s that no foreign firm would ever achieve a substantial share of the American car market, leaving the big three American firms, led by GM, to manage their sales and, essentially, to work out how best to invest their profits. Within less than a decade, the Japanese had arrived and were shaking things up. Following their example, several South Korean firms then also entered the market. Could this happen again? Of course it could: one obvious potential source of such new competitors at some stage in the future would be China. Another could be India.

The car industry may also in future offer a fine illustration of another way in which globalization keeps monopolies at bay: technological innovation. This can open up a market completely, bringing in a whole new set of firms fighting to supply a product. Technological change can have two types of effect: it can bring in new techniques and processes; and it can change the economics of production and development. In the case of cars, the likeliest technological change is the replacement of the internal combustion engine by new power sources, such as the hydrogen fuel cell. This is a unit which uses hydrogen to produce electricity; it produces much less pollution than a conventional engine, but currently costs far more to make. That cost is falling, however. The existing car-makers are all investing in research into and the development of fuel cells, because if change is to come they would rather ensure that they still lead and control the industry. And they may succeed. But they risk failure if, for example, the economics of producing fuel cell motors turns out to favour smaller production runs and thus smaller companies, or if the incumbents try to slow the introduction in order to protect their old businesses, but then find themselves outflanked by new firms which have no old business to protect.

The best examples of how technology can turn an industry upside down have, however, come in the technology industries themselves. There has been a flood of new firms with each wave of change in information technology, taking on the incumbents and shaking things up. This applies to telecoms as well as to computers. Oracle, Microsoft, AOL, SAP, Dell, 3-Com, Vodafone: such firms did not exist twenty years ago, or if they did they merited barely a blip on the radar screen.

British Telecom, AT & T, IBM, Digital Equipment, Xerox, Eastman Kodak, Polaroid, ITT: these firms and many more have had to struggle to survive and some have failed altogether. ITT (originally International Telegraph and Telephone), was the bugbear of those who feared multinationals in the 1960s and 1970s; today it exists only in the component parts of the firm which have all been sold off.

So the pressure towards concentration of business in fewer and fewer hands also faces counter-pressures: new competitors, unleashed especially by open world markets amid globalization; diseconomies of scale and scope, as companies find it hard to maintain their vigour and innovativeness once they become huge organizations; and technological innovation itself, which has the ability to disrupt whole industries, all around the world.

*

As this battle of forces goes on, the basic issue for observers and policy-makers, in all industries and markets, should be the question of whether there is sufficient openness to competition to prevent large firms from exploiting their customers, raising prices and keeping the counter-forces at bay. Big firms are not a problem *per se*; the problems are caused by big firms that can manipulate their markets. In that, globalization helps, considerably. Open trade and open markets greatly increase the amount of competition in any market, by increasing the number of potential rivals for any given set of customers, and by breaking open old walls of protection and privilege. Monopolies have been far more prevalent in closed markets, where big businesses have done deals with governments in return for restrictions on foreign or other firms, than in open, globalized ones.

The more limited the market, and the harder it is for new firms to enter it, the greater the need for laws to protect and police the competition and to prevent monopolies. Anti-trust laws are a crucial part of liberal capitalism. Yet free-market thinkers find themselves in two minds about this issue. On the one hand, they adore incentives as the basic drive towards enterprise; the desire to dominate, to win, is the greatest incentive of all. Remove it, and they risk reducing investment and innovation, as well as being unjust, by taking away someone's due reward. But, on the other hand, they value competition as a discipline, and loathe concentrations of power, whether in government, over-mighty trade unions or dominant companies, for they expect that, in time, the power will be abused and will itself threaten liberty.

The first mind is really a conservative mind; the second is that of the liberal. Whatever the argument about justice, the liberal option is surely the more prudent, since it keeps the abuse of power at bay. Experience still suggests, however, that one of the conservatives' observations needs to be taken into account: namely, that in practice monopolies are hard to establish and sustain, because other firms are drawn in to compete away excess profits and to dream up technological innovations. Governments should therefore be cautious in their interventions, for they generally know much less about the coming technologies than do the various competitors. But if true dominance is established, and new firms are prevented from entering the business, governments must crack down, hard. The price of limited competition will be abuse, higher prices and slower innovation.

If we look at competitive trends in the past century or so, two things emerge. One is that the economy in which competition has been policed most vigorously has also been the most enterprising and the most successful: the United States. This has enriched lawyers, and economists acting as 'expert' witnesses, and enforcement has sometimes followed a false trail. But by and large it has kept prices down and business invigorated, without destroying incentives.

The second is that monopoly has been most damaging when it has been established in collaboration with government, or at least with its collusion, for this magnifies the concentration of power and eliminates the chance of new competition. It is also very likely to subvert democracy, for the rewards of bribing politicians and regulators increase in such circumstances, and the risk of being challenged for it is reduced. That has often been the case in Western Europe, where cartels were backed by the law in the 1920s and 1930s and where states set up their own monopolies as well as licensing others. Later, it came dressed up as the idea that the monopoly is somehow performing a national service by being big and dominant, for then it can stand up and stare foreign firms in the eye. The price for nurturing such national champions has been steep: lack of innovation, high prices, subsidies.

Much tougher issues arise in developing countries. There, too, the benefits of competition, of new technologies and capital being brought in by foreign investors, of the possibility of using a local factory as a base from which to compete in world markets, all make it highly desirable to open the country's doors to multinational investment. But there is a real, extra worry that does not exist in the rich world. It is that in a poor country the institutions of the state and of the rule of law will be weak. This will make it hard for that country to police the fairness of competition or to enforce health, safety or environmental standards.

That worry about how multinationals might dominate the third world has existed ever since the early 1970s, when truly world-spanning, planetary enterprises began to be noticed, and inevitably to be feared. Many third world countries did their best to keep these foreign marauders at bay, either by nationalizing assets, or by protecting certain industrial sectors by law, or by keeping foreign investors out altogether. India, for example, was highly restrictive, permitting foreign activity only when indigenous firms looked unlikely to be able to serve a need (as defined by bureaucrats) on their own.

By and large, during the 1990s the view of multinationals changed completely: third world governments began to welcome them. They trooped to the annual meeting of the World Economic Forum in Davos, Switzerland, to promote their country to the assembled businessmen, journalists and politicians. They relaxed laws that had previously discouraged investment. Some even permitted foreign firms to buy domestic ones. The unsuccessful lamented their failure to lure multi-nationals. And, whereas during the 1970s and early 1980s the typical developing country preferred to receive foreign capital through bank loans or bonds, by the 1990s there was a strong suspicion of loans, bonds and other securities, and a clear preference for direct investment in bricks, mortar and factories by multinational firms.

The reason for that change of heart is that debts have to be repaid, and credit lines or securities investments can easily be withdrawn. Such money is 'hot' and unreliable, as was shown during the East Asian financial crisis of 1997–8, when money flooded out of the doors of East Asian countries, bringing their currencies crashing and leaving governments and private firms holding big, unserviceable debts. Factories, offices and buildings stay put, however; multinationals are, for all their fearsome size, more reliable than are stockmarket speculators or bond investors. But are they exploiters? What of the old fear that they will corrupt local élites and wield political power?

Some of those fears have proved correct. Especially in Africa, and especially in the natural resources business, multinational firms and local political élites have worked together, in each other's interests rather than in the national interest. The success of a natural resources firm called Lonrho, led until his death in the 1990s by Roland 'Tiny' Rowland, often derived from such contacts with the élites. Sometimes, as with the Shell oil company (and other oil firms) in Nigeria, this has not been the multinationals' fault: they simply represented a flow of cash into which the political power-holders could tap. But no matter: it happened. For the most part, however, the record is better. The reasons are a mixture of competition from other multinationals and exposure to the scrutiny of customers and shareholders back home. International firms cannot afford to misbehave abroad, because if they were to be caught the damage it would do to their reputation at home would be too great. They can, of course, misbehave (by home-country standards) in small ways: taking part in low-level corruption, for example, or putting discreet pressure on governments to angle the laws favourably to them. But most know that they cannot afford to be caught in systematic exploitation or misbehaviour.

Indeed, if anything, they behave better than their local competitors. Edward Graham of the Institute for International Economics in Washington, DC, and a world expert on foreign investment, has studied the wages paid by American-owned manufacturing multinationals in developing countries, and has sought to compare them with the wages paid in the same sectors by local, domestic rivals in those countries. He found, in his book *Fighting the Wrong Enemy*, that these American firms pay wages that on average are double those prevailing among local rivals in the lowest-income countries, and roughly 40 per cent higher in middle-income developing countries. This is possible because, with their superior technology and organizational skills, multinationals can achieve much higher productivity than can indigenous firms. A job at a multinational ought to be – and generally is – prized.

Two other issues, however, are more real and loom much larger. One is unfairness in the trading regimes of the rich countries: while Europe,

Japan and America have lowered their barriers against trade in the sort of goods in which the rich countries themselves specialize, they have maintained high barriers against imports of goods in which poor countries tend to be active, such as food, textiles and steel. This is a fair criticism. Subsidies to rich-world farmers help keep poor-world farmers poor, just as quota protection for rich-world textiles firms help keep poor-world textile-makers poor. The other issue is less clear-cut: it is the idea that intellectual property (that is, patent) protection for rich-world firms enables them to keep their goods expensive in developing countries while preventing local firms from competing against them.

This is particularly problematic in the drugs trade. Medicines are cheaper in the third world than the first, but they are still costly by local standards. Pharmaceutical firms argue that they need to make profits in order to make their research into such drugs worthwhile; without patents and profits, the drugs would not exist. Perhaps more pertinent, however, is a fear that if they sell drugs very cheaply in poor countries, traders will buy them up and export them back to the rich world, undercutting the drugs firms' profits there.

Both these arguments are sound. Without profit, the drugs would not be invented. But there remains a question of quite how much patent protection is really needed. And, most important, there remains a question of who should pay to help make drugs cheap in the third world: the drugs firms' shareholders, or rich-world taxpayers. There is a strong moral case for the second, for the use of aid money to bridge the gap between the need for profits to repay research and the difficulty the poor face in paying the bills. This is especially important for diseases that are prevalent only or mainly in poor countries, and thus provide no profits at all in the rich world. Such aid, targeted clearly at medicines and health care, especially for scourges such as AIDS, malaria and tuberculosis, would come with risks. Over time, for instance, the drugs firms might raise the prices charged to the donor governments, thus creaming off more of the aid money for themselves. The risk of smuggling back to the rich world would also persist. But it would still save millions of lives. And the moral point would be clear: it is not capitalism that is at fault in making drugs prices too high and unaffordable in the third world, it is poverty.

*

There are many reasons why people are suspicious of capitalism, some justified, some not, but all enduring. It is alienating, manipulative, greedy, bossy, monopolistic, gigantic. It is also productive, innovative, the source of good wages and salaries, the fount of retirement pensions, the source of all sorts of wonderful products and services. Who can bridge the divide between this hate and this love? Government, of course. It must make capitalism behave properly, rather than improperly. That, according to many critics, is its duty, especially in a democracy. If only it were so easy.

Suspicion of capitalism has, during the past seventy years or so, been one of the biggest factors behind a steady growth in the size and powers of government in the Western democracies. Government may have been viewed with some distaste, but at least it is accountable in regular elections in which voters can kick the latest set of rascals out. The public can detect no such accountability for capitalism in general, so it is natural to try to use the imperfect tool of democratically elected governments to enforce one: through often welcome measures such as health and safety legislation, product liability laws, labour standards, environmental rules, anti-trust laws, accounting rules and all the rest of the panoply of regulations surrounding business.

All this occurred even as communism was advancing in Russia, China, Cuba and elsewhere, and even as the fight against fascism took place. The spread of the welfare state and of controls over business were, in large part, efforts to defuse the time-bomb of opposition to capitalism in America and democratic Europe. They were also ways to discourage the communist alternative.

Those efforts were successful, in the sense that the time-bomb was largely defused, in the 1970s and 1980s. But two new time-bombs were set by this very action. One, which will be discussed towards the end of the next chapter, is that generous welfare spending and tight controls over business came to have a debilitating effect on the very thing that keeps capitalism viable – its ability to deliver rising living standards – while simultaneously stretching to breaking-point the willingness of taxpayers to meet the cost of these things. The other time-bomb is more insidious for the future of democracy itself. It is that, inevitably, as government spending and regulation came to have a bigger and bigger influence over business, so companies tried harder to influence government decisions to their advantage.

There is nothing wrong with that, in principle: free speech and open democracy ought to include the right for companies to have their say. The problems arise when companies' efforts to influence the political process become so pervasive as to appear – or actually to be – corrupting. Financial donations to the electoral campaigns, general party funds or even personal expenses of politicians have been the main conduit by which this influence has been deployed, in America, France, Germany, Japan and, albeit to a lesser extent, Britain. There are other ways, too, in which companies can put politicians in their debt or tempt them to act in the firms' interests. The most common is to encourage them to act, in effect, as export salesmen or as promoters of inward investment into their countries or states. Typically, politicians need little encouragement to do these tasks, as they can thereby associate themselves directly with that most appealing of virtues, the creation of jobs, however misleading or distorting that association may be.

The collapse in December 2001 of Enron, the American energy-trading giant, mentioned earlier in this chapter, was a perfect case study of the problem. Enron was an innovative company, which found new ways to trade in energy-related products and services as well as to produce them themselves; it was led by executives who earned spectacular amounts of money in salary and stock options, but who also became prominent philanthropists. It lobbied the American government to help it win a big power-plant contract in India, and its executives played a big role in advising the current Bush administration about its energy policy. It went bankrupt, however, because it racked up huge debts to finance its various new ventures, which it hid through special partnerships that were kept outside its published annual accounts. It pressured employees into keeping a large chunk of their private pension accounts invested in Enron shares, and prevented them from selling the shares once the company's troubles emerged. Its advisers – auditors, banks, investment banks – had strong financial interests in supporting or acquiescing in what Enron was doing rather than in blocking it. Enron broke laws as well as stretched them. And it spent more than $10 million on political donations in the big election years, spreading its largesse across a wide range of politicians in both the main American parties as well as in some other countries as well. So just about every element of liberal, capitalist democracy was damaged by the affair: faith in the honesty of management, faith in private pensions, faith in accounting and auditing standards, faith in the transparency and reliability of capital markets, faith in the application of the rule of law, and faith in government as the disinterested arbiter of the whole system.

*

On the face of it, this is a very specific, particular problem: malfeasance at Enron, the attempted capture of the political process in a democracy by big business. In a way it is only that: such problems need to be addressed with specific solutions, bringing new controls on campaign finance and new transparency for company accounts. But it is also a very broad problem, which explains why capitalism is destined to remain unpopular and why there will be a constant struggle to benefit from its virtues while restraining its vices.

Companies need to be free to act, take risks, innovate, expand. Their activities need a general, light hand of regulation by government to ensure fair play, safe practices and open competition. Also, however, government has another interest: in any democracy but also in many authoritarian regimes, political leaders want the economic growth, jobs and resources that private investment brings. So there is an almost irresistible incentive for the supposed custodians of business also to get involved in its decisions, in the hope of taking credit for some of them in the eyes of the electorate; and that urge is matched in turn by an urge on the part of businesses to try to win over politicians and other regulators to their side.

This interplay between business and government, which has grown in most rich countries during the past few decades even as privatization has reduced the state's direct role in running businesses, eats at the very heart of liberal democracy. It is corrosive of popular trust in both democracy and capitalism. For whenever a corporate donation is accepted by a political party, it is reasonable to assume that the donor is hoping for something in return. Whenever an export contract is signed thanks to political pressure, or a new factory is built thanks to a government subsidy or licence, the biggest beneficiary of what has occurred is the company itself, and it does not take much imagination to begin to suspect corruption.

In principle, in a liberal democracy, popular suspicion of capitalism and of companies ought to be tempered by the belief that democratically elected governments can and will intervene to prevent excesses, to ensure fair play, to protect the weakest. Separation of powers within government serves to ensure that a democracy cannot be subverted by one or other branch of government; the rule of law, founded on a constitution, provides an equal benchmark and protection for all. But the more that companies appear to control governments themselves, subverting the branches of government from the outside, the less this belief will serve to temper the suspicion and hostility. This is plainly a problem in poor countries in which political and judicial institutions are weak and the processes of government are easily corruptible. But it has also become a weakness of the rich, developed countries too.

In normal times, this struggle between the vices and the virtues of business can play itself out without doing too much damage. The best time, after all, to root out corruption and to restore government's purity and independence is when the economic and social times are good. But one thing can be said with certainty about capitalism: it will always bring bad times as well as good ones. The big danger is that when the bad times come, disillusionment with corruption and collusion between government and business could become explosive.

8

Unstable

Capitalism, challenged though it was, had a remarkable twentieth century. It succeeded in raising the living standards of the rich countries of mankind in a spectacular fashion, achieving the most rapid, sustained rise in living standards in human history. In poorer countries, too, the more moderate rise in living standards that was achieved also meant that, on this measure at least, the twentieth century was their best century in history. This spectacular success was based on capitalism's ability to bring about change, change in the way things are done, and for whom they are done, all in the search for profit. That search generates capitalism's energy, its innovativeness, the temptations it offers people and organizations to risk their money and their effort on new ventures. However, capitalism's success has depended also on a sort of financial chutzpah among conventional banks and stockmarket investors, which is shown by their willingness to lend and venture money they do not physically possess in the hope, indeed expectation, that this sleight of hand will not be challenged and that, in any case, by the time the reckoning occurs (if it ever does), enough money will have been made to cover the loans or investments, with profits on top. It is, one might say, a triumph of the willingness to defy reality, in order better to create a new reality. Or it is a triumph of the willingness to use other people's money to create more for oneself.

But that triumph can so easily turn to failure. The same elements that contribute to capitalism's success – confidence, risk-taking, financial chutzpah, reality-defiance – also bring about its recurrent bouts of failure. This can happen in a variety of ways. Some booms turn to bust because their very success causes shortages of workers or goods and then inflation, forcing central banks to intervene by sharply raising the cost of money or, eventually, making lenders panic for fear that inflation will erode the value of their commitments. That is what happened in the 1970s and 1980s, when inflation was a constant preoccupation in the rich countries, and hyper-inflation a scourge of many poor ones.

Other booms disappear because over-confidence leads to over-investment, as speculators and then companies all spend too much in competition with one another, building much more productive capacity than demand will bear, which then hangs over the economy for several years, depressing future investment. Why build new factories or offices when the old ones are sitting there, unused? That is what happened in Japan when the apparently golden age of the late 1980s turned into a stockmarket crash and stagnation in the 1990s; and it is what happened in America in the late 1990s and early twenty-first century, when a phenomenal, investment-led boom turned to a sudden bust.

Politics, too, frequently intervenes to bring on recession. Sudden political change may be caused by a Middle Eastern war and then an oil-price hike, as in the early 1970s, or by a bout of nationalizations or new regulations in many third world countries in that era, or by a change of regime as in Indonesia in 1998, or the terrorist attacks on New York and Washington in September 2001 – all these changes and more can abruptly alter businesses' expectations and behaviour. They may also damage the confidence of consumers or investors about spending their money in that region, or even in the world as a whole.

Failure has many grand causes. But humbler creatures also share the guilt. The chutzpah-rich financial intermediaries have often made recessions much worse than they need be, for their reality-defiance can easily turn into reverse, as loans are called in and gambles that were made on credit during the good times turn to losses and bankruptcies, producing a chain of financial failures or contractions. In such circumstances the chutzpah typically turns into extreme caution, as lenders and investors sit on their cash rather than taking any risks. Financial panics, indeed, can prove the most brutal recessions of all, for they arise as if out of nowhere, following directly on from a bountiful period in which everything seemed to be possible. What has changed is the psychology, nothing more; but that means that everything has changed, for economic activity is all about human psychology, the confidence to take risks or the cautious desire to avoid them. When the moneymen flee in panic, hoping to minimize their losses or sell their holdings to someone slower and more foolish, whole economies can turn from hope to despair, almost overnight. These things are frequently measured by currency-market panics, or falls in share prices, or property-market collapses, or piles of bad debts and defaults. The real measures, however, lie in people's lives: in bankruptcy, unemployment, falling living standards, debt and even suicide.

Even a short period of unemployment can be painful to those who suffer it, bringing disgrace as well as poverty. But even as capitalism seems to swing naturally from boom to bust, so its rhythms naturally send it swinging back again. At some point during the recession, costs and prices are so low that investors are tempted again by the chance to make profits, or savers are tempted to start spending their money again. And so the cycle begins once more.

It all sounds so natural, almost the stuff of a television wildlife documentary; life and death, renewal and decay, the cycle of the seasons. After sun comes rain, and after rain comes the sun. And yet it was not without reason that Karl Marx and his followers spoke of the recurrent 'crises' of capitalism, and their expectation (or was it hope?) that such crises would, in due course, drive the proletariat to revolt. Marx's forecast, of crises that became ever larger, and of classes that became ever more polarized and alienated from one another, has not come to pass. Nevertheless, his observation that capitalism's greatest weakness is its instability, its tendency to experience business cycles that sometimes turn into crises, is surely correct.

That observation is not, on its own, very helpful, for it fails to answer the most important questions. That economies have ups and downs is not in itself particularly remarkable: so does every other aspect of life. We win in love, we lose in love; we pass exams and we fail them. The important questions concern the way in which such routine ups and downs, such dramas, can turn into crises. The first, crucial question concerns what it is that determines whether a mere economic downturn lasts long enough and becomes drastic enough to become a crisis. And, for a contemporary audience interested in the present and the twenty-first-century future, a second question is whether the modern world economy, with its free-flowing capital but also large presence of government spending, is more prone to such crises, or less. To put it in Marxist terms once again, the classes may be less alienated from one another than he expected. But might he be right that the crises will become ever larger?

*

Certainly, the twentieth century saw one of the biggest such crises that had ever occurred. Before the Great Depression of the 1930s, the conventional view among Western economists, which was shared by businessmen and politicians, was that recessions were nature's purgative. They had to be endured, but one felt better for them afterwards. This was fine for someone with a country house in which to sit out the recession, but not likely to make people love capitalism if they were queuing in a soup kitchen. Even so, the view contained some elements of the truth. But it missed out something important. Purgatives can be made a lot worse than they need to be. And when that happens, they can be life-threatening.

What most people remember about the Great Depression, apart from the Wall Street crash, the dole queues, the dust bowl and the migrant farmers in Steinbeck's *The Grapes of Wrath*, is that at first governments and conventional economists sat on their hands saying the purgative had to be endured, and then John Maynard Keynes came along in Britain to argue that, on the contrary, they should do a lot because public spending was the only thing capable in the midst of a depression of boosting demand. Pay people to dig holes, if you must, and then to fill them in again. But whatever you do, spend. But, like most memories, this is accurate only in parts. And it gets the crucial bit wrong. This is that governments did not simply sit on their hands waiting for the purgative to do its work. Instead, they made things worse – a lot worse.

America's central bank, the Federal Reserve Board, had helped bring about the crash in 1929 by raising interest rates. That may have been correct: America had had a huge speculative boom, albeit fuelled by the Fed's previously loose monetary policy. The 1920s had been a time of great optimism in America, as immigration added to the pool of available labour while new technology, notably electricity, the motor car and mass production, drove industrial growth. Cheap money and financial speculation helped that growth to go into overdrive. As during the 1990s, the United States was said to be enjoying a 'new economy', which brought with it euphoria, enthusiasm and a sense of endlessly sunny vistas ahead. It all came to an end with the Wall Street crash.

Fortunes were destroyed, and along with them many hopes. A recession was inevitable, and began almost immediately. The purge was beginning. But the Fed made things worse by leaving its interest rates high well after the crash. In 1930–31, just when money was getting painfully short, as banks cut lending in a desperate effort to stay in business amid a liquidity shortage, the Fed then reduced its own lending. It raised interest rates again in 1931–2, after Britain's decision to break the pound free from the gold standard led to fears of gold outflows amid an international panic. Other countries' central banks also raised interest rates in order to help stay on the gold standard for currencies.

Why? Two words dominated policy orthodoxy: liquidation and stability. It was firmly believed by senior people in many governments, most notably that of the United States, that what was needed was a liquidation, a purge, of excess capacity, debts, companies, banks and behaviour. Moreover, it was not believed that this should just be allowed to happen; government ought to help it to happen by keeping monetary conditions tight and taking a stern attitude to bank collapses. The other, related, word was stability: the idea that the way to restore investors' and lenders' confidence was to keep currencies stable through the international gold standard and to ensure that government budgets were balanced.

So, just when a bit of extra spending or lower taxes would have helped keep the economy going, most governments cut spending to balance their budgets. This last error, made in the name of stability, is remembered because of Keynes's ideas and because of President Roosevelt's later 'New Deal' spending programmes (though he, too, was loath to borrow to finance them). But although budget balancing was damaging it was probably less important than other mistakes, since government spending was in any case quite small in relation to the whole economy in the 1930s: about 8 per cent of GDP in America, though already 20–30 per cent in most West European countries, including Britain. The corresponding figures today are 30–35 per cent of GDP in America and 40–55 per cent in the European Union (with Britain at the lower end of that scale). So public spending, and budget balances, matter much more today.

Central banks and Treasuries were not the only perverse policy-makers. Congress and the White House joined in. In 1930, just when trade was needed more than ever to keep economies going by spreading demand around the globe, President Herbert Hoover signed the Smoot–Hawley tariff act, ignoring formal protests by more than thirty countries, sharply raising tariff barriers and triggering a world-wide spate of retaliatory protectionism. America had some good reasons to be annoyed with the outside world, as Britain, France and Germany were meanwhile reneging on debts to the United States that had accumulated during and after the First World War. But the results were terrifying: the volume of world trade, already shrinking in 1929, fell by two-thirds by 1933.

There is room for doubt and disputation about which of the various causal factors played the biggest role in bringing about the downturn of the 1930s. However, there is little room for doubt about the fact that what would, but for government, have been a modest, conventional recession was turned into the most searing downturn of the century, probably of all history. Like other downturns, it certainly acted as a purge, but ended up by almost killing the patient.

To a historian, perhaps the crucial policy question is whether the Great Depression was avoidable. The analysis just given suggests that it was, for governments played a critical role in turning the drama into a crisis. But the deeper question is whether, given the knowledge and circumstances of the time, governments could reasonably have been expected to have acted differently. What they did now looks utterly, even criminally crazy, but that is with the benefit of hindsight.

The answer, probably, is that governments can be forgiven one of their sins, but not most of them. The forgivable sin was the main-tenance of currency stability by means of the gold standard. This method of fixing exchange rates to a pre-set value in gold had been successful before the First World War. It encouraged trade, by eliminat-ing currency risk between countries linked to gold. And, at times of crisis, or rather drama, it gave investors some assurance as to the future pattern of prices and the focus of government policy. So investors who had fled as an economic drama began tended to return quickly to snap up what had now, thanks to the drama, become bargains, as long as they felt sure that devaluations of exchange rates were not going to occur.

The sin, with the benefit of hindsight, lay in not realizing that this pre-war credibility no longer held. Investors, it turned out, no longer believed that governments would, or could, hold their pegs to gold, so they speculated upon breaks with the gold standard and on devaluations. Barry Eichengreen, professor of economics at the University of California at Berkeley, and one of the world's authorities on the gold standard and capital flows, blames this change, in his book *Globalizing Capital: A History of the International Monetary System*, on democracy, or at least on the changing institutions and expectations of democratic societies. By the 1920s and 1930s, governments could no longer separate exchange rate policy from domestic politics and so were vulnerable to pressure from groups of all kinds. They could no longer hold the line.

One lesson of economic history, and in particular the successive experimentation during the past century with different exchange rate regimes – the gold standard, floating rates, fixed rates against the dollar after 1945, 'managed' floating, the European Monetary System of target bands, currency boards, Europe's monetary union – is that there is no 'right' answer as to how to manage exchange rates. Each choice comes with advantages and disadvantages, because each comes with trade-offs, most notably in the balance between domestic economic policy and the need or desire to sustain a currency regime. If the currency regime is to be made seemingly unchangeable, as is the case for the countries that have joined the European Union's euro, there has to be a certainty that domestic public and political opinion is willing to accept that in a period of difficulty all necessary economic adjustments will have to be made in other areas and policies, and not in the currency regime (at least, not in the currency regime used with the main trading partners, that is, other euro members).

In America in the 1930s, following Mr Eichengreen's very plausible theory, the political pressures on domestic policy made it less likely that economic management could be made the slave of the exchange rate. To a degree, that is the privilege of a large country and economy: the currency can be treated as a residual variable, rather than a crucial, fixed element, for trade with other countries plays a relatively small role in economic activity. The same is now true of the euro zone in its dealings with other currencies, but not in its internal arrangements. Outside America, it was also the case in the 1930s that governments and all other social institutions had been gravely weakened by the First World War, and, in the case of France and Germany, by the terms of the Versailles Treaty that ended it. So betting against government resilience was a reasonable option, on this as on virtually any topic. Governments, notably Europe's in the 1920s and America's in the early 1930s, were deluding themselves when they thought that they should, would and could still hold the line.

That sin is forgivable because, at the time, it may have felt reasonable to try to re-establish such credibility. The lack of it was provable only by subsequent events, and in the light of a chain reaction of financial problems and political instability. The gold standard had, after all, been a successful way to handle exchange rates and capital flows for upwards of fifty years in most developed countries, so while it may with hindsight have been wrong to try to persist with it, it was not certifiably mad to do so. It offered some promise of a reliable and proven anchor in an otherwise turbulent and unreliable world. The other sins, however, are much less forgivable, for they consisted in the rejection, or the forgetting, of some of the basic economic and financial lessons of the nineteenth century.

The biggest of these was the neglect of bank failures. This took place particularly clearly in America, as banks failed there in a cascade during the first few years of the 1930s. At such moments of systemic crisis, it is necessary for the government to step in as lender of last resort, offering unlimited funds but on penal terms to chosen institutions, in order to punish the managers of the failed banks but to maintain confidence in the system as a whole. Walter Bagehot, a Victorian banker and financial writer who was also editor of *The Economist*, had established this idea of a central bank acting as lender of last resort in the 1870s, in his book *Lombard Street*, and it became a new orthodoxy. That way, good banks need not be pulled down with bad ones, and confidence can be restored. But in the 1930s this conflicted with the mantra of liquidation. So banks were left simply to collapse and die.

Moreover, such neglect also took an international form in Europe with the collapse of Credit Anstalt, Austria's biggest bank, in 1931. The Austrian government acted correctly by stepping in as lender of last resort and guaranteeing the bank's deposits. But this domestic crisis turned into an international one because savers feared there would also be a devaluation since Austria's rescue act was, in effect, inconsistent with its adherence to the gold standard, as the rescue served to expand the money supply. What was then needed was international financial co-operation, a loan from other countries to Austria's central bank to allow it to keep up its role as lender of last resort as well as to maintain the convertibility of its currency. Negotiations took place, but they were slow and then in the end blocked by France whose government wanted diplomatic concessions from Austria in order to make gains at Germany's expense. So no loan was made, Austria abandoned the gold standard – and, in due course, so did other countries. In a conflict with international politics, financial soundness lost.

The second big sin was the renunciation of trade as a motor for economic activity. This was despite all the evidence of the nineteenth century which had showed that trade, and the related free flow of capital across borders, was an essential source of economic growth. Trade, it had been said, followed the flag, which was why so many military efforts were made both by European countries (all around the world) and even the United States (most notably in Japan in the 1850s and 1860s) to secure trade routes and to persuade, or force, other countries to participate in the activity. It may be that, by the 1920s and 1930s, governments had become blinded by that very association of trade with empire, and thus by the halt to the expansion of empires that took place after the First World War. Whatever the reason, they turned their backs on trade through the raising of tariffs and other barriers, with fateful consequences.

The combination of bank failures and the shrinkage of trade meant that what might have been a modest period of deflation – that is, falling prices and wages – turned into drops in both of magnitudes never seen before. In some countries there were drops of up to 50 per cent. Deflation on that sort of scale serves to freeze economic activity, for those with cash will sit on it in anticipation that assets they were thinking of buying will soon be cheaper still; and those without cash cannot get hold of it because there is no employment, or because the terms demanded by banks in return for loans make them impossible for most businesses to obtain. The circle is vicious: spending drops because prices will later become lower, but then incomes drop too, as unemployment rises and wages are cut, and spending drops even further.

The Great Depression does, however, also offer some encouragement for the twenty-first century. That encouragement comes in two parts. The first is that in economic history such events have been highly unusual. Even Karl Marx would have been hugely excited by the 1930s, since in his lifetime (1818–83) nothing of that magnitude occurred (even the depression of the 1870s was less acute than was that of the 1930s). The combination of an economic downturn and the post-First World War fragility of political systems and international relations was deadly, but also very special to the time.

The second encouragement is that the lessons of that dreadful period are there to be learned by all who live after it: that protectionism makes such crises worse; that central banks need to intervene to avert threats to the banking system; that at a time of sharp monetary contraction the government needs to keep supplying more, and cheaper, money; that in extreme circumstances, government borrowing and spending can help restore stability rather than threatening it. Crises can, of course, be repeated. But they are less likely to be as painful, or as long-lived, if the lessons are clear, and regularly re-affirmed.

*

There have been plenty of other crashes and economic dramas in countries all around the world. Indeed, there have been plenty of nasty episodes even in the past thirty years: the collapse of the post-1945 system of fixed exchange rates in the early 1970s, for example; Latin America's debt crisis in the 1980s; East Asia's financial crash in 1997–8; or the very particular local collapses in Russia after the fall of communism in the 1990s, or in Indonesia after the fall of President Suharto in 1998.

But there has really been only one other episode in a big country during the past hundred years to match the financial boom and bust seen in America in the 1920s and 1930s, and it took place in Japan in the 1980s, 1990s and, alas, beyond. In 1924–9, Wall Street's most popularly cited share-price measure, the Dow Jones Industrial Average, rose by 300 per cent (that is, fourfold), and then plunged by 84 per cent in 1929–32. Like America in the 1920s, Japan in the 1980s had been filled with a euphoric sense that old economic rules no longer applied, that Japan had founded a new economy. Japan's industrial and export juggernaut was on the move, and its methods were deemed to be somehow superior to those of its rivals. The Nikkei stockmarket average, the equivalent to America's Dow, climbed by 492 per cent (that is, nearly sixfold) in 1980–89; property prices trebled. Then the crash came: the Nikkei lost 64 per cent of its value in 1990–98, and property prices fell by more than two-thirds.

Despite this, Japan did not follow the American path of the 1930s by entering a great depression in the 1990s. It had a dispiriting time in that decade, with stagnant economic growth and recurrent bouts of apparent recovery, hopes for which were then dashed. More than a decade after the crash began, Japan remains a vulnerable place, vulnerable even to a severe and prolonged recession, as was argued in Chapter 4. But the comparison is still illuminating: even after a boom as big as America's in the 1920s and a bust in financial-asset prices that was just as large, there was no immediate repeat of the 1930s: Japanese living standards stayed high, unemployment fairly low.

It would be premature to declare this episode closed, and the danger passed. But some tentative lessons can still be drawn from a comparison of the 1990s with the 1930s. One is that the Bank of Japan copied the mistake made by America's central bank, though not as zealously. Like the Fed in the 1920s, it had loosened monetary policy in the 1980s and thus fuelled the speculative boom in share prices and property lending. It then helped bring on the crash in January 1990 by successively raising interest rates. But after the crash took place, it was loath to cut rates again for fear of restarting the asset-price boom. This caution may well have made the crash worse.

In two important respects, however, Japan's drama was saved from becoming an immediate crisis because lessons had been learned. One was that neither it, nor its trading partners, followed the Smoot–Hawley example. World trade remained as open as before the crash, as did Japan's trade, which enabled its exports to continue to grow even as domestic activity slowed. At times, most notably during a row with America over car exports in 1995, this openness looked in danger, but the threat passed. Global demand and competition could continue to provide some support and stimulus for the tradable portion of Japan's private sector, even as the domestic and untradable portions suffered from the stagnation.

The second saviour was that the Japanese government used fiscal policy to moderate the downturn. It did not follow the 1930s' nostrums of balancing the budget, and its spending was large enough to make a considerable difference – around 35 per cent of GDP in the early 1990s compared with the American federal government's 8 per cent of GDP in the early 1930s. Moreover, Japan was in good shape to use its fiscal ammunition. In 1990 the general government budget had a surplus of 2.9 per cent of GDP; by the end of the decade successive spending packages gave it a deficit of 9–10 per cent of GDP. This gave Japan a problem of how to sort out its public finances in the future, but meanwhile had prevented the severe contraction that the economy would otherwise almost certainly have suffered.

A third saviour, however, was luck, and it led the Japanese government to act in a harmful way, to make its own sort of mistakes. The open and healthy world economy, combined especially with rapid growth in Japan's nearby markets in East Asia from 1990 until 1997, helped prop up Japan and may have led the finance ministry to conclude that its nastiest problem – a huge pile of bad loans at all Japan's banks – would in time sort itself out as the economy revived. So the ministry chose to conceal the true magnitude of the problem, both in its own reports and by allowing banks to massage their accounts.

In a way, this did constitute a lesson from the 1930s: that the government had to step in to deal with banking collapses. But it was learned in the wrong way: the government dealt with the banking collapses by denying reality and by colluding with misleading accounting, rather than by forcing a restructuring of the financial system. This intervention was in one way true to the form shown in the previous four decades. Compared with America's, Japan's post-war governments were typically fairly interventionist, taking the view that they knew best and that people would trust in their judgement. But in the

1990s, as that intervention came to be seen as both ineffective and corrupt, Japanese people, firms and investors lost their trust in the bureaucrats' judgement. Instead, this form of government intervention became counter-productive. By concealing the truth and consistently making over-optimistic forecasts of economic revival, the bureaucracy succeeded only in eroding consumers' confidence.

As people became more worried about their jobs, they saved more, spent less, and the condition of both the economy and the banks got worse, not better. The finance ministry's luck turned in 1997 when East Asia had its own crash, hitting Japanese exports and damaging consumer confidence in Japan still further. Only since then has a great depression looked a real possibility for Japan, with consumer prices falling, households postponing their purchases and banks beginning to go under. In response to this situation, the government finally began to act, nationalizing some banks and putting a huge financial safety net under the others. Again, the Japanese government made a big mistake, as it heeded only part of Walter Bagehot's orthodoxy: it lent as a last resort, supporting the banking system; but it did not combine this with penal terms in order to force out the old managers, and with a forced restructuring to turn bad banks into new, cleaner ones.

The result of the Japanese crash of 1990 has, in economic terms, been less a collapse than a slow puncture. For the stability of society, that was a much better outcome in the first post-crash decade than the one America went through during the 1930s. Unemployment stayed low, the government helped to prop up the economy, and an open world-trading system meant that big Japanese firms could by and large survive. It was miserable for some: the suicide rate rose sharply, along with the bankruptcy roster. But this policy of muddling through, hoping that something better would turn up, did work, for a while. The question now, at the start of the twenty-first century, is whether, by just muddling through and failing to bring in true change and reform, the Japanese government may have averted one crisis but merely stored up trouble for another. There are some bad portents: in 2001, some of the language used in Japan, even by those favouring radical reform, came to echo language used in America in the early 1930s. What was needed, said Junichiro Koizumi when he became prime minister in the spring of 2001 on a reformist mandate, was pain, a purge, a liquidation. The governor of the Bank of Japan joined in, saying (despite protests) that his central bank would ensure that monetary conditions are kept tight in order to encourage the purging process to take place. The possible implications if this process goes wrong were discussed in Chapter 4.

*

Misguided governments make capitalism's crises worse by their policy mistakes, and thereby determine whether an economic drama turns into a potential tragedy. That has been the argument from the two cases of economic and financial instability cited so far. But some people think this is unfair, that governments merely get tossed around on a far stronger and more malevolent wind: that of financial speculation. Behind most recessions, as in the 1930s and 1990s, there are financial booms and busts. As Walter Bagehot also wrote: 'at particular times a great deal of stupid people have a great deal of stupid money . . . and there is speculation . . . and there is panic.' And surely one of the problems of liberalism is that in these days of globalized, free-flowing capital there is more speculation, larger-scale panics and more chance of innocent bystanders getting hurt.

Certainly, many people concluded from the crash of East Asia's financial markets in 1997–8 that this was the case. It was said to be the first crisis of the era of globalization. The crash began fairly innocuously in Thailand, with the devaluation of the Thai currency, the baht. Plenty of pundits had predicted trouble in specific countries, such as Thailand, Malaysia and South Korea. But few can have predicted the way in which these troubles built upon each other, producing a contagious effect throughout the region. International panic, as investors fled one country and reassessed the chances of others, served to transmit these currency and debt troubles from one East Asian country to another, and then, like a ghastly plague, across the oceans to Latin America and across the steppes to Russia.

It would be wrong, however, to conclude just from this multi-country episode that the 1990s brought in a new and far more frightening era for financial markets. Such panics are, as the above quotation from Bagehot suggests, as old as the hills. They are an integral and always disturbing part of capitalism's instability, but they are not new. Nor is international panic a novelty. Wall Street's 1929 crash was swiftly transmitted across borders, and, as was outlined earlier in this chapter, the damage to the world economy was aggravated by the collapse of Credit Anstalt in Austria in 1931 when foreign lenders withdrew their funds. Many of the banking and currency crises in Latin America at the start of the twentieth century had an international flavour, since Argentina and Brazil were importing large amounts of capital from Europe.

And here's another constant: one type of financial institution is hugely more dangerous than all the rest. It is the one that claims to be the safest: the bank. Its basic danger, though modern pressures on its profits have added others, arises from its age-old asset–liability mismatch. This is a fancy way of describing the commercial bank's financial chutzpah: it borrows short-term money from depositors and doles it out on a fairly long-term basis to borrowers. The trouble is that deposits can leave quickly, while loans tend to stay put, so when a bank gets into trouble it does so in spectacular fashion. Speculators may lurk in the wings of financial crises, but banks always occupy centre stage, usually piled up in a crumpled heap. This was so in Thailand and Indonesia in 1997–8, in Sweden in 1990–91, in America in the 1930s, in Germany and France in 1901 and 1907, respectively, in Japan in the 1990s.

The question, however, is what, if anything, is really new. The best answer has been offered in a 2001 study carried out by Barry Eichengreen with Michael Bordo, another American economist, and two colleagues from the World Bank, in which they compared the financial crises that took place throughout the twentieth century. They did so in the hope of answering one of the questions posed at the outset of this chapter: is our present age particularly prone to financial crises? They embarked on their task with a splendid historical thoroughness, seeking to track down and compare the occurrences of the two principal sorts of financial crisis – banking crises and currency crises – that have occurred in the period since 1880, when the gold standard came into widespread use. Their study also revealed the existence of a third sort of crisis, one in which banking and currency collapses occur together or in swift succession. Because statistics are not available so far back for many countries, comparisons over the full period from 1880 to 2000 were possible for only twenty-one countries. But for the period after 1973 a larger sample of fifty-six industrial and emerging countries could be used. 'Emerging' was the 1990s euphemism for poor countries that stood a chance of getting richer.

Several things stand out. The first is that the period since 1973 has indeed been one of the most unstable phases of the past century or so. Only the inter-war years, with the Great Depression, beats this period for the frequency of currency, banking or twin crises. The period 1880–1913 had only a third of today's number of crises; in the 1950–71 period crises were only half as likely as since 1973. But what does that tell you? Many might conclude that this shows that globalization, one feature of which is the free flow of capital around the world, leads to more crises. But 1880–1913 was also a period of globalization, in which capital was arguably even freer to move across borders than it is today.

The second point is that many of the most painful episodes, measured by the subsequent drop in GDP in the country or countries concerned, occurred during and after twin crises, when banking and currency crises coincided: that is, regardless of which caused which, a moment when international and domestic woes fed upon each other. These twin crises were most prevalent in the inter-war years, but the post-1973 period is close behind. When the Bretton Woods system of fixed exchange rates prevailed in 1950–71, there were virtually no banking crises even though there were some currency collapses when a devaluation was forced. And before 1913, belief in governments' adherence to the gold standard meant that currency rates were left largely unchallenged.

There is an important addendum to this point. It is that almost all such episodes of twin crises took place in so-called emerging or developing countries rather than the richer, developed ones. This suggests that globalization, *per se*, is not the right issue on which to focus, for that affects rich and poor countries alike. What seems to matter most is the fragility of the institutional and political structures in poor, emerging countries, particularly the weakness of bank regulation and supervision, and with it a weakness in law enforcement and the judicial system. So it is the combination of globalized flows of capital with weak structures that causes the problem.

In principle, the correct sequence in which to open up a country to global capital flows would be to make the regulatory structures strong first, and then to open the doors. But in practice many developing countries have tried to do things the other way around. The desire for economic growth, and for the foreign capital and technology that can help fuel it, exerts a more powerful allure than does the more boring effort to develop political, regulatory and judicial processes. This is not particularly surprising: in countries that are now rich, too, good bank regulation was the product of earlier crises, not something that just arose out of brilliant foresightedness. But, although it is comforting to the mind, this is not very reassuring to the heart, for it means that developing countries are likely to develop by bouncing from crisis to crisis.

The third point, however, is that throughout the century, countries bounced back from such crises fairly quickly. Despite the failings of the gold standard in the 1930s, the longer-term lesson is that countries generally bounced back more rapidly at times when they were using a fixed and politically credible currency regime such as the gold standard (and now, it will be hoped, the euro). This is because, even if a currency's fixed rate was temporarily suspended, investors expected it to be restored at the previous rate in due course, so after the crisis came a new inflow of capital betting on the restoration. The semi-fixed rates used by East Asian countries in 1997–8 did not enjoy this self-regulating virtue. And those crucial words, 'politically credible' must be scrutinized carefully: just tying the currency to any anchor, regardless of the possible impact on the economy and the domestic political choices that would imply, is unlikely to remain credible for long. In 2000–2001 that was the predicament Argentina found itself in, for although its fixed currency tie with the US dollar had been effective in curing hyper-inflation the tie itself caused further damage. Only 11 per cent of Argentina's exports went to the United States, so it reaped little benefit from the loss of currency risk in that market but felt all the pain of the US dollar's strength against the currencies of countries with which Argentina traded a lot, such as Brazil. The result was Argentina's default on its foreign debts in December 2001, the collapse of the government and the breaking of that peso–dollar link – all with disastrous economic consequences in that country.

Is the current phase of globalization making things worse? If, as is done by many critics of globalization, the post-1973 period is divided into two in order to separate the phase of most rapid and profound globalization, after 1988, from before, then the facts are quite reassuring. Messrs Eichengreen, Bordo *et al.* found that currency crises were actually more prevalent before 1988 than subsequently. But banking crises were more frequent in the later period, essentially in emerging or developing countries, and they were often combined with currency crises.

What is crucial in making a crisis really worthy of the term, at least from the point of view of jobs, firms and society, is the length of time the crisis lasts. On this question, the study is reassuring: crises have not got any longer as the century has gone on. Nor have they got any shorter. But, in any event, the Great Depression was the great exception to the rule. And how about the depth of such crises, measured by the loss in output during the trouble compared with the pre-crisis trend? Here the answer is even more reassuring. The output loss from currency crises today is only between half and two-thirds what it was in 1880–1913, the previous age of globalization. The loss during banking crises is estimated as 75–80 per cent today of the average level in 1880–1913. Only twin crises have shown a greater severity, and the difference is minimal.

That finding is indeed comforting: if so, modern times are not uniquely prone to financial instability, as George Soros, a great financier, philanthropist and worrier about globalization, has stated in his 1998 book *The Crisis of Global Capitalism*. But we should not be too cheered. For it is nevertheless the case that the problem that brought capitalism close to collapse in the 1930s, close to forcing humanity to choose a terrible alternative, is still with us, more or less unchanged. Capitalism is, indeed, inherently unstable.

*

There is, however, a mitigating observation, although it is not, on the face of it, terribly encouraging to a free-marketeer. This is the fact that the period of the century when there were virtually no banking crises, and few currency crises, was the period from 1950 until 1973, under the Bretton Woods regime of fixed exchange rates, so named because it was agreed upon in Bretton Woods, New Hampshire at the same time as the International Monetary Fund (IMF) and the World Bank were being set up, in 1944. Apart from the fixed rates, the other main financial characteristic was that most governments imposed strict controls on domestic and international transactions, which many did not release until the 1980s. For poor countries, it was not by any means a happy period: capital did not (and mostly could not) flow in their direction. But for the lucky rich it was a golden age. The difficult task is to explain why.

Government must lie at the heart of any such explanation. For, crudely, the lessons learned from the 1930s by governments of developed countries were that high unemployment risked political devastation, that it was a delusion to think that governments should – or could – sit on their hands during recessions, and that central planning had helped both Hitler and Stalin to industrialize and create jobs. The result was a broad expansion in government spending and intervention in all the richer economies. The extent and nature of the growth of government varied (less spending in America and Japan than in Western Europe, more regulation and planning in Europe and Japan than America) but the thrust was similar.

This is a crude description, but the lessons had been learned crudely. The 'full-employment' success of Hitler and Stalin had actually been based on brutality, plus the suppression of wages; and as eventually became clear, any gains from the widespread use of central planning were temporary. Socialist governments (for example, in Britain) also added a dash of Marx, as they nationalized the 'commanding heights' of the economy, such as steel, coal and the railways, to obtain the magic of public ownership, but then found them turning into demanding troughs.

From 1950 to 1973, the developed economies enjoyed their fastest sustained period of economic growth of the whole century, with the fastest sustained rise in productivity and in incomes, and with low male unemployment. This period's productivity growth was faster even than the 1990s in America: the information technology-led 'new economy' of that period was actually merely returning the United States towards the sort of productivity growth rates it had enjoyed during 1950–73. To some, this golden age was thus a time when governments carefully nurtured and restrained capitalism. By contrast, the 1980s and 1990s, during which much talk, and some action, was of deregulation and reducing the role of the state, were to such critics a period that rent the fabric of society asunder, substituting the brutality of market forces for the helping hand of the state.

The other side of the debate stresses some different points. One is that, in a crucial respect, the post-war era featured a big reduction in government intervention. The establishment in 1947 of the General Agreement on Tariffs and Trade (GATT) began a progressive lowering of the high barriers to trade that had been established in the 1920s and 1930s, at least between the developed, non-communist countries, resulting in a rapid expansion of trade and, from the early 1960s, an expansion of overseas investment by multinational companies. Trade and peace, on this analysis, brought growth.

Another point stressed on this side is that the level of government spending was not, in fact, particularly high during the golden age of 1950–73, at least not by subsequent standards. In 1970, taking the twenty-two (as they then were) rich countries of the OECD as a whole, public spending equalled 32.3 per cent of GDP, similar to its current level in supposedly rapacious, market-led America. In France, Germany and Britain it was 38–9 per cent. It was only between 1970 and 1995 that public spending reached its peak, adding a further 10 percentage points in the OECD as a whole, 15–20 in some parts of it. In Western Europe, it continued to rise during the 1990s. On this view, the rise in public spending in the 1970s and 1980s was a response to the slow growth and unemployment of those decades, not a cause of the preceding success. Nowhere has the level of state involvement, measured through spending, been reduced substantially since either 1980 or 1990.

Too much state, or too much market: the argument can easily become raucous. To reach a calmer understanding of the role of government since 1945, and thus to try to chart a course for it for the future as a remedy for or contributor to capitalism's instability, we need to look separately at its various strengths and failings. Since the ideas of John Maynard Keynes, Britain's greatest economist, were a big part of most people's lesson from the 1930s, it is as well to start there.

After his death in 1946, Lord Keynes's writings took on something of a scriptural character; in other words, they were not to be taken literally (or even read at all) but rather to be interpreted according to convenience. He was a self-declared liberal who was tempted by government intervention and favoured capital controls. Yet his most famous prescription, that public spending should be used to create and expand demand, was drawn up for a rare state of affairs: a deflationary depression. A sin he shared with his post-war disciples, however, was an excessive confidence in his own knowledge and judgement.

That led to one big misinterpretation of his views, which did perhaps need experience before it could be shown conclusively to be a mistake. This was the post-war idea that taxing and spending could be used not just to boost demand in a depression but also, in a precisely targeted way, to control the pace of economic growth and the level of employment. The problem with this 'fine tuning' is simple: lack of knowledge. Information about what is happening in an economy is crude and always out of date, and changes in taxes and spending often take a long and unpredictable amount of time to have an effect. The same is true of changes in interest rates. Time after time, governments and their legions of economists got the timing wrong, accelerating when the economy needed some braking, or vice versa. The error with fine-tuning matches the error of the centrally planned, command economy: it assumes an omniscience in government that does not, and cannot, exist.

But another Keynesian idea, that of allowing the natural ebb and flow of spending and revenue to lean against recessions and to restrain booms, does seem to help. The strength of what are called automatic stabilizers (because tax revenue falls during recessions, and spending automatically rises) probably means that the increased size of government tends to moderate the fluctuations of the business cycle. Certainly, the cycles have been less violent since 1950 in the rich countries, though other factors will also have been at work, particularly better banking supervision. A general, broad, fiscal blast can also help: Japan's huge public spending packages during the 1990s came straight out of Keynes. Crises may, as Messrs Eichengreen, Bordo *et al.* have shown, be just as prevalent these days, but their depth seems to be moderated by the size and presence of government spending. While private spending can react to a downturn in a way that aggravates the recession, as firms and people cut their spending to fit their newly reduced circumstances, government budgets naturally lean in the opposite direction (as long as governments allow them to).

There is a further complication, however, that derives from a more wilful misinterpretation of Keynes, combined with the natural incentives of a democracy. Governments, it turned out, did not want simply to use fiscal policy to maintain employment. They wanted to use it to raise everyone's incomes – for, after all, the unemployed are only a small proportion of the electorate. So, rather than running the cyclical mix of surpluses and deficits that Keynes recommended, they hardly ever had fiscal surpluses.

This generated a gradual rise in inflation, which the Vietnam War and the 1974 oil-price hike turned into a rapid one. Combined with a political unwillingness to sacrifice domestic goals for international ones, this led in turn to the collapse of the Bretton Woods fixed rates, and to the use of floating rates instead. From then on, capital controls became hard to sustain – especially given that governments' fiscal policies subsequently fluctuated between deficits and very large deficits for more than twenty years, forcing many to borrow internationally as well as from domestic lenders. Keynes would not have been amused. A solution for deflation had turned into a cause of persistent inflation.

The trouble is that fiscal policy is horribly asymmetrical. In other words, everyone – voters, trade unions, ministries, other pressure groups – can think of reasons why you should raise spending, borrow more or tax less. Politicians who want to create jobs and raise incomes naturally find it easier to do so directly by expanding the public sector rather than by hoping that private businesses will provide. But few people or pressure groups can think of reasons why governments should cut spending or raise taxes. Those who have captured the benefits of previous rounds of public generosity are not keen to give them up. Where this problem can be seen at its clearest is in the welfare state – the collection of public spending and tax policies that, to differing degrees in all the rich countries, seek to provide public services such as education and health, as well as to help the needy through income support, unemployment and invalidity benefit, and retirement pensions.

This is the portion of government involvement that has risen most rapidly since 1960, and has continued to do so, in good times as well as bad. Such transfers and subsidies were equal to 10–15 per cent of GDP in the rich countries in 1960; now they are equal to 25–35 per cent. Much of that rise was driven by the best of intentions. But, though it may have been comforting at times, it has not brought happiness. Despite a spectacular increase in the amount spent on welfare transfers, dissatisfaction with the quality of public services has risen, even in France, the Netherlands, Scandinavia and Germany, where the welfare state is at its most luxurious. Nor has it reduced unemployment: with the labour force expanding rapidly in the 1980s thanks to demographic change, and with labour markets getting more rigid as established groups lobbied successfully for more and more protection, so Western Europe developed a stubbornly high level of unemployment, often more than 8 per cent of the labour force and sometimes as high as 20 per cent, depending on the country. Generous welfare benefits meant that such levels were bearable in the 1980s and 1990s for those on the dole, and that there was no threat to political stability. But those benefits also contributed to the problem by discouraging people from seeking work. And, in the end, long periods without work still lead people to discontent and despair.

This developing dissatisfaction with the state could be waved aside as merely the outcome of rising expectations, or lack of gratitude, if it were not for two other problems. The first is the more unpleasant: that despite all these transfers and subsidies, the condition of the poorest families may actually be worsening in many countries. Explanations for this naturally vary, as do prescriptions for a solution. But those who require more money – and most do, to some extent – hit the second problem. This is that, in the voting booth, people have been resisting both the idea of tax rises and of a reallocation of benefits away from the middle classes and towards the poor. So here is the combined problem: welfare demands are rising, but no one wants to provide the money to meet them.

*

The implications are awkward. The instability of capitalism, seen widely in the 1930s and again in Japan in the 1990s, requires that government should play a moderating, stabilizing role. Much of this is regulatory – ensuring that banks are properly run and penalizing fraud or mismanagement. Some of it consists of doing the right thing during a crisis – being a lender of last resort, expanding the supply of money, keeping trade open. Some of it consists of allowing the automatic stabilizers of spending and borrowing to operate. Most societies, however, also want to provide a safety net to help the poor, and think that certain services – education, health – should be wholly or partly financed by the taxpayer. Democracy, with universal suffrage since 1945, also pushes in the direction of greater government involvement, since the incentive to bribe the voters with their own money is great, and the pressure to offer to do more, rather than less, ineluctable. Yet big government – and no rich country, not even the United States, can claim currently to have small government – brings with it big disadvantages.

One disadvantage is inherent, in principle: higher taxes and more extensive regulations are an infringement of people's economic liberty, which may be a price paid for something else, such as equality, but should also be questioned closely, since even in democracies it is generally imposed by narrow majorities. The other disadvantages, though, are purely practical. One is the already cited problem, that government is not omniscient: despite all those clever economists, it lacks the knowledge to steer and control and achieve brilliant objectives in the way that it promises. The other is that, like any large organization, it is inflexible. Once a course has been set, it is very hard to change it. Eventually, in any society, change will be needed. Capitalism prefers to do this bit by bit. Big government ends up having to do it in great, radical, painful heaves.

As we stride along in the early twenty-first century, we can thus reassure ourselves that government offers some comfort in the face of capitalism's instability: it makes it less likely that future economic dramas will turn into crises. But government has also become a problem itself, acting as a drag on progress and, on occasion, causing its own variety of instability. And it is always being asked to do more, to intervene to solve old problems as well as new ones. In the socialist heyday of the 1960s and 1970s, particularly in Europe, it was always being asked to deal with inequality, another consequence of capitalism. Fashions for socialism may come and go. But anxiety about inequality seems always to be with us.

9

Unequal (1)

People are not created as equals. Liberal, democratic societies believe they should be considered as equals in terms of their political and civil rights, as is aspired to in the American and some other constitutions. But people are not in fact equal in terms of their capabilities, regardless of the political system and ideology of the society within which they live. Some people are strong, some weak, some clever, some less so, some energetic, some sluggish, some prone to sickness, others in fine health, some good at languages, others good at science.

These sorts of differences, being outside our direct control, do not seem to worry us unduly. We may envy those whom nature has blessed, but generally we accept that we can do little about it (though this will change as the science and indeed business of genetic modification develops). Inequality of this sort is considered as just a fact of life. Nurture complicates things greatly, however. People with the same basic genetic make-up develop differently because of accidents not just of birth but of upbringing. Historically, this has worried people much more: an accident of birth that grants someone a large inheritance has caused more jealousy than an accident that grants them a particular set of genes. For inheritance is susceptible to interference by public policy, through the tax system, or by even more overt forms of confiscation.

What is also clear, though, is that inequality is an inherent part of capitalism, as well as of life's struggle. Competition and inequality are opposite sides of the same coin. It is natural for people to compete for advantage, whether for nourishment, esteem, power, sexual partners or wealth (which, at least in the eyes of those who lack it, can bring all the other four as well). Few people think it strange to compete in this way. The drive to work, to invest, to take risks, arises directly from people's desire to prove that they are unequal, different, superior – or, to put it another way, from the desire to overcome disadvantages and to create advantages.

To work properly, indeed, capitalism requires that people should have secure possession of some advantages – specifically, secure property rights – which they may have obtained by work, merit, risk-taking or, indeed, inheritance. Property – that is, land, money, productive assets – is what an investor uses in a new business venture or a trader uses in his business. If there is doubt over the security of that holding, however, the holder will be reluctant to invest, and other people will be reluctant to trust the investors' or traders' promises. So property – that is, actual or potential advantage – is crucial for capitalism, and its use is threatened if its holders feel at constant risk of its seizure, penal taxation or other restriction, even if on the grounds of remedying an inequality. Proudhon's claim in 1840 that 'property is theft' was thus simply a claim that capitalism is theft.

The important question, however, is one about degree rather than kind. There will always be inequality, and there will always be jealousy and competition; and such things are not only inherent but also constructive. But how much inequality is too much? How much is considered just and how much is unjust? At what point does too wide a degree of inequality cause the social binding of a country to snap? These proved to be serious questions during the twentieth century, or at least questions the answers to which can have serious consequences. What is more, this issue is widely considered as one of the biggest weaknesses of capitalism, and its planetary expression, globalization: the growing inequality brought by globalization, it is commonly believed, could threaten the whole process.

In principle, this worry is surely correct. Large gaps in means, in living standards, in opportunities, can indeed threaten the stability of a whole society, because they are liable to call into question the conventional means of obtaining and using resources. The have-nots (or have-a-lot-lesses) are tempted to drop their normal, acquiescent behaviour and instead to band together to challenge the haves, and thus to better their condition by seizing a greater share of income or wealth. This may occur through taxation and regulation imposed through the democratic process (the have-an-awful-lots are generally a small minority) or it may occur through the imposition of more direct, coercive, even violent means. Or, to give the subject an international scale, the have-nots could be tempted to move house, country or continent, to go and live where the grass appears to be greener in order to share somebody else's advantages – or they might, in their rage over their inferior condition, simply seek to hurt those who are better off than themselves, through terrorism. Or their governments may decide that it makes sense, in the national interest or just that of the political élite, to seize someone else's territory or resources by military means in order to take a short-cut towards greater prosperity and power. Saddam Hussein wanted to remedy the inequality, as he saw it, between his power and others' by seizing Kuwait and its oilfields in 1990.

Among these possible responses to inequality the common theme is that, in some circumstances or beyond some point of acceptability, the gap can become so large as to provoke an unconventional and disruptive reaction. But at what point and with what consequences? To grope towards an answer to this question, the issue needs to be divided into two parts: inequality *within* societies or nations, and inequality *between* societies or nations.

The same principles apply to both. Yet a simple contrast of two facts will offer a clue as to why it makes sense to separate them. On the one hand, *within* most countries in the world but particularly within the richest thirty or so, over the course of the twentieth century societies became more equal: the distribution of both income and wealth became more even. It fluctuated, of course, during that period, and in the past twenty years incomes and wealth have typically become more unequal again. But still, comparing 2000 with 1900, the extent of inequality had been greatly reduced. On the other hand, the picture *between* countries looks completely different. During the twentieth century, the gap between the richest and poorest countries widened, virtually continuously. The only times when it narrowed were periods when the incomes of the rich countries were falling or barely growing. A few countries have certainly caught up with the rich. But most have fallen further behind, at least until very recently.

The pattern of experience of these two categories – *within* and *between* – has thus been utterly different. The factors that drive inequality, and the political or social responses to it, are different between these categories. Indeed, what this differing pattern of experience chiefly tells us is that inequality *within* countries is much more important, as a continuing influence on policy, politics and behaviour, than that *between* countries. Concern about inequality *within* has forced things to change, in such a way as to regulate the degree of inequality over time. But that has not happened on an international scale. For that reason, in this book the issue will be addressed in separate chapters: this one will be devoted to the issue of inequalities within societies, while the following chapter will address inequalities between them.

*

Why should inequality have diminished within the richer societies during the past century or so? The statistical picture is patchier and more complex than that bald statement implies. Countries have all gone through different phases of inequality and equality. Much depends on exactly what is being measured: the picture changes depending on whether it is the distribution of individual earnings, household earnings, income of all kinds, pre-tax or post-tax income, or wealth that is being considered. But one does not need to make a statistically pure examination in order to draw broad political and social conclusions. Over a long period of time, the social and political divisions within rich societies have narrowed. They began to widen again in the 1980s, but, taking a long view, they have narrowed.

A good source for data backing up these statements is a British expert on inequality, A. B. Atkinson of Nuffield College, Oxford, and his article 'The Distribution of Income in the UK and OECD Countries in the Twentieth Century', in the *Oxford Review of Economic Policy* winter issue of 1999. He explains in this article how patchy the data are, especially before 1950. Nevertheless, in Britain the evidence is that the biggest bursts of equalization of incomes came in the first two decades of the century, and then from 1940 until the late 1970s. In the United States, the data are just as poor, but Atkinson concludes that income inequality there declined from roughly 1929 until the early 1950s, followed by a further decline during the 1960s. Inequality began to rise again in the United States from 1970 onwards.

In France there was a similar period of equalization which in that case lasted until the mid-1980s, following which there has been little sign of change, whereas in West Germany incomes did begin to become more unequal again during the 1980s, even before unification with East Germany in 1989-90.

The poor quality of the data makes it hard to draw firm conclusions about why income gaps narrowed, especially conclusions that hold good across a wide range of countries. Nevertheless, some general statements can be made, which may not apply in all cases but are indicative of the broad trends. Income gaps narrowed, first of all, because education became more widely available and more widely exploited, closing the gap in marketable skills between the richest and poorest, and bringing about social mobility. They narrowed also because the incomes and wealth of those at the very top of society, who were typically land-owning and bond-holding aristocrats or other sorts of gentry, have fallen, thanks to land reform in some countries, to the decline of agriculture and to rising costs in maintaining big estates.

Changes in the customs (and in some cases, laws) of inheritance have also affected the élite. Previously, a tradition of primogeniture (one heir inheriting everything) tended to keep huge estates and collections of wealth intact; a practice of spreading legacies more widely in a family tends to break up and reorganize wealth quite rapidly. Differences in the custom of inheritance help to explain the big difference in the flow of wealth in America compared with Western Europe: like the Rockefellers, Vanderbilts and (today) Bill Gates, many European aristocrats of the nineteenth and twentieth centuries made their fortunes in business, but then used them to create estates that were primarily passed on to a single heir who often saw his duty as one of preservation and stewardship rather than reinvestment. The children of America's super-rich in the twentieth century also became wealthy through inheritance, but in smaller parcels rather than one huge chunk, which served to encourage the wealth to be deployed more widely and even to be spent. European inheritance practice has become more like that in America, but largely only in the past half-century.

This drop in the levels of wealth at the top of society went into a sharp reverse during the stockmarket booms of the 1990s, albeit creating a different sort of super-rich. Over a longer period, however, the gap between the rich and everyone else has narrowed because, thanks to technology and competition, prices have fallen, in relation to all incomes, both for basic goods and for the things people buy for their leisure, while the prices of people (that is, wages) have risen. The sort of individuals who pay wages are only those at the very top, whereas poorer people devote a larger proportion of their incomes to spending on basic necessities.

The divisions have narrowed because public services, not just of education but also of health care and welfare support, have become widely available. They have narrowed also for non-financial reasons: work practices and, in some countries, legislation have meant that poorer people have received paid holidays and paid maternity or even paternity leave, perks they would not have dreamt of getting at the turn of the twentieth century. Airline flights, motor cars, telephones, home entertainment, golf courses: all these amenities are now within the reach of middle- and low-income families, albeit not the very poorest.

Dora Costa, an economist at the Massachusetts Institute of Technology, studied this phenomenon of the spread of leisure in a 1997 paper for the National Bureau of Economic Research. Evaluating the distribution not of income but of living standards by looking at recreational spending, she used consumption surveys for America going back as far as 1888. In that year, the average family of industrial workers surveyed spent less than 2 per cent of their income on leisure, while they spent three-quarters of their income on the basic necessities of food, shelter and clothing. By 1991, the average household was having to spend only 38 per cent of its income on those necessities, and could devote 6 per cent to recreation.

Overall, spending on leisure – which is hard to define, but includes travel, entertainment and holidays – grew from roughly 2–3 per cent of GDP in America in the early 1900s to roughly 10 per cent now. There has been a big drop in working hours for the ordinary man, even if they may recently have risen for the high-flying professional. Where at the turn of the century a Briton worked for 2,700 hours a year, by the 1990s the hours worked in rich countries had dropped to 1,400–1,800 a year. Paid holidays became the norm after the 1940s, ranging from two to three weeks a year in America and Japan to six weeks a year in Germany. From the 1960s and 1970s, ordinary people began to join the jet-set.

Another important sign of greater equality is the evolution of domestic services. A hundred years ago, even a moderately well-off family would have had a couple of servants, generally living in the attic or basement of their house. Truly well-off families had households consisting of dozens of live-in servants. Now only the mega-rich have such servants living with them, and few of those have large staffs. The use of occasional cleaning help, or child-minding, now extends a long way down the income scale in rich countries, but it is not anything like as intensive, or extensive, as was the use of servants at the turn of the twentieth century.

Technology has in part been responsible for the change. The vacuum cleaner, the washing machine, motor cars, gas and electric ovens and hobs have all been cases of machines replacing people. Cars and better public transport also help to explain why even the cleaners, nannies and other child-minders of today rarely live with their employers. They help explain why chauffeurs are not as plentiful now as some pundits thought likely when the motor car first sputtered into life in the early 1900s: cars are easy to drive, and their maintenance can be outsourced to specialist garages – unlike that of horses and carriages, where the 'maintenance' was labour intensive and mostly had to be done on-site.

Education, too, has had an influence: the supply of cheap young maids and servants, in their teen years, disappeared with the spread of full-time, publicly funded, secondary and tertiary education. But the other big cause has been a narrowing of the gap between incomes – that is, the rise in the cost of employing such servants, as a proportion of the incomes of the better-off. When the gap was large, wealth gave some people a great command over others. Now that the gap has narrowed, the wealthy mainly have command over things – their boats or gadgets or fancy cars. In terms of the domestic conveniences provided by servants, the moderately well-off in India or South Africa, for example, are able to feel the benefit of their wealth much more keenly than their equivalents today in Germany or America, where they are now much less likely to have servants.

These are all symptoms, however, not causes. Why has education become more widely available? Why has the wage gap narrowed sufficiently to make domestic servants viable only for the very few? Why have public services become more widely available? The broad answer is that these things have arisen from two forces: first, the operation of democratic politics – which itself has been stimulated by pressure from the mass urban working and middle classes, demanding change; second, the commercial pressure of economic development, which has led businesses to demand more mental skills from their workforces and has pushed societies towards being meritocracies rather than stratified, hierarchical structures.

A paper in Harvard's *Quarterly Journal of Economics* in November 2000, by Daron Acemoglu and James A. Robinson, provided empirical evidence to support what common sense would suggest had been the case: that the major democratic reforms (extending the franchise, and so on) in Britain, Germany, France and Sweden in the nineteenth and early twentieth centuries all coincided with peaks in inequality. In other words, a widening of inequality brought about social and political pressure for reform, which the established élites responded to by providing the discontented with greater democratic representation. The elastic stretched, and for fear that it might break, bringing on violence and turmoil, political reforms were offered and accepted.

This, in turn, has had a levelling effect. For, in time, democratic reform influences those in government: those seeking election will make sure that their policies are of broad benefit to those who they hope will vote for them. Hence, the provision of, and improvement of access to, public education and other services; hence, the granting of steadily greater rights and protections for ordinary workers; hence, the gradual introduction, even without pressure from socialists, of progressive taxation, by which governments could draw more of their revenue from the few than from the many. The effect of this on post-tax incomes is complex, since taxes alter people's behaviour. But, as a general rule, it has narrowed the gap between post-tax incomes.

The other big effect of democracy on inequalities of income and wealth has been to make societies, or rather political establishments, less tolerant of high levels of unemployment. 'Let them eat cake' is no longer a viable or acceptable reaction. The result has been that, in the democracies, efforts have either been made to try to reduce unemploy-

ment, or to make unemployment less disastrous financially by expanding welfare benefits. That has been less true of the United States
than of Western Europe or Japan, but, beginning with the 'New Deal'
of the 1930s, it has nevertheless been the American trend too.

It would be wrong to suggest that the connections between inequality, democratic reform and the levelling process are either direct
or exclusive. Indeed, what seems to have happened, and to be happening still, is more of an interplay between that political process and the
broader forces of economic development. Growth and technological
change have steadily raised the demands made by employers for skills
and education levels, while also, over time, providing governments
with the tax revenue necessary to finance education and other public
services. Marx could not have forecast it in the 1840s, but far from
requiring an ever-larger, more oppressed, more *lumpen* mass of manual
workers, the maturing modern economy has instead required ever-
larger injections of knowledge and brain-power, as it has switched its
emphasis from physical labour and raw manufacturing to higher-
technology goods, imaginative design and analytical or creative services. Mass education has served capitalism, as well as being made
affordable by it; and in turn the need for education has helped to
save capitalism from itself, by leading, over time, to a reduction in
inequality.

This move to a 'knowledge economy' and 'knowledge workers' has
been a theme of at least a hundred years or more. As early as 1910
Norman Angell, a British socialist, made the claim in his bestselling
book, *The Great Illusion*, that 'brainpower has replaced manpower,
horsepower and material power as the main force of our age'. Peter
Drucker, the doyen of management gurus, claims that he coined the
term 'knowledge workers' in the early 1960s; Tony Blair, Bill Clinton
and a generation of other politicians caught on in the late 1990s.
Internet enthusiasts, keen on discerning the arrival of a new 'information age' or 'weightless' or 'virtual' economy, made this sort of
observation with new vigour, as if it were a revelation. But it is old
news. The drive towards knowledge, through mass secondary and
tertiary education, has been an equalizing force throughout the past
century or more, even though the nature of the knowledge that is in
demand has altered as the decades have passed and as society and the

economy have changed. There is also an important caveat, however. This is that education is a levelling force among all those who have access to it or who manage to exploit it. But it provides a new dividing line between those who do exploit it and those who do not or cannot.

*

It is fashionable instead to lament a new 'digital divide', between those with personal computers and the skills to use them, and those without. That notion may have some force when it is applied to inequalities between countries, for it may signify the fact that some types of investment are hindered in poor countries because of a lack of information technology infrastructure. But within countries, the issue is more straightforward. In reality, the digital divide is just a fancy way of describing a long-running educational divide. The important divide is not set by computer literacy, for such literacy has become easy to obtain and computers have become much easier to use. It is set by literacy itself, broadly defined.

The problem for those on the wrong side of the digital divide is not just lack of access to a computer and of a subscription to an Internet service provider. If that was the issue, public libraries could provide the answer. The problem is a lack of the educational skills (that is, basic literacy and numeracy) to use the computer in the first place; the lack of those and other broad educational skills that are necessary to gain a job that pays reasonable wages; possibly compounded by some other factors that make work hard to obtain, such as a criminal record, poor transport facilities or sickness of some sort. All those factors do in turn make people unable to buy a computer or connect to the Internet. But in fact those 'digital' aspects are no more than a symptom of the underlying problem. The problem is not lack of information or lack of technology. It is the lack of the wherewithal, in a modern economy, to earn money.

The implications are twofold. One is that there has been for many years, and always will be, a need for government to improve and extend the public education system. Such improvements and extensions are of specific benefit to voters, at least voters with children, for they receive the educational service being supplied; but it is also of general benefit because there is a broad economic and social gain to a society from having a large supply of well-educated adults. A by-product of that benefit is the reduction of the inequality that results from the educational divide itself.

The second implication, however, is narrower and more awkward, and may militate against such a solution. It is that, in a mature, rich-country democracy at least, those on the wrong side of the educational divide are going to be a minority rather than the majority they once were, a hundred or even fifty years ago. In modern parlance, the trickiest issue of inequality has, in this sense, shifted from being one concerning broad divisions between classes to become one of a gap between the mass of people and an 'under-class' of the 'socially excluded'. This group, which is variously estimated in America as being anything from 10 to 20 per cent of the population, and about half those levels in Western Europe, poses a humanitarian problem, one of pity and decency, as well as one of crime.

That makes inequality in some ways a less potent issue than it once was: it is no longer a question of pitting the lucky few against the less fortunate many, and no longer a question that puts fierce pressure on politicians hoping to secure a majority in national elections. But it also makes it more intractable. For most of the solutions to poverty require public money, and the providers of that money are the majority of the electorate. Instead of democracy working to serve the interests of the majority, what is now going to be needed is for the majority to agree to help out the minority. One of the biggest social and political questions of the next quarter-century will be whether or not they are willing to do so.

*

This returns us to the theme outlined at the end of Chapter 8, that of the limits to governmental activism. One sort of limit is strictly empirical: direct efforts by governments to redistribute income to the poor have not been successful. Welfare benefits are not enough, and tend only to make people dependent on them, and permanently poor. In any case, in a democratic society, politicians do not generally concentrate most of their public spending on a small minority of voters, which is what the poor now are. Rather, they channel much of their money to the middle classes, while offering only a small slice to the poor. That way, they are more likely to be re-elected.

Another sort of limit, however, is the debilitating effect that equalizing measures, or high public spending, may have on economic growth as a whole. Poor growth not only affects the state's ability to finance these welfare measures, but it also then makes it less likely that the non-poor – that is, the middle and upper echelons of society – will be willing to vote for an egalitarian, high spending government. Such unwillingness can even affect the type or magnitude of spending on education: the pressure from the majority may be for more spending on higher or secondary-school education, while the needs of the under-class for more spending on basic or remedial education are ignored.

Is that why, in most countries, but particularly in Britain and the United States, income inequalities widened again in the 1980s and 1990s? Did the political balance switch away from redistribution and towards lower taxation, and did that in turn result in inequality?

The full answer is complex, and differs from country to country. For example, in the United States, high levels of immigration occurred, which increased the supply of unskilled labour; this did not happen in Britain. In Britain, a greater impact was made by the reduction of state benefits for the unemployed and other recipients of public welfare, a move which coincided with high levels of unemployment in the 1980s, in particular. The same sort of change was made in some continental European countries, notably the Netherlands, but also, more recently, Germany. Taxation of income also became less progressive in all countries, though the effect was moderate: the highest marginal rates of income tax were eliminated, but the high rates nevertheless tend to apply to moderate incomes, so that a disproportionate amount of tax revenue is still paid by the better-off.

Much of the explanation must also be found at the higher end of the income scale. Booming stockmarkets up until 2000 boosted the wealth of those who own shares, and shareholders are overwhelmingly people who are already moderately or very wealthy. The effect was amplified in the United States in particular by the fashion among companies to pay senior managers partly in shares and share options – not, in general, as a substitute for basic pay, but as a substantial supplement to it. Market fever and a desire to align managers' and shareholders' interests partly explain this, but also accounting rules mean that the full cost of options did not have to be carried in companies' profit-and-loss accounts, so companies competed for staff in a way that did not damage their reported profits. Or, in the case of Internet start-ups, companies were thus able to compete for staff even in the absence of profits and of cash.

This phenomenon brought back to prominence, in newspapers, intellectual essays or political forums, a public discussion of the acceptability and justice of such extremes of wealth and income. Such a debate could have revealed (or brought about) a willingness among the richer classes to help the under-class. But so far it has not done so, for this sort of discussion typically fails to provide simple or clear answers as to what is, or is not, considered to be acceptable or just. The issues are not simple. Their complexity is perhaps best illustrated by the apparent social attitude, reflected or reinforced in the mass media, to luck.

If a sports star earns hundreds of millions of dollars (or pounds, or virtually any currency) a year, is that fair? Probably not, if the measure of justice has something to do with effort, attainment, application and so on, proportionate to the efforts of others. Those who do not reach the top often try just as hard as the stars, but their earnings are much smaller. The star's gifts may be thought of as principally that: gifts of nature, though doubtless honed by psychology. And the economics of broadcast television have served to amplify the rewards of the star, by reinforcing their celebrity and enabling millions and millions of people to watch them. In what has thus rightly been called a 'winner takes all' society, the gap in earnings between the top handful of stars and the second or third layer of the merely excellent has become huge.

So, again, is that fair? Is it fair to have such a gap either between rivals in the same generation, or between stars of equivalent skill in different generations? Babe Ruth was not as rich as a modern baseball star; Stanley Matthews was a pauper compared with a modern European soccer player. Well, if it isn't fair, nobody seems to care very much. People do not seem to consider this sort of luck to be particularly objectionable. The great thing about sports, or indeed about the movies, by and large, is that the gift to do well in them could have landed on any of us. Or, at least, that is what we appear to think. It is the same with winnings from public or private lotteries, or other forms of gambling: a millionaire winner is not to be resented. He or she is just lucky. If resentment arises it is generally because of what they choose to do with their money, not because of the luck itself.

There does, however, appear to be some distinction between social attitudes to the rewards of entrepreneurship and to luck in conventional employment. If Bill Gates of Microsoft or Larry Ellison of Oracle becomes extraordinarily rich through the rise in the stockmarket value of their software companies, it does not seem to cause a lot of resentment. Their ideas, and their successful application of those ideas, make the wealth seem deserved, whether or not you think the reward might be disproportionate to the effort and genius involved. It could have happened to any of us, if we'd had the luck to have Bill Gates's ideas, and then the determination to make them work. If, however, a mere chief executive, an employee, earns hundreds of millions in pay and stock options, there is sometimes a rumble of discontent, because he or she is not an entrepreneur, not a risk-taker, not a provider of new ideas or apparent genius. This differs between countries. The vast pay given to Michael Eisner of Disney is accepted in America with barely a murmur, while it would raise a lot of eyebrows in Britain, France or Germany.

One issue is whether the reward has arisen because of some perceived abuse of position – in other words, by the person rigging his or her own pay – or whether it comes from a mixture of luck and corporate performance. Indeed, during the 1990s expectations appeared to change about what the British newspapers call 'fat-cat salaries'. Huge payments caused little fuss if they appeared to have been tied to particularly strong results for the executives' company. Actually, many of the really big pay packets on either side of the Atlantic in the late 1990s arose because of what was more or less a windfall: pay was tied to rises in firms' share prices, and this was a period in which virtually the whole stockmarket rose substantially in value. So those executives who happened to be sitting in the top seats in the late 1990s and 2000 found themselves becoming rich beyond their dreams, and well beyond the riches earned by their predecessors in the early 1990s or 1980s. Although it was possible to do badly, it wasn't easy to do so. Much of the earnings arose from luck, just as much as for sports stars or lottery winners; and the lucky recipients justified their receipts largely by the fact that other managers were also hitting the jackpot at the same time. In other words, this was mainly the market at work, and it was bringing luck. It was not only that, however: as corporate scandals that emerged in America in 2002 at firms such as Enron, WorldCom and Tyco showed, top executives also used their power to amplify their luck, by distorting profit-and-loss accounts to show figures that enhanced their bonuses, or by persuading tame boards to vote them gigantic awards of stock options and to lend them huge sums of money that were later 'forgiven' and thus simply turned into pay.

While that was happening at the top end of the income and wealth ladder, the poor were not getting much richer, if at all, either in Europe or in the United States. One group was getting a little better off: those who had been unemployed and who now found work in a buoyant economy. But for the most part, the lower-income groups did not do well. They did not become worse off, on most measures. But the gap widened, greatly. An under-class had always existed, but now its apparent numbers increased.

*

If the past is a guide, this might be expected to mean that a new democratic reform is about to take place, under pressure from the dispossessed. But that is unlikely, to say the least, in America and Western Europe, because everyone already has the vote and equal civil rights in those countries. No new extension of democracy is available to be offered to buy off the dissent. The same is true of Japan. In developed, undemocratic countries, which essentially means some of the tiger economies of East Asia, though also parts of Latin America, the pressure for democratic reform will build, however. If those governments do not find ways to release the pressure, it could become explosive. And the same will be true, in due course, of China, as was argued in Chapter 3. For as that huge country develops, inequalities within it will cause social and political trouble if there is no political channel within which they can be resolved peacefully.

Does the widening of inequality nevertheless mean that democratic governments will feel obliged, under the pressure of voters' discontent, to redirect their cash and legislative resources towards the reduction of inequality? To return to the question with which this chapter opened, is inequality again going to be one of the big political themes of the first decades of the twenty-first century, just as it was in the early twentieth century?

To find an answer, the democracies need to be separated from the others. Full democracies have the channels and the means to defuse any such pressure gradually, well before it becomes explosive. That does not prevent inequality from being an important issue: it could just exert its influence over a long period rather than in a big bang. But there is also plenty of reason to wonder whether inequality is going to be a very important issue at all. That might sound complacent. It is not intended to be; rather, it is intended to be analytically precise. Poverty, pain and sacrifice are perfectly likely to become big political issues in the West, whenever they are suffered by large numbers of people. If booms turn to bust, people suffer and they become angry about it. They may even have stored up some resentment against those who benefited most from luck during the boom times. But at such times the fight will, in reality, be about jobs and poverty, or about stamping out corporate abuses that enabled executives to get more pay than they merited. That is not the same as a fight over inequality *per se*.

The reason returns to the point made earlier, that, thanks to mass education and the knowledge economy, the hurtful divide in society is no longer between mass groups, still less between the unlucky many and the lucky few. It is now a divide between the lucky many and the unlucky few: between the fairly comfortable masses and the socially excluded under-class.

There is certainly also a divide between the comfortable masses and a small band of super-rich. But that does not feel like a dangerous divide, as long as societies obey one important condition: meritocracy, or something approaching it. As long as entry to the top band appears to be open to all, on merit or luck, rather than being restricted or protected in some way by the top band's members, then the divide is likely to be accepted. It will not necessarily be welcomed or liked; tastes change on this point according to the economic circumstances, and differ between countries. But resentment of the super-rich is unlikely to drive political action to any great extent because there is no reason for the majority to conclude that it would gain much, if anything, by grabbing all or part of the wealth of the top band (for, spread among the majority, it would not go very far). And the thought that they, or their children, could one day belong to that super-rich band acts as a further disincentive against grabbing the money or harming its holders.

The real potential problem for democratic societies in the next few decades will be the divide between the lucky many and the under-class. This divide is most clearly defined by education (the poverty rate among high-school drop-outs in America is seven times that among college graduates) but is not limited to it. Nor is it a problem of fixed size. In periods when capitalism reminds us of its inherent instability, the number of members of the under-class will rise, as those in unskilled jobs start to lose them, and find it impossible to find new ones. The distinction between those in unskilled work and those in the under-class is not at all sharp; indeed, statistical surveys suggest that there is a considerable amount of movement between the two categories over time, as people fall in or out of low-paid work. During recessions the rich lose more money than the poor because their assets fall in value, but they are still left with plenty. The poor lose less, but they have less to lose.

They also have less to lose if they seek to challenge the political, social and judicial system of the society in which they live. After all, they are not getting much from it in the first place. And they are a minority, so they are not going to be able to gain resources through the normal democratic methods, unless the middle classes vote with them for fear of instability or out of humanitarian concern. The incentive to cause trouble, either as a group or just as individuals, will be strong.

*

The question, then, is whether this is likely to be a big, century-defining problem, or just a constant headache. The latter is more probable than the former. If poverty really did become an explosive issue, it would be because the whole economic system was failing, as it did in the 1930s, not because it was serving the majority fairly well and a minority poorly.

Short of such an economic disaster, however, there will be a headache for the modern, rich societies for as long as the existence of a sizeable, alienated under-class is able to threaten the safety and living standards of the majority. It will be a headache for policing, for the justice system and for prisons, and will raise the costs of all of these. It will be a headache for representative democracy: dealing with minorities is never something that democracy can do comfortably, as has been shown through the decades in any country in which a large ethnic minority resides alongside a homogeneous majority (as in many of the countries of Central and Eastern Europe, and in the Balkans).

This headache, however (to repeat the point for extra emphasis), is not directly the result of inequality *per se*. It will not become worse as the broad distribution of income becomes more dispersed, nor better as the distribution becomes more even. The true problem is independent of the general degree of inequality in democratic societies. It is, and will continue to be, a problem of a dispossessed, dispirited, alienated under-class, which will at times be aggravated by the expansion of that group during economic slumps.

The solution to this problem, in the long term, will lie almost entirely in improvements in public education, and in associated efforts to ensure that all parts of a country can share in the fruits of economic growth. The challenge for elected politicians will be to persuade their middle-class voters to pay for this educational investment even when it does not bring benefits to them directly. But whether in booms or in slumps, the gap in wealth between someone in that group and someone like Bill Gates will not be what matters. What will matter is the gap between the under-class and everyone else. In other words, the confrontation will be one in which the poor few are ranged against the well-off many. And this is the opposite of the questions posed by the growing inequality between the few rich countries and the many poor ones.

10

Unequal (2)

The world has never been richer. To put it another, more accurate way, the rich people in the world have never been richer, more numerous and more productive. But, as a proportion of the world's population, the rich (a term which in this chapter takes in everyone living in the industrialized, developed countries that are mainly in North America, Western Europe and Japan) make up a fairly small minority. Defined generously, they are probably around a billion of the world's 6 billion people. Of the other 5 billion, 2.8 billion live on an income of less than $2 a day, according to the World Bank. Of those, 1.2 billion live on less than $1 a day. More than 40 per cent of those 1.2 billion are in South Asia – that is, India, Bangladesh, Pakistan and Sri Lanka; 23 per cent are in East Asia, which includes China. Never mind the digital divide between those who can use the Internet and those who can't: there are billions of people who have never even used that late-nineteenth-century technological breakthrough made by Alexander Graham Bell, the telephone.

The poor, said Jesus Christ, are always with us. Yet some basic economic principles suggest that they might not have been, at least not in such large numbers. In 1900, if an economist had been told what technological progress was going to be made during the century, especially in world-shrinking transport and communications, he (for an economist then would certainly have been male) would first have fainted in disbelief. But then he might well have made the following forecast: that the gap in wealth and income per head between rich countries and poor ones would therefore narrow as the world shrank and ideas crossed borders. About how much it would narrow, he would have been uncertain. But narrow it would.

An obvious reason why there are so many poor is that there are so many more people than before. But even the proportions of rich and poor outlined in the opening paragraph above would have seemed outlandish to any economist who had truly been convinced that the world would see the sort of fast economic growth it has enjoyed, and that there would be so much technological progress. In a sense, Karl Marx has been proved right: the world has become more and more divided between the few rich and the many poor – except that, rather than glowering at each other within the same country, the two groups live apart, not only in different countries but in different continents.

The international gap should have narrowed for two simple reasons. The first is that ideas can easily cross borders, spreading productivity gains far and wide. It is hard to invent electricity, or a new way to make a plough, or a new high-yielding variety of rice. But once the invention has been made, it ought to be easy to apply those ideas all over the world, wherever the benefits from doing so are potentially the greatest. And those benefits should be greater in countries that are more backward, because the incremental gain from the new idea ought to be larger in such places. In principle, this should mean that countries which develop later ought to be able to do so more rapidly and should thus be able to catch up with the richer, earlier developers.

One obstacle to that process, it might be suggested immediately, is the ownership of those new ideas, through patents, trademarks and copyright laws. That is true. But the second reason to expect incomes and wealth to narrow between countries can then counter this objection. This reason is the instinct, in capitalism, to invest money wherever the potential returns are highest. For new ideas, they should be highest in the more backward countries, again because there the incremental gain from applying new ideas should be greatest. So all the incentives for holders of patents, trademarks and copyright protection – intellectual property, as it is collectively known – should lead them to invest in the now-poorer countries or license their inventions to others who wish to invest there, helping those countries to narrow the gap with the richer ones. The opening of borders to trade and investment should mean that patents and other rights have now become even more valuable, because there is the chance of world-wide exploitation. The very nature of capitalism ought, on this analysis, to mean that the international gap between rich and poor should narrow.

These reasons are simple, but also simplistic – which is another way of saying that they have proved to be wrong. On their own, both principles are plausible and even, in a limited sense, correct, but they do not operate on their own. Other factors have blocked the flow of ideas or have made the returns available from implementing them in poor countries much less attractive than they might have been.

*

The hard fact is that the gap between rich and poor has not narrowed. Instead, the gap has widened substantially. According to a study by Lant Pritchett of the World Bank, in the summer 1997 issue of the *Journal of Economic Perspectives*, in 1870 the world's richest industrial countries, Britain and the United States, had an income per head roughly 9 times that of the poorest country. In 1990 America's income per head was more than 45 times the income per head of Chad or Ethiopia, say. Mr Pritchett calculates that in 1870 the world's seventeen richest countries had an average income per head 2.4 times as high as all the other countries; in 1990, the top seventeen countries were 4.5 times as rich as the rest. More recently, to cite a different measure, the World Bank has calculated that the average income in the world's richest twenty countries is 37 times the average in the poorest twenty, and the gap has doubled in the past forty years. Hence the title of Mr Pritchett's study: 'Divergence, Bigtime'.

This is especially surprising given one of the first big political events of the century: the naval defeat of Russia by Japan in 1905. This was taken as a sign that the balance of world power might be moving away from the Europeans; or, more neutrally, that the industrial revolution could now take hold in other, non-European cultures. Japan had, since 1860, been importing technology and, although it had quite a high living standard before then, it was keen to catch up with the West and did so in industrial terms, first by the 1930s and then again by the early 1960s. Ideas crossed from Europe and from North America, and were applied successfully in Japan. This non-European country, far away from either Europe or North America, managed to catch up with the West and even (during the 1960s, 1970s and 1980s) to overtake all the Western countries, barring the United States, in terms of overall GDP.

After 1950, this same gap-narrowing trick was achieved by a small group of other countries in East Asia: first South Korea, Taiwan, Singapore and Hong Kong, and then China, Malaysia, Thailand and Indonesia. None has yet caught up to the same degree as Japan, but all have narrowed the gap and have raised their living standards in a spectacular fashion. For that reason, the number of people in East Asia living on less than $1 a day fell between 1987 and 1998 from 420 million to 270 million. But in other parts of the world – notably sub-Saharan Africa, Eastern Europe, Central Asia and South Asia – the numbers in such abject poverty rose. The combined total fell, thanks to those big gains in East Asia, but only slightly. Overall, inequality was as bad as ever.

Perhaps, as with so many things, it is only economists who find this surprising. Plenty of people think the dice are loaded, and always will be, to help the lucky get luckier and to make sure that the poor stay poor. Yet there have also been times, in the 1920s, for example, and the early 1990s, when richer people have been scared that their luck was about to turn: that mobile capital plus low transport costs meant that their industry was about to move to wherever the wages were lowest. Ross Perot, scourge of the North American Free-Trade Agreement (NAFTA) that in 1994 bound together Mexico, Canada and the United States in a free trade zone, spoke of a 'great sucking sound' that was going to pull American jobs down south, across the border into Mexico. His reasoning relied on that simple rationale used earlier: that, once there were no trade barriers between the United States and Mexico, it would always be cheaper to produce things in Mexico and so any rational businessman would take his technology and capital down there. Mexico would do well out of the deal, while American unemployment would soar and American economic growth stagnate. To put it another way, Mexico would narrow the economic gap with the United States.

In fact, in the years since NAFTA was born, both countries have fared well. Mexico began with a devaluation crisis in 1995 and a recession, contrary to Mr Perot's warnings, but then recovered rapidly. The United States, far from having the jobs sucked away from it, has enjoyed falling unemployment and, if anything, has sucked Mexican labour northwards across the Rio Grande, through legal or illegal immigration. NAFTA did not cause the late-1990s buoyancy in the American economy and all that job-growth; its effects on the whole economy were marginal. But they were marginally positive rather than negative.

Indeed, faster growth in poor countries would not be a threat to the rich; it would be good for everybody, since if it were to occur we would each buy more of each other's goods and services, and have the chance to become richer still. So sunnier people have also periodically predicted that the latest new technology was at last going to bring that benign trend about. One of the latest such forecasts was in *The Race to the Intelligent State*, a 1993 book by Michael Connors, a British fund manager (previously a labour economist), which argued that information technology could well take hold faster in poor countries than rich ones, as well as helping the poor subvert their dictatorships. It has not happened so far, at least not to a great extent. But if it were to do so, it would be a welcome change.

*

These are the bleak facts. Inequality between countries has increased rather than diminished, over a long period. For the most part, this has been because the rich countries have become richer rather than because the poor have become poorer, although it is also the case that poor countries have had faster population growth in recent decades and so the poor have become more numerous. And some countries in sub-Saharan Africa have in fact become poorer in absolute terms as well.

To become a little more optimistic about this subject, we need to leave history behind a little and focus on the more recent past. In the last twenty years, some measures show that income inequality has begun to diminish again, as more countries in the poor or once-poor world have begun to grow rapidly, especially those East Asian gap-narrowers already cited. That 'especially' gives the clue: the reason why inequality seems to have diminished in this period is because the world's largest country, China, has been growing rapidly since 1980, lifting hundreds of millions of Chinese out of absolute poverty. India, too, has begun to raise its economic growth rate since 1990. That phenomenon of faster growth in the world's two most populous countries swamped all others in the final decades of the twentieth century. If it were excluded from the data, we would return towards the long-run trend: that inequality has been increasing. But it is crucial to include it.

The measures for inequality that are in use by economists and commentators vary widely. Incomes can be compared by country or weighted for population, or by using normal exchange rates, or by adjusting for differences in purchasing power. The bleak, basic figures that were deployed above used normal exchange rates. But this over-states the gap, for by using normal currency rates we are, in effect, comparing the ability of an American and a Malawian to buy the same bundle of goods and services in New York City, whereas what really determines the gap between the two standards of living is the respective abilities to buy comparable goods and services in their home countries. Hence, the fairest measure of income inequality between individuals would be a measure adjusted to achieve purchasing power parity (PPP), because such adjustments smooth out currency fluctuations and also take in the costs of the many goods and services that are not traded across borders but which make up a large part of people's spending. If, at market exchange rates, incomes of the richest 20 per cent of people in the world were 74 times higher than the poorest 20 per cent in 1997 (according to the UN), in purchasing-power terms the gap narrows hugely to only about 15 times.

According to an article in *The Economist* in April 2001 by Robert Wade, professor of political economy and development at the London School of Economics, if we use what he considers the fairest measure, that is, with PPP and weighted by population, and include China, then in the past twenty-five years we find that there has been little change in income inequality, overall. That is at least an improvement compared with the previous seventy-five years, during which time inequality increased on this measure. He also, though, argues that China distorts the picture. If we deal with the underlying economic and social reality of China rather than the formal borders, he argues, then China ought to be thought of as at least two countries, China-urban, counting the coastal cities where most of the recent growth has occurred, and China-rural, where there has been far less progress.

Xavier Sala-i-Martin of Columbia University disagrees, however. In an article for the National Bureau of Economic Research in 2002, 'The Disturbing "Rise" of Global Income Inequality', he argues that such adjustments distort the true picture. Thanks to Chinese and Indian growth, the proportion of the world population living on less than $2 a day really has fallen, from 44 per cent in 1970 to 8 per cent in 1998. Inequality must therefore be decreasing.

*

Even so, poverty and inequality remain huge, whatever the correct measure. This leaves us with two questions. First, in what ways should they worry us? And, second, why do they endure? To which can be added a third question: What can be done about them?

Why does inequality matter? At the simplest level, world income inequality matters for humanitarian reasons. It is tragic that the lives of so many people are blighted by a lack of resources and modern technology, when those resources and technology sit only a phone call, or a few hours' flight, away. It is not only a tragedy, it is an apparently avoidable tragedy: if the rich countries know how to get rich, as well as how to cure all sorts of diseases, it is a tragedy that so many of the poor have been unable to emulate them. Moreover, this very modern technology also means that it is possible for the rich to become aware of such poverty much more easily than in the past, thanks to jet travel and to television, so famines and squalor are more noticeable. The humanitarian pressure to try to do something about poverty ought therefore to grow and grow.

Put in a more self-serving way, such inequality also matters because it represents a huge missed opportunity: if the poor were more de-veloped and wealthier, we could all become even richer together because of all the extra trade, investment and technological innovation that would take place. This might alarm environmentalists who fear development (of whom more in Chapter 11), but it should not alarm people on any other grounds. There is a parallel here with the 1940s and 1950s, when America was far and away the world's richest country, and Europe's economy had been devastated by war. Ameri-cans came up with the Marshall Plan to channel investment funds to Europe in the hope that Europe would thus become richer, which in turn would help America prosper too. The rich world has an interest in helping the poor world to become more prosperous because it will benefit as well.

There are other self-serving reasons to be worried about inequality and its handmaiden, poverty. One is that a poorer country is more likely to have weak political and social institutions, which are then more likely to collapse into chaos or civil war. That is especially likely when the country is poor in terms of the direct economic activity of its citizenry but is nevertheless home to some valuable natural resources, such as the diamonds of Sierra Leone. Forces within, and forces from outside, are liable to fight to get their hands on those resources. Chaos and civil war are essentially local troubles that need not affect the rest of the world, but they are liable to draw in neighbours, risking a wider regional conflict as countries or factions vie to exploit the vacuum left in the collapsing state.

Poorer, unstable countries are also likely to harbour and to foster two other ills: disease and terrorism. Disease may well contribute to poverty rather than being a consequence of it, but it is also the case that a poor country is likely to lack the infrastructure as well as money to be able to deal with epidemic diseases such as the human immunodeficiency virus that causes AIDS, or Ebola, and those diseases might then be able to spread across other borders.

The danger of terrorism is more obvious: discontented, otherwise hopeless people may wish to take out their sense of grievance on the luckier rich, and will be likely to find plenty of willing recruits for dangerous or even suicidal terrorist missions. The terrorist attacks on 11 September 2001 confirm this only indirectly, since the terrorists concerned were neither poor nor hopeless. But they and their followers did, it seems, feel that Islamic countries in general were poor and lacking in hope, following centuries of humiliation at the hands of the West. And the argument applies directly to Afghanistan: if that country had not been dirt-poor, it would have been unlikely to have acted as a host to the al-Qaeda terrorists. Rich countries can give rise to terrorism too, even without the separatist movements found in the Basque Country and Northern Ireland; Germany had its Baader–Meinhof gang in the 1970s, Italy its Red Brigades and even America had the Symbionese Liberation Front. But they have not been numerous enough to pose a danger to their governments or to any other country.

Poverty and despair act as a more powerful recruiting sergeant for terrorists than do mere alienation or beliefs in anarchism.

A more direct reason why people worry about inequality is migration. Over time, immigration has been of huge economic benefit to the rich world, because it has brought new energy, new skills and cheap labour into their economies and societies. In the short term, though, it can cause political and social hostility, for fear of sudden changes to local communities, pressures on jobs and welfare, and mere cultural dislocation. The larger the gap in incomes and living standards between countries, the greater the incentive for people in the poorer countries to migrate to places where the opportunities may be greater. When the twentieth century began, great movements of people were taking place, principally between Western and Central Europe, and the new frontier countries of the United States, Canada, Argentina, Australia and New Zealand, where the opportunities seemed much greater, both economically and socially. Now, the poor man is again knocking at the door of the United States, which in the 1990s welcomed its largest wave of immigrants ever, and also of European countries. In the case of the United States, most of the poor men knocking are from South and Central America. In the case of Europe, most are from Africa, Eastern Europe (especially the Balkans), the Arab world and even China.

History does not, however, suggest that there is a simple, linear relationship between inequality and migration. The motivation to move home and even family from one country to another is more complex than that, for the incentives to stay put are strong: language, culture, existing networks of friends and family, and relative costs of living, even before legal barriers to departure or arrival are taken into account. If income gaps were all that mattered, then most of the population of Russia would surely have jumped on a train and headed westwards during the 1990s.

To explain the flow of migrants, common sense requires a combination of circumstances: permissive laws; economic and social opportunities in the host country; a sense of despair and hopelessness, beyond mere disappointment or resignation, in the home country. It even appears to be the case that a modest amount of growth at home can encourage migration, for it gives people the wherewithal to pay for their travel to a new potential home and to feel just about able to afford the considerable risks that are involved. That is not, however, a reason to oppose growth in the poor world, but rather a reason to want it to be sustained and more vigorous. If the poor world were, in a broad, sustainable way, catching up with the rich world in the manner of Japan in the 1960s and 1970s, there would be many fewer migrants knocking at the doors of the rich – or else those who did migrate for a time would soon be returning to exploit the new opportunities at home.

Other people worry about inequality because of a fear of war: the fear that countries which feel that they are unable to advance their living standards and sense of power by conventional economic means may be tempted to use military methods as a short-cut. As a general proposition, this argument is unconvincing, for a poorer country is also often militarily weak, though that still made the Soviet-led Warsaw Pact countries a formidable enemy to NATO during the cold war. By and large, however, the rich will always be able to defeat poor countries in anything other than a guerrilla war – and such fighting methods may be common in civil wars or in wars of liberation, but they do not put other countries themselves in physical danger, except from terrorism. But in some circumstances this argument may hold good. North Korea, for example, has long used the threat of military attack either on its southern compatriot, or on Japan or the United States, as a means by which to blackmail the rich. Iraq invaded Kuwait in 1990 in order to grab its oil as well as merely to make a territorial point. Inequality, in other words, may lead to an increase in the number of unpredictable dictators – slightly euphemistically known as rogue states (even more euphemistically known, by America's State Department, as 'states of concern'). These rogues have become more dangerous as technology has advanced sufficiently to make long-range missiles cheap enough to buy and develop, and to use as a threat. They could become extremely deadly if any obtain the means to develop and deploy nuclear, chemical or biological weapons.

Inequality may also bring a risk of environmental degradation, for poor countries may be unable to deal safely with toxic pollutants, or may be so desperate in the face of population growth and poverty that they permit actions, such as deforestation, that have a damaging influence on the global climate. In general, rising incomes bring better control of environmental damage, as Chapter 11 will argue. A few extreme environmentalists raise concern about any and all economic growth in poor countries, for in the short term that growth could bring on new environmental challenges, such as the burning of coal and other dirty fuels in Chinese homes and factories. But it would surely be intolerably selfish to deny poor countries advancement on those grounds. The bigger ground for concern is pollution out of desperation: the resort by the poorest to short-sighted forms of agriculture or industry, in the absence of any other means of survival.

That difficulty of balancing one sort of environmental fear against another raises a broader difficulty about the subject of inequality between countries. It is that it is hard to work out what weight to put on this issue. There are, as the above shows, plenty of reasons to worry about international inequality. Anyone with a heart or a conscience should wish, dearly, for poverty to diminish and the life chances of billions of people to improve. But wishing and doing are different things. What all those worries about inequality have in common is that none of them really produces a strong, hard-to-resist pressure for change. Whereas *within* a country inequality forces political change for fear of rebellion or a democratic overthrow, there is no such reliable or irresistible mechanism *between* countries.

Indeed, it is hard to avoid the conclusion that if inequality between countries really mattered, it would long ago have set forth pressures that would have led to its own correction, or at least mollification. The steady widening of inequality is testament not to its importance as an *increasing* threat to global stability but rather to its unimportance in such a context.

That is a pretty sanguine, perhaps complacent, view, especially given the terrorist attacks on 11 September. But, at least as a description of the past, it holds good. It is possible that recent changes in the world will make the future rather different, in this respect. Globalization has made the world increasingly open, with both transport and communication far cheaper than ever before. This has steadily improved poor people's knowledge of standards of living in other parts of the world, as well as increasing their ability to migrate there or to conduct terrorist attacks there. And advances in miniaturization and in computer processing power have made it easier for both terrorists and rogue dictators to develop and transport weapons of mass destruction.

On the other hand, globalization is also setting in train some forces that operate in the opposite direction. Improved knowledge of the rich world can also make poor people less susceptible to rabble-rousing radicals at home, for they are less easily fooled by efforts to demonize the West. It also, as will be argued in the remainder of this chapter, makes it possible for the poorer countries to modernize, narrowing the gap with the rich world. Rather than inequality bringing about instability and terror, that modernization could be at least as dangerous, for it will threaten to overthrow traditional institutions. Iran in 1979 had an Islamic revolution, which brought in a conservative theocratic regime. Now, more than twenty years later, gradual modernization of the economy is weakening the grip of the theocrats.

That fits with past experience. World-changing, destabilizing military conflicts have, in the past, tended to occur mostly when countries have been *rising* in absolute and relative economic strength rather than weakening. Germany, in 1914, would not have invaded Belgium and France had it not had the wherewithal to contemplate a war, and if its economic progress had not also led to frustrations about its status and sense of its own security. The Russian revolution of 1917 took place in the depths of a humiliating war, but it followed a period in which Russia had been faring quite well, economically. The Tiananmen Square protests in China in 1989 came at the end of that country's best decade of economic growth in the whole of the twentieth century.

Inequality between countries does not yield a clear and conclusive set of dangers for the world in the twenty-first century. Globalization and technology could make it a bigger concern for the rich countries. But there are also forces working in the opposite direction: globalization and technology may be simultaneously problem-causers and problem-solvers.

Rather than focusing on inequality, it is more useful to focus on poverty itself and the moral challenge it poses. Inequality is primarily caused by the success of the rich, not the failure of the poor. Nothing would be achieved by insisting that the rich become less successful, even though there would be less inequality if they did. But the continuation and even spread of poverty casts a moral shadow over that success. It also serves to define a huge opportunity, that of sharing the rich countries' success, and the ideas and methods that brought it about, more widely. If the rich world's success were really to be shared, the rewards would, in the long term, be mutual, as the welfare of the whole planet would increase greatly, accelerating the progress of mankind both in today's rich countries and tomorrow's. It would be a beautiful outcome in both moral and practical terms, one that would even help to decorate that ugly word, globalization. Can it be achieved?

*

Let us try a different question first. Why haven't more poor countries caught up? Most answers to that question are essentially tautologous. They don't have the skills, their education systems are inadequate, history stands in the way, they have too little capital, their culture is not entrepreneurial. These are just detailed ways of saying that poor countries are poor.

Out of that list of tautologous but sadly commonplace generalizations, the one which history condemns most clearly is the one involving culture. Rather than working hard or founding businesses, Mexicans have been said to prefer sleeping under trees, or even cacti, wearing their sombreros. Apart from the sombreros, and perhaps the cacti, you could substitute any number of nationalities in that dismissive sentence and stand a certain chance of echoing a statement made about that poor country by someone, probably an expatriate European or American, quite possibly sitting at a dinner party in their home country's embassy, at some point in the not too distant past. 'Trouble is, these Nigerians/Indians/Mexicans/ Papuans don't want to work; never have, never will . . .'

Yet you could also take any of the recently successful developing countries – Japan, South Korea, China, even Italy or Spain in Europe – and find similar cultural dismissals in the past. Thanks to their culture, they could never make it. But they did. As recently as the 1980s, many supposedly learned articles were being written explaining that China's fragmentary, individualistic form of Confucian culture was the reason why its economy had failed to grow while Japan's group-oriented culture showed why it had prospered. The Chinese had lost the ability to co-operate, to work as a group, a trait the Japanese had fostered so fruitfully in all their wonderfully productive factories. Yet even as those articles were being written, China's so far twenty-year period of economic take-off was getting under way. Doubtless, articles can now be found that attribute China's new success to its individualistic culture, or to something else. There are certainly plenty that now blame Japan's bad decade of the 1990s, on its group-oriented culture.

The trouble with 'culture' begins with the catch-all nature of that word. But it also arises from the fact that cultures are not static; they change, along with changing circumstances. Certainly they may affect the way in which nations respond to those circumstances, but they are also themselves altered by such circumstances. They are, in short, useless as an independent, explanatory idea for why particular countries stay poor.

Are there any useful explanatory ideas? Given that the question of why some countries stay poor and others grow rich is one of the most fundamental issues in economics and economic history, it would be foolish to pretend that there is universal agreement about the answer. All attempts at answers are by their nature over-simplifications, and the remainder of this chapter will be no exception. But, especially as the legacies both of colonial rule and of communist central planning recede into history, the picture is at least becoming clearer.

The findings of history are quite simple, even if it is not becoming any easier to implement them. To believe them, however, one must first believe in capitalism and in the fact that it has been the only successful generator of sustained improvements in human welfare that has so far been discovered. The next thing is to work out what it is that makes capitalism tick. Or, put another way, one must find out what is different about the places where it ticks and the places where it doesn't.

That is what an international study, *Economic Freedom of the World* has sought to do every year since it was first published, in 1996, by eleven economic think tanks around the world led by the Fraser Institute in Canada. The correlations it finds between sustained economic success and aspects of capitalist circumstances suggest that most of the explanations lie in how poor countries are governed, rather than in natural disadvantages or unfairness by the rich. Those suspicious of free-marketeers should note that conclusion: it is government, or the lack of it, that makes the crucial difference.

The aim of the study was to see whether countries in which people had more economic freedom were also richer and grew more rapidly. But the study also sought to define economic freedom, in the hope of capturing and measuring the things that matter in making capitalism work. Broadly, economic freedom means the ability to do what you want with whatever property you have legally acquired, as long as your actions do not violate other people's rights to do the same. Goods and services do not, alas, fall like manna from heaven; their arrival depends on property rights and the incentives to use and create them. So the issues surrounding those are what matter: are property rights legally protected? Are people hemmed in by government regulations and trade barriers, or fearful of confiscation? Are their savings under attack from inflation, or can they do what they want with their money? Is it economically viable for parents to send their kids to school?

The study's authors initially found seventeen measures of these things, expanded in the 2001 update to twenty-one, and rated 102 (now 123) countries on each of them, going back, if possible, to 1975. They then had to find ways to weight the measures according to their importance, and used a panel of economists to do so. The conclusion was abundantly clear: the freer the economy, the higher the growth and the richer the people. This was especially so for countries that maintained a fairly free economy for many years, since before individuals and companies will respond to such freedom they need to feel confident that it will last.

This is not, to repeat, an argument for raw *laissez-faire*, anything-goes economies or societies. Rather, the study indicates that government is what matters most. Economic freedom is a broad concept, which seems to require a great deal from government if it is to prevail and to work its living-standard-enhancing magic. Government needs to set a clear, predictable, regulatory and macroeconomic climate: protecting property rights, enforcing the law, avoiding inflation and, just as important, not taking all the money for itself. Things must be arranged in a way that gives people an incentive to invest. This does not just mean the building of new factories or farms, but also, for example, the decisions of parents about education or workers about training. To the people and households involved, those are considerable investments, involving the devotion of a lot of time and money many months or years before any financial benefit is reaped, and involving the forgoing of other income and opportunities.

People do not react well to being told what to do, and the instructors – central planners, as they were known in communist countries – never know the right answers in any case. Nobody could, for the task is beyond human calculation. What people do require, if they are to invest their time and resources productively, is secure ownership of those resources, the ability to borrow money on the basis of that ownership, and a reasonable expectation that the fruits of their investment (if there are any) will not be stolen from them or inflated away by the debauching of a currency. Hernando de Soto, a Peruvian economist, has shown how a quite simple thing such as the lack of established legal ownership of houses can be a great obstacle to entrepreneurial development. If (as is the case in many developing countries) people do not have legal rights to their land or house, they will be unable to borrow much money, and then unable to expand their business activities very much. Absurd, time-wasting, resource-sapping bureaucratic red tape also holds back enterprise disastrously in many countries.

In post-communist Russia there is a market economy, and property rights are fairly well established. But high inflation, currency restrictions and credit controls have been getting in the way, as well as crime, corruption, unpredictable or arbitrary regulation and political instability. Hence, despite what critics consider to be the country's ridiculously free market, established supposedly at the behest of 'fundamentalists' from Western universities and the IMF, Russia ranked 116th out of 123 countries in the 2002 survey of economic freedom. It may have markets, but its people do not have genuine economic freedom. India, too, has some of the prerequisites, and its economic freedom score has improved since 1990, but government licensing rules, price controls and state ownership, currency controls and high barriers to trade all still stand in the way, as does rampant corruption. Its ranking in 2002 was 73rd, better than in the previous year but below freer developing countries such as Mexico (66th) and the Philippines (38th).

Apart from the objection that this analysis is too simple, two sharper criticisms have been put forward against the view that what a poor country needs is stable government, the rule of law and economic freedom. One is the idea that, regardless of government or freedom, importing technology costs too much. Patent rights held in the West act as prison guards for the poor. But the facts of history refute this. As Mancur Olson argued in an article in the spring 1996 issue of the *Journal of Economic Perspectives*, the experience of South Korea in the 1970s, when that country's growth accelerated, shows that royalties and other technology payments were trivial compared with the growth achieved. This technique – of importing technology by buying licences – also played a big part in Japan's long-term success during the twentieth century. The other common objection is the notion that 'over-population' unavoidably holds countries back. Olson rebutted this idea in the same article, by showing that, when large numbers of people migrate away from densely populated areas, the incomes of those who remain do not rise, which would be expected if pressure on land or capital were truly the problem.

*

There is a better objection, however: these observations are all very well, but, like the tautologous explanations produced earlier, they still do not get anyone very far. What, after all, are the reasons why so many governments fail to provide all these life-enhancing freedoms and assurances? It all sounds so simple: set up a government, provide legal protection for property rights, establish a police force and judicial system to enforce the law, avoid debauching the currency – and hey presto, the country should grow and grow.

The objection is a fair one. For the connection between economic, social and environmental weaknesses and the instability or non-existence of governments all too often becomes a vicious circle. Jeffrey Sachs, of Harvard University, has shown how tropical disease is correlated with poverty and instability; by weakening populations it helps obstruct any efforts to enter the virtuous circle of growth and stronger government. It is not an absolute barrier: Singapore was a malaria-infested swamp before it was developed as a port in colonial and post-colonial times. But it is a big disadvantage.

Broadly, the countries that fail to grow and to improve their people's living standards beyond even a basic level can be divided into two groups. In one, the problem is that there is no real or sustained government, thanks to anarchy, civil war or broader war. In the other, the problem is that government stands in the way, either because it steals money or because it fails to provide the necessary freedoms and opportunities.

The first of these categories – what scholars of international relations call 'failed states' – is the hardest to assess. Examples of countries in this category include Sudan, Sierra Leone, Afghanistan, Somalia and Congo. Others hover on the border of this category, such as Georgia, Algeria and Colombia. Outsiders, whether they are countries, the United Nations or non-governmental organizations, can and should seek to help, but whether they can succeed in rebuilding the country's institutions will depend on the co-operation of local factions. The second category is easier to analyse and to provide prescriptions for. But that does not make success much easier.

Things are looking better for this group, which includes most of the other developing countries except for the most autarkic dictatorships such as North Korea, Iraq, Myanmar and Libya. Many countries were held back by the false road of socialism, which deepened poverty. But since the Soviet Union collapsed in 1991 many more countries have taken a new, more liberal road and many have begun to succeed: these include India with its improvements in economic freedom from a low base, as well as former communist countries in Eastern Europe and the authoritarian countries of Latin America which from 1950 to 1990 attempted their own brand of government-led autarky. Privatization has been all the rage and it has worked well as long as public monopolies have not simply been replaced by private monopolies. Investment in public education is on the rise. The control of inflation, scourge of Latin America, has become far tighter. This is a time of hope for many such countries around the globe.

Yet having a government and having successful examples to emulate do not guarantee success. Governments frequently do not choose to offer economic or indeed political freedom, and they waste the resources at their disposal. Often, as in Mobutu's Zaire (or in the renamed Congo led by his successor, Laurent Kabila), or the generals' Nigeria of the 1990s or the junta's Myanmar for the past several

decades, this is because their interest lies in personal power and enrich-
ment rather than in national advancement. These are gangster-states
rather than nation-states. Sadly, states that appeared to be properly
run can later descend into gangsterism: Robert Mugabe's Zimbabwe
is an example.

In other cases problems arise precisely because liberalization is
disruptive; it redistributes power away from the currently fortunate
(such as, in India, state-enterprise workers, or holders of licensed
monopolies), and such losers lobby against change, vigorously.
Hindustan Motors, sitting in the nominally communist Indian state of
West Bengal and for many years a near-monopolist car maker for the
whole country, stands as a monument to such inertia. It still makes a
barely upgraded version of a 1950s Morris Oxford, the Ambassador.
The local government is wondering how on earth to deal with the
losses the company is making, now that it faces competition from
companies making cars people actually want.

India is perhaps the greatest symbol both of the uphill struggle that
is represented by the effort to eliminate poverty and of the potential
for doing so. It is an uphill struggle because of sheer weight of numbers
of population; because of the blocking tactics of those interest groups
who benefit from the rigid, unfree status quo; because of the way
illiteracy and disease block the path of progress; because of the environmental damage that can simultaneously be caused by population pressure, poverty itself and development. But then the potential becomes
clear: the potential in this country packed with talented, eager entrepreneurs, crowds of whom can be seen at any railway station hustling and
bustling to try to make a sale or provide a service; the potential in this
country where democracy, plus the trappings of a judicial system,
offers the chance to enforce the rule of law; the potential in this country
that has, for fifty years, shut itself away from trade, foreign capital,
foreign investment, much foreign technology and most foreign
markets. The potential for the alleviation of poverty and the raising of
living standards is simply huge.

*

Potential, potential, potential. The old joke about Brazil, most often
told by Brazilians themselves, is that 'it is the country of tomorrow,
and always will be'. At the start of the twenty-first century, it is not

enough to know that there is potential for an improvement in the standards of living of countries such as India. Our question is, or ought to be if we care about this issue: how likely is it that that potential will be fulfilled?

The important thing to keep clear in one's mind is that the principal source of answers to that question lie at home – that is, the poor countries' homes. The need is for a domestic government that presides over an open, competitive economy, maintains a stable macroeconomic framework, sustains the rule of law, raises public money for health and education and spends it well, removes price distortions, builds infrastructure and maintains peace and consent perhaps through a Western-style democracy – a country with such a government is, history suggests, likely to enjoy sustained economic growth. But the rich Western world can have an important effect too: by fostering financial stability or instability; by maintaining open markets; by assisting with some disaster relief or infrastructure spending, and helping to solve special problems such as AIDS, malaria and other devastating diseases; by maintaining global or regional peace; by running strong economies themselves.

The experience of the twentieth century, admittedly, is not terribly encouraging. For most of that period, most poor countries stood still in economic terms. They did not get appreciably poorer, but nor did they get wealthier. They became more populous, and any increased wealth was merely shared out among a larger group of people.

Yet there is also cause for some optimism about the twenty-first century. The conditions have never been more favourable for more countries to grow: world trade and investment flows are bigger and more open, technology transfer is rapid and widespread, global peace prevails. These conditions have been emerging since the 1970s but really only took solid form in the 1990s, with the fall of the Soviet Union. The dozen years since that event is too short a period to allow optimism to become deeply entrenched. It is also dispiriting that so soon during this period of greater globalization campaigners have taken to the streets calling for restraints on growth and trade and development. Doubtless in the apparent cause of easing inequality, such demonstrators are making it more likely that inequality will continue to widen. But the argument between globalizers and antiglobalizers will go on and must go on, for in reality it is an argument about how and whether the poorer 5 billion of the world's population can get richer even as they also become more numerous. The important thing is to win that argument about globalization, and then to keep on winning it. The prize is huge. The promise, for the twenty-first century, of economic and social development for the world's poor, is real.

I I

Unclean

'The world's environment is surprisingly healthy. Discuss.'

If this were an examination topic, most students would tear it apart, offering a long list of laments, from local smog to global climate change, from the felling of forests to the spread of new roads and cities, from poisonous harbours to the extinction of species. The concern would be perfectly legitimate. Yet the real surprise is how good things are, not how bad. And that is not just a clever way of saying that things might have been even worse. For many people in the world, and for almost everybody in the rich world, the environment has actually been getting better in recent decades. There are important exceptions to that statement. But they are just that: exceptions, not rules.

Certainly, things have changed. After all, the world's population has more than trebled in the past hundred years, and world output has risen even faster. So it is only natural to expect that the earth itself will have been affected. But one would also expect people's behaviour to have changed in response. People depend on the earth for their food, air and water, and for other less vital resources too. So they have a strong incentive to protect their environment in ways relevant to their needs, comfort and survival, and a strong incentive to learn both from bad experiences and from new scientific discoveries. If people typically lived, consumed and produced things now in the same way as they did in 1900 (or 1950, or indeed 1980), the world would be a pretty disgusting place: smelly, dangerous, insanitary, toxic and worse.

But they don't. The streets of London or other big, rich cities are no longer full of horse manure, or blanketed in smoky fog, or full of open sewers; houses are no longer full of harmful smoke (not even from cigarettes, one of the biggest killers), and water is cleaner both from the taps and in the rivers and seas. The reasons why people in the rich, developed world have changed the way they live, and why the environment has not in fact been turned to rack and ruin, have to do with prices, technological innovation, social change and, in democracies, government regulation in response to popular pressure. And those reasons are why today's much larger environmental problems in the developing countries ought, in principle, to be solvable.

In contrast to this upbeat view, many people believe that the world's environmental problems are growing by the day, as man's appetite for economic growth coincides with a growing human population and crashes headlong into the finite, fragile resources of this small, lonely planet. An advertisement placed in American newspapers in 2001 for a television series that was shown on America's Public Broadcasting System, presented by a very thoughtful and respectable reporter, Bill Moyers, encapsulated the worry perfectly. Called *Earth on Edge*, the series was advertised as follows: 'Half the world's wetlands lost. Half the forests chopped down. Half the fisheries depleted. We live on a planet pushed to the edge by the demands of a single species. Ours.' The claims sound dramatic. If half of this or that has been used up, and if one reminds oneself that the industrial age began only a couple of hundred years ago and that the world's population has grown merely in the past hundred years from 1.6 billion to 6 billion, and is heading for 9 billion, then it cannot be long before the other half of all these resources is used up. And, most probably, this rate of usage applies elsewhere, too. The day of reckoning must be approaching. After that day, the old sci-fi vision of spaceship-loads of humans touring through space in search of raw materials and places to live could become reality.

This sort of worry, and style of argumentation, is not new. In 1972 an environmental group called the Club of Rome produced a bestselling book, *The Limits to Growth*, which claimed that man would soon run out of many resources: gold would run out in 1981, silver and mercury in 1985, zinc in 1990, petroleum in 1992, and copper, lead and natural gas by 1993. Human activity was likened to a water lily on an ornamental pond, regularly doubling its size, so that its final doubling would cover the whole pond. Never mind that the lily would require genetic modification to achieve this. The point is that selfish, short-sighted man will one day swamp the planet – or, rather, exhaust it.

The Limits to Growth is, rather obviously, far too easy a target. None of those predictions came true. Today they look comical. But, one might retort, they will come true one day: the warning could still be worthwhile, even if the dates are somewhat awry. That view is inherent in the modern fashion for the phrase 'sustainable development', which implies that much existing development is in some way unsustainable. Moreover, economists are hardly in a strong position to criticize others for making inaccurate forecasts.

Yet in fact these forecasts are unlikely ever to become true in any meaningful fashion. The Earth is really rather large. There are plenty of untapped resources buried in it. Man keeps on finding new ways to find and extract more of them, which is why, since the Club of Rome's 1972 prediction, the known reserves of all the resources it listed have grown larger, and the price of them has fallen. Even when those start to run out (if they ever do), many minerals could be extracted from sea water, for instance, or taken from the bottom of the oceans. There is a very long way to go, even for a rapacious beast such as man. In the case of oil and other forms of carbon, the real danger is actually the opposite of that worried about by the Club in 1972: it is that oil will remain so abundant, and hence cheap, that there will be too little incentive to limit its use and to try to develop new, cleaner sources of energy. The wrong worry, in other words, is resource depletion. The right worries are global warming and pollution.

At the same time, however, the environment has offered a seemingly plausible and, to some, compelling argument for why, whatever the recent and current data, disaster could strike in the future. This depends upon the notion that the planet's eco-system is a delicate thing, whose balance could easily be tipped over. It then proceeds with the observation that economic and population growth since the industrial revolution have already had a big impact on the planet, leading to the digging up of minerals and harvesting of other resources, and the spewing out of gases and chemicals of all sorts while processing and using these resources. Indeed, humanity's impact on the planet, measured in almost any way, has been greater during the past two-and-a-bit centuries of the industrial revolution than in the previous thousand years, or possibly the whole of human history. This is not surprising, given that roughly a fifth of all the years lived by humans since the beginning of time were lived during the twentieth century alone. Professor J. R. McNeill of Georgetown University, in his book *Something New Under the Sun: An Environmental History of the Twentieth-Century World*, estimated that more energy had been used during that century than in all of human history before 1900.

The keenest environmentalists proceed from these observations to point out that sometimes, once change passes a certain threshold, it brings about what scientists call a 'non-linear effect': in other words, a dramatic change rather than a gradual, proportionate one. The clearest example is the relationship between ocean temperatures and the climate. When the water temperature of the tropical Atlantic is below 26 degrees Celsius, there are no hurricanes in the area; above that temperature, a whole series of hurricanes will suddenly occur. This fear is featured prominently in the more extreme concerns about global warming. Another version is put forward by an eminent biologist, E. O. Wilson, who has given warning of a massive extinction of species at some point in the future, but without evidence of any linear relationship between cause and effect.

In his book *Earth in the Balance*, first published in 1992, Vice-President Al Gore used the analogy of a sandpile to illustrate this purported phenomenon, which he calls 'self-organized criticality'. As grains of sand are gradually added to a pile of sand, for much of the time the pile merely grows in size, interrupted only by minor avalanches. But the balance of each grain depends on all the others. A time comes when, as more grains are added, the pile reaches a 'critical state' and much larger avalanches occur. Mr Gore uses this theory to explain his worries about the climate, but then takes it a huge stride further. He writes:

Apart from our growing threat to the integrity of the global ecological system, the dramatic changes now taking place within civilization itself are also likely to pose serious threats of their own to the integrity and stability of civilization itself. The accumulation of another billion people every ten years is creating a whole range of difficult problems, and all by itself the exploding population is liable to push world civilization into a supercritical state, leaving it vulnerable to very large 'avalanches' of unpredictable change.

We are not just on a sandpile of a planet; we humans are forming a sandpile, too.

This sort of argument, whether from melodramatic politicians or from respectable scientists such as E. O. Wilson, is hard to confront because facts from the present and past play no role in it. The science of sandpile collapses is thin. It is a theory which is untestable, because it depends on the very idea that the future might suddenly become drastically different from the past. But how probable are such drastic changes? Could they happen across large areas of the planet by some means other than the familiar, external shock such as a crash of a meteor or asteroid into the Earth? By definition, we cannot know: we cannot predict the unpredictable. It is a brilliant as well as infuriating argument, reminiscent of the Marxist ploy of 'historical materialism', or false consciousness, discussed in Chapter 7: nothing can refute it.

*

We can, however, assess some facts, in order to separate real and known environmental problems from the false ones, as well as to see why no environmental issue is ever a matter of black and white. A convenient place to start is the alarming set of claims cited in that advertisement for the *Earth on Edge* television series. Were they true, or even nearly true?

Have 'half the world's forests' been chopped down? No. It is, admittedly, hard to be sure how much land was covered by forest before man started to remove it, and hard to agree when that comparator date should be. Clearances began during the Bronze Age, or even earlier. As a result, estimates vary widely for how much deforestation has occurred since the dawn of agriculture. Professor J. R. McNeill estimates in *Something New Under the Sun* that the reduction since agriculture began is about 26 per cent. Other respectable academic estimates range as low as 7.5 per cent. The World Resources Institute, an environmental think tank, cites an exceptionally high figure of 46 per cent, which may be the source for the advertisement. But such a high figure appears to depend on very bold guesses about what forests might once have existed in places about which little is known, such as much of Africa; it is not based on known clearances of known forests, thanks to economic development.

Perhaps a more recent starting-date might help, since historical records could offer a more reliable comparison. It will still not be foolproof, because, for example, if you take AD 1700 or even 1850 as the starting-date, records of forest cover in Africa remain poor. Professor McNeill has a table in his book showing estimates for how much of the world's land was accounted for by forest and woodland on various dates. He estimates that 62 per cent was covered in this way in 1700 and still 60 per cent in 1850, but coverage had declined to 48 per cent in 1990. So is it now declining quickly? Measures vary because definitions vary, but according to figures from the Food and Agriculture Organization (FAO) of the UN, the world had 40.24 million square kilometres of forest in 1950. The UN's *State of the World's Forests 2001* report says that total world forest cover in 2000 was 38.7 million. So there had been a drop, but not a drastic one.

What has been happening, however, is that the type of forest has been changing. Forests in temperate countries have been expanding, as agriculture has taken up less space and land has reverted to natural woodland, and as plantations have been created (for example, to provide woodpulp for the paper on which this book has been printed). In 1895 a mere 5 per cent of Britain was covered in woodland; according to the country's Forestry Commission, the figure now is 11.8 per cent. Tropical forests, however, have been shrinking. The FAO estimates that net deforestation in the tropics proceeded at a rate of 0.8 per cent a year in the 1990s.

It is probably true that a large proportion of 'the world's wetlands' have disappeared, though whether the right figure is half, or 70 per cent, or 30 per cent is highly debatable since again there is no clear definition and no agreed-upon historical records. Professor McNeill thinks about 15 per cent of the world's 10 million square kilometres of such lands were drained during the twentieth century alone. The better question to ask, however, is whether this matters, or at least why. Should a caring, environmentally aware person want to demand the immediate evacuation of most of the Netherlands and the reflooding, or digging out, of all the polders in that former wetland? The same would apply to the entire floodplain along the Mississippi River, and to much of the modern parts of Singapore. 'Wetlands' have disappeared because people have drained swamps and bogs, have reclaimed land from the sea or from lakes, and have tamed (with varying degrees of success) the floods of great rivers. By doing so, they have obtained some excellent agricultural land, as well as creating new places on which to build towns and airports. They have thus made the land much more useful for them, but have displaced other creatures and life forms that lived in the wet. Whether you consider this tendency benign or malign depends on your view of this trade-off.

Are 'half the world's fisheries' depleted? According to the FAO, about 35 per cent of the world's total fish catch comes from fish stocks whose yields are declining. That is a fair measure of the word 'depleted': too depleted to sustain constant or rising yields to fishermen. Some studies suggest that quite a few marine species were driven to extinction by being harvested by local humans centuries ago, well before the rise of industrial fishing but also well before the accrual of scientific knowledge about what sort of catches were sustainable. Similar things happened during the nineteenth and early twentieth centuries to some whale species. Where man had long since transformed himself from a hunter-gatherer into a farmer on the land, on the sea the hunter-gatherer spirit persisted.

Today, however, the farming idea has spread to the seas. Total fish production is rising despite these falling yields because an increasing proportion of the total consumption of fish, world-wide, is coming from fish farms. This point can be discounted if fish from farms are not thought of as 'real' because, perhaps, they are not naturally reared. (It is worth noting, however, that in that case the world probably has both a 'sheep crisis' and a 'cow crisis' since very few sheep and cows live in the wild any longer. Clearly, the world's sheeperies have been sadly depleted.) If the farming of fish takes some of the pressure off natural fisheries, it must be beneficial, at least in that regard (though as some farmed fish are fed on fishmeal from conventionally harvested fish, the relief may be modest).

There is certainly a 'problem of over-fishing of natural stocks', for it is a familiar truth that when a resource is collectively owned, or not owned at all, those using it have little incentive to conserve it and much incentive to harvest it as quickly as possible, lest others get there before them. So policing of fishing, particularly co-operative policing between nations, does matter and is necessary. There are also the marine equivalents of land-based endangered species, which like tigers and elephants are generally singled out for their size and their looks: whales and many types of turtle.

All the specific claims in that advertisement were thus false or highly misleading. Perhaps it shouldn't matter: advertisements typically exaggerate, and it was just one television series. Yet the view which it put forward was not at all exceptional or unusual. The specific list of claims may have been the series' own, special choice. But its general thesis, that the planet has been 'pushed to the edge', is shared by many people. Before looking at solutions, therefore, it is worth exploring some more of the claimed problems.

First, the loss of species, and of what is known as biodiversity. This rather fundamental issue is again complicated by a lack of knowledge of (or at least agreement on) the starting-point. The trouble with species is that they are very hard to define and then to count, even in the present day, for the vast majority consist of insects. Since we do not know how many there are now, it is also impossible to know how many species there were 100, 500 or 1,000 years ago. Roughly 1.6 million species have been counted, and scientists' estimates of how many there really are varies between 2 million and 80 million, according to a book by a Danish statistician and former member of Greenpeace, Dr Bjorn Lomborg, called *The Skeptical Environmentalist*; or between 3 million and 100 million, according to Professor McNeill. On the other hand, some are clearly dying out. Since 1600, according to Professor McNeill, some 484 species of animals and 654 plants have died out. Some have been hunted into oblivion. Some species have been introduced, across the world, into alien habitats and have driven competitors out. And some species, propagated or encouraged by agriculture, have multiplied greatly (those sheeperies again).

The rate of species extinction is well above what scientists call the 'natural background rate', that is, the rate that would occur anyway given evolution and changes to climate, terrain and so on. But how worrying is it? According to the UN's Global Biodiversity Assessment, something in a range between 0.1 per cent and 1 per cent of species are becoming extinct every fifty years. At this rate, even over two centuries a maximum of 4 per cent of species would have been lost. Dr Lomborg, citing a biologist's study, plumps for a rate of 0.7 per cent every fifty years. Given that he is a statistician and not a biologist, that may be the wrong choice. Nevertheless, if (a big if) the current total were to be 1.6 million, that would mean the loss of 11,200 species over fifty years.

Some think this could be too low an estimate because of the destruction of tropical rainforests, since roughly half of all terrestrial species live in those forests. If the forests continue to be hacked down, there might be a sudden, catastrophic extinction of species living there. According to the World Conservation Union, about 20 per cent of what is thought to be the original extent of tropical forest cover has disappeared. About 14 per cent of the Amazonian rainforest, the world's biggest, has been cut down. The rate at which the Brazilian forest (about two-thirds of the Amazonian rainforest is in Brazil) was being cut down in the 1980s and early 1990s caused widespread concern. Now, the rate of deforestation in the Amazon has slowed to about 0.5 per cent of the total land area each year. If that were to carry on unchecked, however, it would mean that the whole forest would be gone in two hundred years' time. That is very unlikely to happen: legislation is already restraining further deforestation; that, combined with further pressure from Brazilian voters, is likely to push more timber firms into methods of logging that leave more of the forest intact. Corruption and crime could slow that improvement down, but they have not prevented an improvement from taking place over the past decade. Even so, the evidence from other tropical forests, such as that cited by Dr Lomborg for Puerto Rico, is that species extinction does not occur in any catastrophic, or even extreme manner when part of the forest is cut down. The main reason is that much of the forest does not just disappear: it is replaced by fresh woodland and other vegetation in which many species survive. Only if it were comprehensively cleared and concreted over would a dramatic loss of species take place.

Air pollution, as we shall discuss later in this chapter, is bringing about the genuine, and genuinely worrying, question of global warming and of climate change. The average world-wide atmospheric temperature appears to have risen because of human actions, and is still rising. But meanwhile pollution is not making the air that we, in the richer countries, breathe any dirtier. Far from it: that air has mostly become cleaner, and is becoming cleaner still, in the developed countries.

The air in the cities of North America, Western Europe and Japan became steadily dirtier in the nineteenth and early twentieth centuries as more and more factories and residents burned wood and coal for their power and heat, and as people came to live near the factories themselves. Two things then changed, which have made the cities steadily cleaner: companies and people switched to a cleaner fossil fuel such as oil and gas, or to electricity, which can be produced many miles away from the factories and houses that use the power. Alarm about the damage to health from bad air gave rise, in democracies, to legislation which put tight restrictions on the right to pollute. The result has been a big fall in all measures of airborne particles and chemicals of all kinds, including smoke, soot, lead, nitrogen oxides, sulphur dioxide, ozone and carbon monoxide. The dates at which those falls began vary, from the early 1950s (smoke) to the 1970s (lead, and nitrogen oxides and carbon monoxide from vehicle emissions). They have taken place despite a big increase in all rich countries in the numbers of cars and other motor vehicles, and in the degree to which they are used. In the United States, for example, according to the US Environmental Protection Agency (EPA), between 1970 and 2000 the aggregate emissions of the six principal pollutants tracked nationally were cut by 29 per cent. During the same period, according to the EPA, American GDP rose by 158 per cent, energy consumption rose by 45 per cent and the miles travelled by vehicles rose by 143 per cent.

The story with water pollution is similar, though the first big improvements were made longer ago than was the case with air. The discovery of bacteria and of their connection with human illness gave rise, during the nineteenth century, to the first modern urban sewerage systems, and to treatment plants for drinking water. It was not until the 1950s, however, that serious efforts were made in America, Western Europe and Japan to clean up urban rivers and nearby lakes, which had become seriously polluted by both commercial and household wastes. This was done both because of worries about safety and for broader, aesthetic or environmental reasons. The increased use of leisure time made the ability to swim in rivers, lakes and coastal waters more important, and made more people concerned about the lack of fish and other creatures in those waters.

One persistent concern is about the use of artificial fertilizers and pesticides in agriculture and fish-farming, which then contaminate watercourses and, in the end, perhaps drinking water. They can cause direct worries about cancers and other long-term ill-effects, or indirect ones, because nitrates and phosphates can encourage algae to grow, which in turn can reduce the oxygen level in the water, hurting other organisms. These are fairly new fears, and consequently the scientific research required to prove them to be reasonable or unreasonable is also fairly new. This issue offers a fine illustration of the trade-offs that occur in many environmental questions: if fewer artificial fertilizers were used, then to produce the same amount of food would require more agricultural land, which would mean that more forests would be chopped down, and so on. It may also, in some places, illustrate what is in effect a law of unforeseen consequences: that often the intensive use of fertilizers is a response to a subsidy, which rewards farmers for producing more food from less land. If more food were imported from the developing countries, where land is often abundant, less fertilizer would be used and the poor farmers would become richer.

*

This list of facts is not intended to mean either that all has been well, or that all will be well. The twentieth century featured plenty of man-made environmental disasters: destructive world wars; two nuclear bombings; nuclear meltdown at Chernobyl; the horror of Minamata disease, in Japan, from mercury poisoning; the disaster at the Union Carbide factory at Bhopal in India; ghastly oil spills from the *Exxon Valdez* (1989) or *Atlantic Empress* (1979) tanker wrecks, or from the deliberate release of oil from Kuwaiti refineries by Saddam Hussein in 1991; the destruction of the Aral Sea in what was then Soviet Central Asia; appalling air pollution in many cities by smoke, factory fumes and car exhausts. All these environmental problems – in a few cases, catastrophes – resulted from man's economic development, from man's propensity for conflict and from man's ability to invent new ways to explode, to destroy, to kill. And all that is without even mentioning global warming. The twentieth century was the warmest century in the second millennium, with a rise in the global average surface temperature of about 0.6 degrees Celsius. Much of that rise – scientists do not know how much – was probably caused by human activity.

The first lesson from the twentieth century, however, is that it proved possible for mankind to learn how to deal with such disasters: to heal the land or the sea (or, sometimes, to allow them to heal themselves), and to find ways to make such events less likely in the future. Both nature and man proved to be good at adapting and recovering. The second lesson is that although, inevitably, economic development brought about many of the problems or changes, wealth ultimately proved to be the solution, not the problem. Today the cleanest, most environmentally safe societies are the rich ones; indeed, those societies enjoy air and water that is cleaner than it has been for hundreds of years. The dirtiest, most environmentally unsafe societies are the poor ones.

To have any idea of what the future, in the twenty-first century at least, might hold it is necessary to try to understand why this has occurred. The first reason is not, at an initial glance, terribly comforting. It is coincidence. The coincidence is that the worst sources of air pollution – both in the open air and, even more dangerously, inside dwellings – arose from inefficiency. Particles of soot and smoke that were in the air were, by definition, waste. An efficient process would have converted those particles into useful energy. As a result, the eventual drive for efficient – that is, cheaper and more reliable – sources of power resulted in the discharge of fewer of these particles into the air, and hence into lungs. The switch to oil entailed a switch to a more efficient source of power and heat. Legislation designed in some cities (notably London) to encourage a shift to 'smokeless' fuels thus coincided with an economic incentive to move in that sort of direction anyway. This force is likely to be repeated in developing countries. For inefficiency costs money, and the technical methods of reducing it are already available, off the shelf, in the rich countries. China, today, burns a lot of coal, both in commercial and in residential buildings. The desire for efficiency gives us cause to be optimistic that countries such as China will switch to cleaner fuels and technologies much more quickly than the rich countries did.

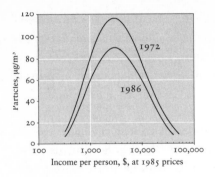

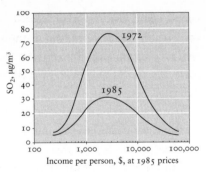

Figure 1. The connection between national income per head and particle pollution in 48 cities in 31 countries, 1972 and 1986. Source: Bjorn Lomborg, The Skeptical Environmentalist

Figure 2. The connection between national income per head and SO$_2$ pollution in 47 cities in 31 countries, 1972 and 1985. Source: Bjorn Lomborg, The Skeptical Environmentalist

Studies by the World Bank have shown two comforting things. One is that there is a very clear connection between wealth and air pollution: the amount of particles and gases in the air increases until a country has reached a certain income per head of population, and then declines rapidly. The second is that the level of pollution at which this transformation takes place has declined substantially over time. Figures 1 and 2 show the connection between air pollution and income levels in 1972 and then in the mid-1980s. The later connection is reassuringly shallower than the earlier one: pollution has been declining at lower levels of income.

This requires an additional explanation, however. For the coincidence of rising efficiency with cleanliness is an exception to the most fundamental environmental rule. This is that the reason why firms pollute and otherwise despoil the world is that they do not suffer the costs of their despoliation. If those costs formed part of their calculations about how and what to produce, they would behave differently in an effort to reduce the costs and increase their profits. Instead, other people bear those costs, whether of cleaning up the waste, or of enduring an aesthetically ruined scene, or of suffering directly from poor health or other injuries to life. Those costs are often borne quite locally rather than by society as a whole; the firm's bosses and owners may live in splendid cleanliness but those living near their factory breathe in the pollution. The costs are a species of what economists call 'externalities'; they are borne externally from the direct activity or transaction concerned. Externalities can be positive (that is, beneficial) or negative (that is, costly); these are the negative sort.

Put simply, the environment becomes cleaner when firms and people can be persuaded to absorb (that is, deal with) more of those externalities in their internal (that is, private) activities. The clear experience of the twentieth century is that this persuasion takes place quite readily in democracies but with great difficulty (if at all) in dictatorships. Those bearing the social costs have a means, in democracies, of getting their complaints heard and of persuading elected law-makers to alter the law in order to clean up the environment. If those bearing the costs are something like a majority, they will have a pretty good chance of forcing change to take place.

In dictatorships, such changes depend either on the benevolence of the dictators, or on mass demonstrations successfully forcing the dictator to take action, or on the dictators themselves feeling affected by whatever scourge is under consideration. Naturally, therefore, successful cases of environmental improvements are much rarer in dictatorships. Communism, in which governing officials were completely unaccountable, proved far dirtier than democratic capitalism. Thus, one can be optimistic about the possibility that China will increasingly seek to make its use of energy more efficient, and thus less prone to causing particle pollution, because that stimulus is purely economic. But one cannot be so optimistic that China will seek increasingly to deal with the externalities or social costs caused by other sorts of pollution, where the issue is not one of inefficiency but rather of who bears the costs.

The improvement in rich countries' environments has been closely correlated with the growth of democracy in those countries. The first stringent anti-pollution laws were introduced in the 1950s, when democracy was blossoming in many countries. Japan had the dreadful Minamata disease from mercury poisoning in the late 1950s; that and a series of other pollution disasters gave rise first to citizens' protest movements, but then, belatedly, to new laws to control toxic effluent and air pollution. In their imperfect way, democracies are able to give voice to the social costs of dirt and danger, and their political systems offer a rough and ready mechanism to make the trade-offs between those who win or lose from such costs or from their prevention. This is especially true when local democracies – for example, in an American state such as California, or a Japanese prefecture – have control over local environmental laws which can override or supersede national ones.

This does not readily occur when governments are authoritarian and can afford to turn a blind eye to pollution. So the rise in democracy, all around the world (details of which will be explored in Chapter 12), gives a cautious case for optimism. Most of the rich countries were not democracies during the periods of their early industrial growth. As more poor countries become democracies, so the possibility looms that their citizens will opt for cleaner growth at an earlier stage of their development than was the case in Western Europe, America or Japan.

*

That is a hope, not a dependable forecast. That is all it can be, for we are talking about the future. There are numerous variables involved: will poor countries continue to switch to democracy? Will their citizens develop the same taste for a greener environment that rich-country citizens developed? Will they make the same choices when presented with the trade-offs that the environment involves? Or might their environmental preferences conflict with those of the rich world's citizens, provoking conflict? Might this whole, gradualist hope be subverted by military conflict itself, for it is at times of conflict that the greatest environmental damage is wrought? None of these questions can automatically be given a favourable answer. But the cause for hope is nevertheless strong. History does suggest that, at least in the absence of war, democracies become greener, and that the pollution level at which societies make that sort of switch is declining. If poor countries do grow and become much richer, and it is sincerely to be hoped that they do, then the increasing number of democracies among them is likely to mean that their economic development will become greener, much more quickly than was the case for the already-rich countries.

This is not the end of the tale, however. For there are two other issues to explore. One is the mega-issue of global warming. But first there is another, more personal, local issue, that of everybody's favourite toy: the motor car. The car is worth exploring because it throws in stark relief the sort of choices that must be made. They are not between pristine nature and industrial grime. They are between different sorts of human activity, and different sorts of human effect on the environment. Pollution is involved, but it is not the main issue: the issue is what sort of freedom, and what sort of urban development, people turn out to want. And as they get richer, typically they have wanted more freedom and more motor cars.

'O bliss! O poop-poop! O my! O my!' Those words are especially dear to an Englishman, being a quotation from Mr Toad, in Kenneth Grahame's *The Wind in the Willows*, a charming children's book published in 1908. Mr Toad's exclamations of the joys of motoring – the freedom, the sense of power, the pleasure of forcing others to get out of your way – perfectly encapsulate the appeal of the car. He spoke of 'the poetry of motion', and surely only the hard-hearted would deny that this is indeed what many people feel when they are driving their cars. In the book, though, Mr Toad also gets into a lot of trouble: he crashes, is arrested and so on. Which is also fitting, given the amount of anguish the car causes these days.

It causes that anguish because of its effect on the environment, which really means its effect on other people. As machines go, the car is not terribly noisy (certainly compared with supposedly environmentally friendly scooters), nor terribly polluting, nor terribly dangerous; and on all those dimensions it has become much better as time has passed. It causes difficulty because of its ubiquity and the social costs that ensue from the use by everyone of something that would be fairly harmless if, for example, only the rich were using it. It is a price we pay for equality.

However, before becoming consumed by gloom and traffic fumes, it is worth recalling why the car has been arguably the most successful and popular product for the whole of the past hundred years – and remains so. That begins with the environmental improvement it brought to big cities in the 1900s. In New York City in 1900, according to *The Car Culture*, a 1975 book by James Flink, a historian, horses deposited 2.5 million pounds of manure and 60,000 gallons of urine every day. On average, the city authorities had to remove 15,000 dead horses from the streets every year. Compared with all of that, the car seemed more or less antiseptic.

Then there was the car's flexibility. The initial solution to equine pollution and congestion was the electric trolley bus. But that required fixed overhead wires, and rails and platforms, which were expensive and ugly and inflexible. The car required merely the asphalting of roads, which improved them, and the development of a network of places where you could buy fuel. It could go from any A to any B, and allowed towns to develop in all directions, with low-density housing, rather than with a string of houses squashed along the trolley or rail lines. Rural areas benefited too, for they no longer seemed so remote once cars became commonplace. Postmen could deliver the mail; farm children could go to larger schools.

Most of all, however, the car brought freedom and represented equality. It spread far more quickly in America because incomes were higher and more equal there, spaces were bigger and the market was more competitive. By 1927, America accounted for 80 per cent of the world's stock of a machine that had originally been developed in France, and had one motor vehicle for every 5.3 people. It also spread rapidly in other countries with space, European immigrants and a fluid society: New Zealand (10.5 people per car in 1927), Canada (10.7), Australia (16), and Argentina (43). France and Britain both had ratios of 44 people per motor vehicle. Economically troubled Germany was miles behind, at 196.

That sense of independence, of the ability to get up and go where we please, to do what we please, has stayed with the car to this day. In Japan in the high-growth 1960s, when the war was finally being left behind, the basic aspiration of an ordinary family was described as the achievement of 'the three Cs': car, cooler and colour television. A new Japanese phrase appeared: *mai car suru*, to drive around in your car at weekends. It was a statement about freedom, about independence. Similar phrases will be popping up in today's developing countries, once incomes per head go above the $6,000 level beyond which sales of cars seem always to rise sharply.

Another constant is that ever since pollution became a concern in the 1950s, pundits have predicted – wrongly – that the car boom was about to end. Mr Flink's *The Car Culture* argued that by 1973 the American market had become saturated, at one car for every 2.25 people, and so (because of land shortages) were the markets of Japan and Western Europe. Environmental worries and dwindling oil reserves would prohibit mass car use anywhere else. The political strength of the industry was on the wane, he said: the industry still provided one in every six jobs in America, but government now provided one in every five. 'Projections for a vast increase in the number of motor vehicles on our roads over the next several decades . . . have lost credibility,' wrote this automotive historian.

But they hadn't. Between 1970 and 1990, while America's population grew by 23 per cent, the number of motor vehicles on its roads grew by 60 per cent. There is now one car for every 1.7 people there, one for every 2.1 in Japan. About 50 million new cars are made each year, worldwide, and around 550 million are already on the roads, not to mention all the lorries and motorbikes. Will it go on? Undoubtedly, because people want it to. India has only one car for every 350 people. If, as is to be hoped, its people become richer, freer and more equal, many more will want cars – or, at least, they will want some means of personal, independent, reliable, reasonably rapid transportation. Is this the tyranny of the motorist? Hardly. We are all (or almost all) motorists now.

*

As a result, it is as certain as anything can be that free choice and the popular vote will keep the car rolling on. But the popular vote will also want to change the way the car rolls on, to try to moderate the three different sorts of difficulty that it poses: pollution, congestion and development.

Governments have been grappling with all three, under popular pressure, mainly since the early 1970s; sometimes governmental actions have outpaced the car, but then it has overtaken them again. Planning regulations and green belts have limited development; quotas and tolls have been used, a little, to try to reduce congestion, even as large sums have also been invested in new roads, especially ring roads around big towns and cities; bans, laws, targets and taxes have been used to address pollution. Why not just attack the car directly, with laws, bans or huge taxes, to try to deal with all three problems simultaneously? Because it would offend everyone at once, which politicians in a democracy try to avoid. But also because the three types of problem are separate – in their economic characteristics and, therefore, in their political ones.

Congestion is a lot less likely to be addressed than pollution. Almost all the direct costs of congestion – delay, frustration – are carried by the people sitting in the traffic jam themselves, though some are carried by those buying products whose delivery has therefore become costlier or lengthier. These direct costs are shared by others who might have wanted to drive from one place to another, but who were discouraged by the likely traffic jams. But if people want to avoid traffic jams, they can make their own choices: not to drive, or to go at a different time, or to install a mobile phone so that they can do something useful while jammed. One of the attractions of cars is that, maddening though a jam might be, the interior of the car can be made quite a comfortable place in which to pass the time, with a phone, music, air conditioning, comfortable seats and all the rest. In a few highly congested city centres, if popular pressure builds up to clear them, road pricing will surely be used to smooth out traffic use. But congestion will have to become a great deal worse, and more widespread, before a broad swathe of voters supports a lot of road pricing.

The indirect cost of congestion is localized pollution: all those cars, lorries and buses sitting below your window, belching out fumes. Road pricing, to smooth out traffic flow, might reduce that. But this would not have a big effect on pollution, for the real worries about that arise from the continuous presence in the air of exhaust gases. Most of the cost of the pollution is not borne by the particular people sitting in the cars; it is borne by everyone breathing in the air, principally in cities, which makes it more likely that politicians will be driven to try to deal with it, just as they did with smoke and soot from fires and factories.

Since 1970, very little has been done about congestion in the rich countries, beyond building a few more roads, but quite a lot has already been done about pollution, because it is a greater social evil. So far, most of the action has been in the form of rules: about exhaust emissions, catalytic converters, inspections and so on. Almost certainly, there will be more such rules in future, chiefly to try to accelerate the introduction of electric cars, run by batteries and, the greatest hope of all, fuel cells, which convert hydrogen into electric power. Yet rules to force the pace of technical change are unlikely to be enough.

The reason is that most of the pollution comes from existing cars. Fuel cells and batteries may well start to enter commercial use within the next few years. But they will take time to be widely accepted by motorists, given the need for a network of rechargers or hydrogen-refuelling stations before such cars become useful. So if governments are serious about reducing pollution, they will have to levy taxes on the ownership or use of older, petrol-driven cars, to try to make people use them less and to switch to newer, cleaner ones; or the taxes will be levied on the petrol itself, as is already the case in much of Western Europe. The refusal of politicians to impose higher taxes on petrol in the land that epitomizes free choice and democracy, the United States, does not bode well for their widespread imposition elsewhere, either.

That is what control of the car will depend on: the willingness of voters to accept controls, and to vote back into office politicians who impose them. This also applies to the issue of urban development: new houses, new roads, new schools, new hospitals, new office buildings, new shopping malls. As and when these things are built, concreting over some part of the countryside, spoiling somebody's view and generally attracting new crowds and congestion to an area, the action takes place because somebody stands to benefit from it. The direct benefit goes to the property developer, certainly, but the indirect benefit goes to all those who live in the new houses, shop in the mall, use the schools and hospitals and so on. Others, however, lose. Urban development (or, to use the derogatory term now in common parlance, urban sprawl) is not a simple, ethical issue, of nature versus man, of capitalism versus the environment. It is always a matter of political choice, between different goals and competing interests.

Environmentalists often argue that one of those competing interests ought to be that of future generations. By paving paradise, as Joni Mitchell put it in a song, and putting in a parking lot, today's developers and drivers are depriving future generations of that natural scene over which they have poured concrete. This is true, but lacking in any practical force. We cannot know what future generations might prefer. Only when large numbers of us feel able to put ourselves in their shoes is it possible for the interests of grandchildren to be brought to bear on a decision. We can know, for instance, that they would rather not live by a lake full of mercury, as it would be potentially deadly. But we cannot know whether they would prefer that lake's shore to be pristine and untouched, or for it to have a smart (or even unsmart) promenade built along it. That choice can only be ours to make, not theirs.

Only one thing can be predicted with certainty about urban development. It is that the battle, the need for political choices to be made, will continue. This is not an issue that either the environment, or economic growth, can win. It is a question of a series of compromises, of choices, between costs and benefits, between one person's gain and another's loss, between the value people put on nature and the value they put on human constructions and amenities.

*

Something similar must be said about global warming. There are political choices to be made. The awkwardness about this very real environmental issue begins with the lack of knowledge about the true dimensions of the problem. It continues with a lack of knowledge about the consequences of global warming. And then it hits the hardest problem of all: that although this is an issue with global causes, it is also one in which there are big losers, small losers, big winners and small winners, with the losses and gains varying at different times in the future. If it were possible to say, starkly, that this is a shared problem from which we all stand to suffer equally, it would be fairly easy to sort out a solution. But it isn't.

Whole books can be, and are being, written about the topic of so-called greenhouse gases, global warming and what to do about it. It is thought of as the most important environmental issue of our times, which certainly means for the twenty-first century as a whole. And it is surely important. But it can actually be discussed quite simply and even briefly.

Scientists gathered together under the auspices of the United Nations, in the Intergovernmental Panel on Climate Change (IPCC), have said, in their latest (2001) report that current trends, plus the possible future effect of future emissions and accumulations of greenhouse gases, will probably mean that the global average surface temperature will rise during the twenty-first century by somewhere between 1.4 degrees Celsius and 5.8 degrees Celsius. They may be right or they may be wrong, but in any case this is the best estimate that is currently available. It should be compared with an estimated rise in the same measure during the twentieth century of 0.6 degrees Celsius (which, in turn, followed a particularly cold period of the world's climatic history, known as 'the little ice age', so, to some extent, the temperature has been rising from an unusually low level). The lowest estimate for the twenty-first-century rise is, we should note, more than double the estimated rise during the twentieth century. But the range in the estimates is extremely wide, because of a very high degree of uncertainty about the science of climate and temperature, about the modelling, and about the future course of greenhouse gas emission.

Faced with a rise in temperature of this range of magnitude, the first question to ask is: why does it matter? There is no such concept as the ideal global average surface temperature, so we cannot know what temperature trend we should prefer. A hotter earth would imply a higher sea-level, as ice in various places turns to water. But, depending on its size, that would hurt only a few places: low-lying islands and communities on vulnerable coasts. The IPCC thinks that, in economic terms, the effect of a rise in temperature of up to 2 degrees might well be positive, overall, for the existing developed countries. Most of them are in northern, temperate zones which would have milder winters. And, as these countries are already rich, they would be able to adapt fairly easily to changing conditions. But the IPCC believes the effects on developing countries of such a rise in temperature would be negative, because these poorer countries are less able to adapt, and because most of these countries already have fairly unwelcoming climates which would become even less easy to work and live in. So, if the IPCC is correct, the problem at the lower end of the temperature range is not one of clear, overall damage to the globe: it is one under which the poor countries become worse off and the rich ones slightly better off.

Above that rise in temperature, things become simpler, according to the scientists: everyone, overall, would be worse off. But, again, the rich would be better able to adapt to the new conditions. And, as with everything about global warming, there is a very high level of uncertainty.

When the IPCC says that some would gain and others lose, the next important question is: how much? It is not easy to say. One reason is the complexity of the effects, on agriculture, energy use, forestry, human health, water provision and treatment and so on, as well as possible effects on settlements from a rising sea-level. Another is the possibility that as temperatures rise, the effects on weather systems could be non-linear: in other words, that we might start getting more hurricanes, floods or droughts, all of a sudden. A particular fear, with no clear scientific foundation, is that a rise in temperature might lead to a change in the ocean currents in the Atlantic, for example, producing a sudden change in weather patterns elsewhere. This would mean that the overall costs would rise in a non-linear way, too: a one-degree rise in temperature could impose much greater costs when it represents the difference between a three-degree rise and a four-degree one, than when it is the difference between a two-degree and a three. But all this is speculative. The scientists do not know.

Gradual changes in temperature and climate make little economic difference, overall. This is because people can adapt what they do and how they live, as the climate changes. For example, it would be useless to try to calculate the economic cost of the twentieth century's rise in global average surface temperature by 0.6 degrees. To make any sense, such a calculation would have to be based on the assumption that people lived, worked and produced things in the same way in 1999 as they did in 1900. But that assumption would itself be nonsense, for people have changed their behaviour in a huge number of ways, a few of them stimulated by rising temperatures but many of them not. Inventions such as air conditioning, and progress in disease control and health care, have made it far more possible to live productively in Singapore, or Houston, Texas. Much the same should be expected in the twenty-first century. Changes in technology and behaviour will alter, in ways that we cannot now even begin to imagine or to feed into our computer models, the lives of people in different parts of the world and the economic calculations surrounding different activities in different locations.

What points, then, should be considered reliable enough to act upon? One is the fact that the global temperature is indeed rising, and that even at the lower end of the IPCC's estimated range it is rising at a rate that is a lot faster than during the past century. That hundred years itself saw quite a lot of variation, with fairly rapid warming from 1910 to 1945, some cooling from 1945 until 1976, and then a new period of warming which is still continuing. During this recent period of warming, the temperature rose more rapidly than it did in 1910–45. A second point is that man-made greenhouse gases do contribute to the rise in temperature. How much is uncertain. We know that gases such as carbon dioxide, nitrous oxide and methane act to trap heat in the atmosphere, like the glass roof of a greenhouse. Life on earth depends on this greenhouse effect, as otherwise the temperature would be far too low. But the quantity of greenhouse gases has increased thanks to mankind, which is helping to increase the heat. Scientists on the IPCC believe that the amount of carbon dioxide in the atmosphere has increased by a third since 1750, and that by 2100 the amount will be 90 per cent higher than since the same date. They also conclude that 'most' of the observed warming over the past fifty years is likely to have been due to an increase in greenhouse gas concentrations.

A third reality is that once it has been released into the atmosphere, a greenhouse gas stays there. If forest cover were suddenly to expand dramatically, the trees might absorb large amounts of carbon dioxide and thus reduce the greenhouse gas accumulation – but extra forests cannot be planted and grown rapidly enough to make an appreciable difference during a reasonable planning period (for example, thirty years). They may, and probably will, make some difference, but not a lot. Other factors in the atmosphere that serve to cool the earth – such as cloud cover, or the airborne particles known as aerosols – could, in theory, increase in their quantity and effect and thus counteract the warming; but their effect could also diminish, accelerating the rise in temperature. Recently, the scientists say, their effect has been considerably outweighed by the effect of the accumulation of greenhouse gases.

Thus, we know that the temperature is rising; that greenhouse gases are at least part of the explanation; that it will probably continue to rise for a long period, but that the further ahead predictions stretch the less reliable they become; that the rise in temperature will impose costs on certain parts of the world, especially the poor ones; and that the higher the rise, the more the costs will be incurred by most of the globe's population and, probably, that those costs could become very large if there prove to be more extreme weather conditions.

We cannot, however, put a sensible, reliable number on the overall costs because of all the uncertainties involved. Dr Lomborg, despite the fact that he called his book *The Skeptical Environmentalist*, produces an estimate for the total cost of around $5 trillion. It will certainly be incorrect. Even so, it gives us some sense of the magnitude: roughly equivalent to the value of the current annual output from the world's second largest economy, Japan, or roughly half the annual output of the United States, the world's largest economy. But that sum is spread over a long period.

Not that this figure should be taken literally: it is a broad, probably crude, indication. Many dispute it. Yet a cost of, say, $50 billion a year, whether it is half the truth or double it, still tells you that the possible cost is noticeably large: it would be equivalent to reducing Japan's GDP by 1 per cent each year. It therefore follows that it is worth trying to reduce the man-made component of the rise in temperature, either to halt the rise or to slow it down, but not by measures that plainly exceed this cost. If it could be slowed down, then people would be better able to adapt to the change in climate. The chance of a substantial increase in the frequency and severity of such disasters as hurricanes, droughts and floods would then be much smaller.

To reduce this cost or, avoiding such utilitarian arguments, simply to reduce the impact of global warming for its own sake, countries must find ways to encourage their households and industries to reduce their emissions of greenhouse gases. This entails either replacing energy sources that emit greenhouse gases with others that don't; or finding technologies that can trap and break up the gases before they disappear into the atmosphere. When it was realized that a hole was forming in the ozone layer, high in the atmosphere but above the Antarctic and the southern cone of Latin America, it was quickly agreed that the way to deal with this was to try to get rid of the substances thought to be acting to destroy the ozone layer. These were chloro-fluorocarbons, or CFCs, which had been thought to be cheap, clean and safe substances for use in aerosol spray-cans and refrigerators. An international deal was struck at Montreal in 1987 to eliminate the use of CFCs, which was achieved successfully and remarkably cheaply during the next decade. Substitutes were found, and they were no costlier at their tasks than CFCs. So the danger of a widening hole, bringing with it more harmful rays from the sun and hence skin cancers and other maladies, was averted. Put simply, the same sort of thing needs to be done for greenhouse gases.

Responsibility for emissions and global warming

	Per capita GDP (1995 $)	Per capita CO_2 emissions (tonnes, 1995)	CO_2/GDP (kg/$)
United States	26,980	20.5	0.76
European Union	19,050	7.9	0.41
Russia	4,820	12.2	2.53
China	2,970	2.7	0.91
Africa	1,760	1.1	0.63
India	1,420	1.0	0.70

Source: World Resources Institute, quoted in Marina Cazorla and Michael Toman, 'International Equity and Climate Change Policy', *Resources for the Future*, December 2000

The task, however, is far from simple. One reason is quantity: carbon dioxide, which is produced by burning fossil fuels such as coal, oil and natural gas, arises from far more industrial and residential processes than did CFCs. The task of substitution is far more complicated. And the task of deciding which countries should cut emissions the most is a fraught one. The table shows how tricky it will be to agree on an apportionment between countries. The United States is clearly the biggest emitter of greenhouse gases, both because it is the world's largest economy (it accounts for a third of total economic output) but also because it produces a lot of emissions per head of population. But compared with Russia (especially) and China, its industrial processes are cleaner: those two (massive) countries produce more carbon dioxide relative to their GDPs. In terms of ability to bear costs today, clearly the United States is in a better position to do so. Yet we should remember that the problem is not that the globe is too hot today, but rather that it could become so in the future. A big part of that threat arises from the hoped-for economic growth of countries like China, India and Russia. So one of the biggest solutions would be for those countries to ensure that their future growth was carried out in a way that produced fewer tonnes of greenhouse gases. Experience, as cited earlier in this chapter, suggests that they will anyway become greener as they get richer; global warming may offer a reason to persuade them to accelerate the process.

The apportionment will also be tricky within countries. Basically, the need is to switch from dirtier fossil fuels to cleaner ones, and from all fossil fuels to other sources of energy that do not emit greenhouse gases. So firms and households already committed to the use of coal or oil will suffer from a change; so will producers and processors of those fossil fuels, in the mining, distribution and refining industries. And since the most obvious initial way to cut emissions is to discourage the use of the dirtier fossil fuels through a carbon tax, every user who has to pay that tax will suffer from higher costs, until such time as they are able to switch to an alternative source of energy at a similar or cheaper price.

As a result, all international and domestic deals to try to cut greenhouse gas emissions are likely to be tentative and fiercely disputed, which is another way of saying that initially they are bound to be inadequate. That is what has happened since governments first gathered to discuss global warming at the Rio summit in 1992, and again in Kyoto in 1997. They agreed upon a framework deal under which the rich countries would begin to cut emissions, but made no provision for the future involvement of the developing countries. As a result, and thanks to disputes over exactly how emissions reductions could best be achieved and enforced, the Kyoto deal was rejected by the United States, first in a unanimous vote in the Senate during the Clinton administration's time in office even before the Kyoto talks took place,

and then as one of the early official proclamations of the Bush administration in 2001. Other countries proceeded without the United States'
co-operation to find ways to cut their own emissions. But the resulting
plan looked unambitious, and lacked conviction.

*

Nevertheless, what is absolutely clear is the direction of change. There
is no serious disagreement over whether greenhouse gas emissions
need to be curbed. At issue is the speed, how the change is distributed
around the world and how countries deal with the balance at home
between gainers and losers. The best plan, from an economic point of
view, would provide incentives for users to switch to cleaner energy
sources and for producers to invest more in research into those sources;
a plan that allowed users, and indeed countries, to trade emissions
rights in order to explore the value of those emissions and of conservation, and to channel resources to the most efficient users; and a plan
that progressively included the developing countries, in a way that
added to the incentive in those countries to move to less carbon-
intensive energy sources more quickly.

What will happen in the future? Three things can be said with
reasonable confidence. One is that the actual plans deployed are likely
to fall short of the ideal. But, given agreement on the direction of
change, the gap, at this stage of the development of global warming,
is unlikely to be so large as to be frightening.

The second confident forecast is that technological change will
dominate the process, and may well overtake it as the decades pass.
Already, even at current prices and current lack of political urgency
over greenhouse gas emissions, there are signs that the energy business
is going to be turned on its head by technological change. Fuel cells,
which convert hydrogen into power and do not emit greenhouse gases,
are firmly on their way towards large-scale commercial applications.
As was noted earlier, the need for a new network of fuel storage and
supply means that this cannot happen overnight. But on the timescale
of global warming, it could be fairly rapid. Carbon taxes, stiffer
regulation and increased public pressure will also encourage more
research and development of other energy sources, particularly solar
conversion and even forms of nuclear energy. Well before someone is
sitting writing a book called '21:22 Vision', the world may well have

moved firmly out of the carbon age, and even the oil age, into a new era dominated by different energy sources.

The third confident forecast is that as this transformation of the energy business occurs, it will have geopolitical consequences. Sheikh Yamani, famous as Saudi Arabia's oil minister during the 1970s and early 1980s, once pointed out that the Stone Age did not come to an end because the world had run out of stones. The oil age will not end, as some environmentalists have forecast, because the world has run out of oil. It will end because new, cheaper or more acceptable sources of energy have been discovered or invented. This process may be complicated by fluctuations in the price of oil, which either accelerate or discourage that process of the search for a substitute. But, given the pressure of global warming, the move away from oil is still likely to occur. And as it does, those countries that depend on sales of oil for a large part of their incomes and – in particular – for a large contribution to their military budgets will find the money and the power seeping away from them. Mostly, that means the Gulf states of the Middle East, including (as Sheikh Yamani was warning) Saudi Arabia, but also any others still excessively dependent on oil. Currently, that list would include Venezuela and Nigeria, but also (albeit to a declining extent) Mexico. Economics and politics can never be entirely separated.

One could readily add a fourth forecast. This is that, on global warming as on other laments about the environment, people will continue to claim that everything is getting worse, that nothing is being done and that the world is going to hell in a carbon-propelled handbasket. Such laments are likely to be wrong, and in some cases could do real damage by diverting attention from genuine problems, such as poverty. Even so, the laments will continue to be made. Man is never satisfied.

EPILOGUE AND
PROLOGUE

12

Paranoid Optimism

The questions were simple. Will America continue to lead the world and keep the peace? Will capitalism's strengths outweigh its weaknesses sufficiently to encourage people and their governments to keep faith with it, through thin times as well as thick? The answers were not so simple. They can be summarized briefly: to the first, fortunately yes, albeit with some friction and tough opposition; to the second, probably, but with a lot of potential for rebellions, reversals and revulsion. Such summaries conceal a raft of other ifs, buts and maybes. It is in those vital qualifications, in the opportunities and risks that the preceding chapters have described, that the secrets of the twenty-first century lie awaiting our discovery.

The most important thing as we look ahead is to try to understand those opportunities and risks. We cannot know what will happen during the twenty-first century, any more than someone writing early in the twentieth century could have foretold the events that followed. But it ought to have been possible in 1900 to see that dangers were being posed by the growing rivalry between the most powerful countries in the world, and by the declining ability of Britain to keep the peace and maintain international order. It ought also to have been possible to see the danger that capitalism's instability and inbuilt tendency towards inequality could bring about a political and social backlash in the twentieth century. There were indeed commentators who warned of one or other of these dangers; and in some countries governments responded to some of the warnings. It was much harder, however, to see how the two sorts of danger might feed upon the other: the way in which conflict between the great powers enfeebled capitalism and amplified its weaknesses, and in which an unstable and weak international economy in turn led to political extremism, disillusionment with capitalism and democracy, and then further destructive conflict.

The same difficulty haunts our view of the future today. While we can try to analyse international relations and economics in separate compartments, and can even make a stab at predictions and recommendations in each field, the truth is that the two will be intertwined. Developments in one, for good or ill, will have consequences for the other, and vice versa. As in the twentieth century, trends and changes in each field can greatly intensify trends and changes in the other. To put it simply, that is why the world is capable of galloping off for decades at a time in new and unexpected directions.

The broad trends of the twentieth century were quite clear and consistent. If we look at the century's first decade and its last, we can find strong common threads between the two, as if one had led inexorably to the other: America's economic and political ascent; the development of Germany as a new, rich, unified country; Japan's emergence as a modern, industrialized society; the spread of democracy; the growth of global trade and investment; the rise of stock-markets and modern corporations; the fall of aristocracy, and the rise of social mobility and meritocracy; the spread of material development and scientific knowledge to more countries around the world; the development of the technologies of communication, transport, energy, biology and destruction. And during the twentieth century mankind made more material progress than in any previous century, and ended the period with more individual freedom, longer lives and more ability to preserve, nurture and extend human life than ever before. Yet the eighty years between the century's first and last decades contained a number of episodes of diversion and regression, to put it mildly. If the common threads can be taken as representative of powerful long-term forces, there were also powerful forces pulling in the direction of instability and volatility.

The same sort of thing could well happen in the twenty-first century. It is possible, even probable, that the very long-term trends will again be positive and powerful: that democracy will spread further; that China, India and other now-poor nations will develop and emerge as modern, richer, industrialized societies; that this will be facilitated

by further growth in global trade and investment; that new technologies will be developed which will again transform work, production, energy, transportation and even life itself; that the individual
autonomy that emerged during the twentieth century in many of the
richer countries will develop further as social organizations fragment
and as education gives individuals more choices and freedoms; and
that such individualism will also spread in poorer countries as their
economies grow. Indeed, the prospects for such long-term trends look
even better than they did in the early twentieth century because of the
favourable answers given to the two big questions addressed in this
book.

The United States of America is able to, and willing to, offer much
stronger leadership in the cause of world peace and security, and of
unimpeded trade, than could Britain in the early 1990s. Britain then
was being matched and challenged in terms of its economic strength
both by the United States and by Germany, and the burden of maintaining its world-wide empire was huge. America has no world-wide
empire, though it does have world-wide obligations and a world-wide
network of military bases, albeit less extensive than Britain's in 1900.
Like Britain then, the United States now does not have anything like
enough power to solve all the world's political and economic problems.
But it does have enough military muscle to deter any country from
seeking to impose its will on others, or to cause mischief at a regional
or global level. Germany's miscalculation in 1914 that it could gain a
swift victory in Western Europe could only be made by a lunatic today,
in the face of American supremacy.

There is a theoretical possibility that American supremacy could
eventually be countered by a large alliance of other powers, ganging
up on the hegemon. Such an alliance could consist, for example, of
India, China and Russia, or of a European Union by then able to
conduct a common foreign and defence policy. The trouble with this
theory, however, is that to occur it would require circumstances in
which America's interests and the interests of a hypothetical alliance
were in such contradiction that it brought about an actual clash. This
need not be a full military clash, but it would need to be a situation so
full of adversarial fervour that it led to borders being closed, defences
being built, rival organizations being developed and so on. Yet it is

very hard to see America's interests themselves bringing about that clash: unless America itself changes, its basic commercial and political desires have long been for the very peace, democracy, openness to trade and capital, and international rule of law that any such clash would challenge. There will be plenty of friction over specific issues, including those caused by Americans straying temporarily from these general values. But as long as it sticks broadly to these basic interests and values, and as long as it desists from building a formal empire, America is unlikely to pose a direct threat to any group of countries large enough to challenge it.

Indeed, there is a basic paradox about American leadership that is likely to make it essentially benign, at least until much later in the century. This is that the values it espouses and seeks to establish overseas would, if adopted by other countries, make those countries stronger, not weaker. It is not a repressive or exploitative power, but rather an enabling one. Only if China or India, for example, successfully introduce a blend of the economic and political freedoms that America epitomizes could either of those budding powers ever hope to get anywhere close to matching America's military or economic strength. The United States is the first pre-eminent power in history whose ideas, if they triumph, would bring about the loss of its own dominance. It is possible that as that moment comes closer, Americans will change their minds and seek to prevent this process from bringing about their relative decline. But that time is a long way off, and the possibility a remote one.

All the foregoing, however, has been an analysis of international politics in isolation from economics. As the twentieth century showed, such isolated, compartmentalized thinking is often mistaken. Merely within 2002, the danger of ignoring the interplay was shown. At the same time as the fight against terrorism was drawing attention to America's political and military prowess, bringing about a mixture of awe, envy and trepidation, under the surface of America's economy something less admirable was stirring. Week after week, new scandals emerged from corporate America, as company after company was shown to have manipulated its financial accounts and even to have committed outright frauds. What had seemed during the Internet boom of 1997–2000 to be an unstoppable economic force, a model to be emulated by every other country, began to look a lot weaker and less admirable. This threatened to reduce America's economic influence around the world, as its super-capitalist system showed its flaws, and even eventually to reduce its political and military influence, if economic weakness were to make Americans less willing to bear burdens overseas.

It is too soon to be sure where this re-evaluation of American capitalism will lead. One of the great strengths of American capitalism has long been its flexibility, its ability to adapt quickly once problems emerge or new opportunities appear. But the re-evaluation is a salutary reminder that the themes of the second half of this book remain powerful, in the twenty-first century just as in the twentieth. Capitalism is unpopular for its greed and ruthlessness. It can be frighteningly unstable. It brings about inequalities in incomes that have the ability to cause political backlashes. It causes resentment. Periods when it falls into disfavour tend also to be periods in which the role of government grows, as public opinion begins to support tougher regulation of the capitalists and more intervention by the politicians and bureaucrats. History suggests that such swings of the pendulum are inevitable, but that they also bring on their own flaws, as the new regulation chokes off enterprise or as the interventions turn out to be misplaced.

There are, however, reasons to be optimistic about the prospects for capitalism in the early decades of the twenty-first century, just as there are about American leadership. Although it will never be loved, capitalism is already a lot better regulated in all the rich countries than it was a hundred years ago and in an increasing number of poor ones, making it less likely that periods of instability, inequality or even environmental damage will be devastating. They may well cause short-term damage, and require the search for and introduction of new remedies. But the role of government is already large enough, and the body of regulation already extensive enough, to justify optimism about the duration and severity of such episodes of damage. Politically, moreover, in almost all countries there is a strong inclination to stick with today's reasonably (but far from fully) open capitalism, including its reasonably (but far from fully) open trading system, because memories of the effects of communism, socialism and other variants of tight governmental control over economies are so fresh.

Some winemakers have a term for this balance between positive expectations and a keen awareness of risk. It is paranoid optimism. This, a winemaker once told me, consists of confidence that each vintage is going to be better than the last, based on the progress that he has made over the years. But it is tempered by the fear that something – too much rain, sun at the wrong time, a vine disease – could come along to spoil things. His paranoia helps him to make preparations to try to limit or at least cope with the dangers. Yet it does not alter his basic optimism.

*

It does not take much of an imagination to think of grounds for paranoia, in politics, economics, ecology or society. Many of them have been explored in this book. Nuclear terrorists could destroy our cities, China could descend into civil war, refugees and other migrants could flood across borders, economic growth could turn into depression, the climate could change, our food, air and water could become poisonous, new Dr Frankensteins, armed with modern genetic science, could create monsters of which even Mary Shelley could not have dreamt, our individualistic societies could become rife with crime and disorder as under-classes or other alienated elements turn hostile. The question, however, is whether such paranoia should lead towards pessimism or, as in this book, become an essential guardian for one's optimism.

There are plenty who draw gloomier conclusions. Some base their pessimism on a speculation about the future: a view that species may suddenly vanish in their millions, as the dinosaurs once did, or that the nuclear bomb will eventually bring our own species to an end. Many more, however, base their pessimism on a bleak view of the present and the recent past: the idea that things are already bad, and that present trends will bring us to disaster. To this optimist, however, such a view relies on a perverse twisting of the facts – under which, indeed, the more successful the human race becomes, the more it is accused of actual or impending failure. It is the species' version of the 'Catch-22' that Joseph Heller invented in 1961 for soldiers in the Second World War. In Heller's novel, which is concerned with the futility of war and with conscripts' desperate efforts at survival, the squadron's rules allow an airman to be sent home on grounds of insanity. But they also stipulate that anyone who asks to be sent home on such grounds has thereby defined himself as sane.

Humanity suffers from a similarly topsy-turvy sort of linguistics. For all other species, for example, biologists see rising population numbers as a clear indicator of success: success against predators, success against natural disasters, success in finding food and water, success in reproduction. During the twentieth century our numbers nearly quadrupled, from around 1.6 billion people alive in 1900 to more than 6 billion alive as the twenty-first century dawned. Population growth had already accelerated in the nineteenth century to a then unprecedented speed of 0.5 per cent per year, world-wide, but surged to almost 1.4 per cent per year in the twentieth century. Conquest over diseases, along with new techniques to produce far more food as well as to make more land habitable, have enabled human numbers to grow more rapidly in the past fifty years than in any other period in history. Life expectancy, a basic measure of success from the point of view of an individual (even if a matter of indifference from the point of view of a species, or at least of its genes), greatly increased during the twentieth century, from 45–50 years in 1900 to 70–80 now in the richer countries and from 20–40 to 50–60 in the poorer ones, and it is still rising.

Yet this population growth, despite being a consequence of good things, has in aggregate been feared as a very bad thing: as a population 'explosion' that threatens to overwhelm the earth's resources, and cause overcrowding, conflict and perhaps catastrophe. It still might do so. But of those fears it is conflict that poses by far the biggest danger. The remarkable fact is that, even though the earth's population has more than tripled in a century, price – the best measure of the scarcity of resources – has fallen virtually throughout that time for just about everything that is extracted from or grown in the earth, and yet has risen, in the form of wages, for the one thing that has become far more abundant: people.

Moreover, the likelihood of a population explosion appears to be receding. Part of that, alas, is due to the devastation being wrought by AIDS in Africa. But mainly it is because fertility levels are dropping sharply in most poor countries and all rich ones. The current rate of world population growth is thought by the United Nations to be

1.2 per cent a year, below the twentieth-century annual average. The latest 'medium variant' forecast from the UN for world population in 2050 is 9.3 billion, with an annual growth rate by then down to 0.47 per cent. ('Medium variant' assumes mainly medium levels of fertility, along with other factors affecting births and deaths.) Even those figures could prove to be over-estimates. Such is the sensitivity of long-run demographic forecasts to small changes in birth rates and mortality that they could be under-estimates, too. And 9.3 billion is a huge number of people. But on optimism's side is the evidence that, all over the world, people seem to react to better welfare and improved chances of survival by having fewer children. And they react to the challenge of population by finding new ways of growing food, new ways of making a living. Much depends, therefore, on whether the welfare of the poorer countries will in future improve, or whether economic growth might pass them by and be limited to the richer nations.

In material matters, humanity as a whole has never been wealthier. Output of goods and services is larger than ever before, has been growing consistently for longer than ever before, and is also larger per head of the world's population than ever before. This is true of every region of the globe. As the table opposite shows, even Africa achieved growth in output per head of 1 per cent per year in real terms from 1900 to 2000, more than double the rate it is thought to have achieved during the previous century (though the data for nineteenth-century Africa are even less reliable than those for the twentieth). It was the slowest-growing large region of the world taking those 100 years as a whole, but those who worry that recent falls in economic output mean that Africa is forever doomed could gain some reassurance from the fact that in the first half of the century a different region was the slowest. That dishonourable title was taken by Asia (excluding Japan), where output per head grew by just 0.1 per cent a year, barely a tenth of the growth rate in Africa. Beset by war, political instability, colonialism, disease, climate and, allegedly, cultural barriers such as China's apparently anti-capitalist Confucianism, Asia's prospects looked as dim in 1950 as Africa's do now. In the century's second half, Asia was far and away the region that created wealth most rapidly, with an annual average growth rate in output per head of 3.5 per cent.

One of the great tasks of the next few decades will be to try to find ways for Africa to emulate Asia's twentieth-century turnaround.

Growth of GDP per capita
(average annual percentage change)

	1820–1900	1900–1950	1950–2000	1900–2000
OECD*	1.2	1.3	2.6	2.0
Eastern Europe	0.7	1.3	1.2	1.2
Latin America	0.6	1.7	1.5	1.6
Asia (excluding Japan)	0.2	0.1	3.5	1.8
Africa	0.4	1.0	1.0	1.0
World	0.8	1.1	2.5	1.9

Source: Andrea Boltho and Gianni Tonolo 'The Assessment: The Twentieth Century', *Oxford Review of Economic Policy*, vol. 15, no. 4
* North America, Western Europe, Japan, Australia, New Zealand

Mankind's economic success would even have surprised one of the greatest economists of the twentieth century, John Maynard Keynes. His thinking was honed in the economically troubled years of the 1920s and 1930s in Britain, and he spent much of his time preoccupied with the question of how mankind could solve what he called 'the economic problem', the challenge of increasing production, on a sustained basis, to a level that would satisfy people's basic needs. In fact, the world long ago surpassed the level that Keynes would have defined as sufficient. Despite that, our needs remain unsatisfied, even in the rich world, for the very reason that capitalism creates new wants in order to provide the profits that stimulate its activity, and because in any case our idea of what is meant by 'basic' is constantly shifting. Beyond the barest minimum, our concept even of material need is psychological rather than physical. Material things do, or can, provide spiritual or emotional comforts. And yet the idea still quite often nags in the back of our minds that the good of all this materialism might really be a bad.

Although the world as a whole – or, rather, the world's human population as a whole – has become richer in material terms, some parts of it have become a great deal richer than others. As Chapter 10 described, the gap in incomes and wealth between the richest countries in the world and the poorest has been getting wider during most of the past century. With all that material wealth, there is arising an ever wider gap in circumstances. This produces guilt, but also it produces envy, and the guilty can easily be made afraid of the envious. Yet this growth in inequality is another case of 'Catch-22' linguistics: it has arisen entirely out of success, not failure. The poorest of the world have not, in general, become poorer. What has happened is that the rich have got a lot richer while the incomes and wealth of the poor have grown more slowly.

A new version of this concern is what is known as the 'digital divide': the idea, described in Chapter 9, that there is an increasing inequality in access to, or use of, information technology in general and the Internet in particular. Such technological inequality is scarcely a new phenomenon: had people at the time only thought of it (and perhaps some did), there were presumably railway, electric telegraph and steamship divides in the nineteenth century, and then a telephone divide, a motor car divide, and even, for a time, a radio divide during the twentieth century. These are just fancy ways of saying that some people are richer than others, and that possession of new technology has at times reinforced the advantage of the rich. For the digital divide has not occurred because the poor have changed the way in which they communicate or handle information. It has occurred only because the rich have found new ways of doing these things. If only there hadn't been so much success, we could have avoided this failure.

The growth of inequality has, however, been a failure for a group of professionals who have otherwise had a steady rise in their circumstances during the past century or so: economists. For it is not what most economists would have expected to have happened. As Chapter 10 agreed, ideas are believed to be the basis of economic growth. And good ideas are hard to come up with but easy to copy. So although the first big benefits of technical progress should go to those who first came up with the ideas, it ought to be easy for others later to catch up. As successful techniques cross borders by being licensed or copied, inequality ought to diminish rather than increase. One great case study in the validity of this notion is Japan, which caught up with the West spectacularly in the late nineteenth century and throughout the twentieth century, by just such methods. But copycat Japan was an exception, merely followed later by a few other countries in Asia. Most countries, most of the time, didn't catch up. They fell further behind.

There are many explanations for this. But one is inherent in the catch-up theory itself: the fact that for decades barriers between countries prevented the flow of technology across borders, as well as of the capital which enables the technology to be used and that the goods in which the technology is embodied. Indeed, such barriers were lamented for other reasons too. For more than forty years after 1947, the world was divided into two essentially closed camps on either side of the Iron and Bamboo Curtains, separated by ideology, animosity and weaponry. And, even within what called itself the 'free world', much was made of the ills of nationalism, of the excessive closing of borders, of narrow-minded parochialism, of the dangers posed by the nation-state, and of the contrary merits of unity, of open minds and open exchanges of ideas, of treating the world and its people as one. This anger at petty nationalism even took on romantic clothing, gathering a following among the young in the rich West. In his song 'Imagine', John Lennon spoke of a world with no countries, in which all the people shared all the world.

Right now, in the first years of the twenty-first century, such an appealing world is at last becoming genuinely imaginable. The long and winding word for it is globalization, and it consists of the removal of barriers to trade, cultural interchange and (sadly to a lesser extent) the movement of people, the diminution of the prominence of countries, of nation-states, of borders. Since the 1980s and early 1990s, the idea of such freedoms has had its most successful period ever, as much of the world, especially the developing countries, began to choose to open borders as well as minds, in the hope of attracting money, trade, technology, the cleverest people and the support – financial, moral or political – of the rich West. The world's two most populous countries, China and India, both decided during the 1980s and early 1990s to open their borders in this way, and as a result the degree of income inequality in the world as a whole began to fall after 1980. The gap between the very richest and the very poorest continued to widen, but the incomes of the larger mass of the world's population started to converge. In its latest manifestation globalization is a fairly new phenomenon, one that has inevitably brought bumpy change as well as its broader benefits, but it holds great promise for the next few decades. It is one of the biggest single justifications for optimism about the twenty-first century.

And lo, that success in at last creating a movement towards globalization, towards a unified world in which governments did less to divide people, has come to be defined by protesters as a source of impending failure, as the modern successors of John Lennon took to the streets, the television studios, the op-ed pages and even the music charts to complain that if this were to continue then soon . . . there would be no countries . . . that globalization threatened to harm the poor, to change or even destroy local cultures, to bring in foreign influences and dependencies, to damage the planet irreparably by spreading the wasteful habits of the rich among the much more numerous poor. They marched in Seattle in December 1999 and on every available occasion thereafter against the World Trade Organization, a body entrusted and empowered by its 144 member countries with the task of enforcing a common set of rules by which '. . . all the people' could share a common trading system for '. . . all the world'. And they marched against other internationalist bodies, such as the International Monetary Fund and the World Bank, and against summits of rich-world leaders.

Most probably, if he had still been alive, John Lennon would have been among the sceptics about globalization, for he was not noted for his support for anything in which large companies could become enthusiastically involved. Even though the Beatles were themselves early and extremely powerful cultural imperialists, who built a global brand and a following that made them, as he once put it rather unsubtly, 'more popular than Jesus Christ', and more profitable than most companies, John Lennon would surely have sided instinctively with globalization's opponents. Like him, they want to see themselves as being on the side of the oppressed, against exploitation and in favour of peace, love and the planet. Capitalist success must inevitably involve exploitation, and something other than love, and certainly brings changes to the environment. Such success must therefore really be failure.

*

Is this just mankind's natural cussedness? Might it be this very sense of being eternally dissatisfied, constantly worried about where things might be heading, about what problems might shortly need to be solved, that accounts for mankind's string of successes? At the simplest level, the answer to both those questions must surely be yes. The most dangerous and least sustainable moment for humanity would be when most people felt it was time to declare victory, to pat each other on the back, to sit down and put their collective feet up.

But there is more to it than this. At the heart of today's success, or today's prospect of success, lie some inherent sources of instability that do call the future into question. For, as this book has argued, they certainly call the past into question. The highly successful century that has just closed was, after all, also a highly unstable one: with two world wars, sundry famines, the slaughter of millions of people by their own governments, the threat for many decades of an even more destructive war, and with one deep world-wide economic depression but also a number of unpleasant regional or national economic set-backs. Our paranoia permits us, quite rightly, to imagine that such things could occur again, or that new and even worse threats could come along. History suggests that it would be wrong to turn that paranoia into a generalized pessimism. But our optimism that prospects are better today than in 1900, must, nevertheless, include a strong dose of realism, on two especially important counts.

One is that the parts of the world where the biggest opportunities lie for further progress in raising living standards are also the parts that host the biggest problems. It is a tragedy that India, a country of more than a billion people, full of technical know-how and entrepreneurial vigour, has hundreds of millions of people living in poverty, and has a literacy rate (in the 2001 census) of just 65 per cent (though up from barely 50 per cent in 1991); neighbouring Pakistan, with

141 million people, has an even worse literacy rate of 45 per cent. Developing countries such as these, and even more so those states of Central Asia, the Middle East and Africa that lack proper governments, suffer the worst civil disorder and violence, and some of the worst pollution. For such countries, the size of the problem also defines the size of the opportunity, but grasping that opportunity will be far from easy.

The second dose of realism is connected to the fact that the main source of optimism arises from globalization – in other words, from the fact that liberalization and integration with the world economy have recently spread to many poor and formerly communist countries. But what such globalization entails is change. And change is destabilizing. Its very intent is to bring about a series of cycles of what Joseph Schumpeter, the Austrian economist cited in Chapter 2, called creative destruction. The first of those two words is always going to be more welcome than the second. When there is change, there is the chance of social and political instability.

Will globalization stick to its current course and, in time, create higher living standards for the billions in the poor world? It is too soon to be sure. The liberation of developing countries from communism, central planning, authoritarianism and closed borders – that is, globalization and the spread of democracy – is quite new. Many developing countries had barely escaped from colonial servitude in mid-century when their governments gave them a new sort of servitude, a new straitjacket of communism, socialism or some variety of authoritarian rule. China's adoption of capitalism began only in 1978, and it has yet to adopt democracy. India has long had democracy, but began to open its borders to trade and to release enterprise from the shackles of the 'licence raj' only in 1991. For Russia and all its former communist satellites the same starting-date applies. For Latin America, the overthrow of authoritarian regimes and the adoption of a more open capitalism began with the region's debt crisis in the 1980s.

As a rich-country phenomenon, globalization is old news. John Maynard Keynes, writing in 1919 about Europe before the First World War, said in a famous passage of his polemic *The Economic Consequences of the Peace*, that at that time:

The inhabitant of London could order by telephone, sipping his morning tea in bed, the various products of the whole earth, in such quantity as he might see fit, and reasonably expect their early delivery upon his doorstep; he could . . . adventure his wealth in the natural resources and new enterprises of any quarter of the world . . . He could secure forthwith, if he wished it, cheap and comfortable means of transit to any country or climate without passport or other formality . . . The projects and politics of militarism and imperialism, of racial and cultural rivalries . . . appeared to exercise almost no influence at all on the ordinary course of social and economic life, the internationalisation of which was nearly complete in practice.

Keynes was, of course, writing only about the opportunities for an élite. But even so, many of the most dramatic causes of global shrinkage had already happened. The electric telegraph had the biggest effect, especially once reliable transoceanic cables had been laid. New York and London were linked in 1866; and cables reached Buenos Aires in 1878, Tokyo in 1900. By 1914, it took less than a minute to transmit a cable message from London to New York, and financial-market prices for the same liquid security or commodity on the two sides of the Atlantic had become identical. Telephones made communication even easier, and steamships moved people and things around the globe.

Keynes's intention was to warn that all this progress was now in danger. He was right. This economic integration was not well matched in politics, and as a result in the 1930s integration became disintegration. High trade barriers were imposed, as were immigration controls (note that Keynes did not need a passport); foreign investment was banned in various countries; and there were even bans on cultural interchange. All these measures considerably reduced integration until the 1950s, when barriers between Western Europe, North America and Japan began to be lowered. It was only in the 1960s that the amount of trade, relative to GDP, returned to pre-1914 levels. But politics still kept much of the rest of the world separate, thanks to ideology and beliefs about self-sufficiency. The developing countries as well as the communist world were left out of the rich world's post-war globalization, and did not share in the rich world's fastest ever period of economic growth.

The demise of those political barriers is what has brought on the past decade's acceleration of global integration, and its extension to many (but not yet all) parts of the poor world. That point is worth dwelling on for a moment: the widespread decision, during the 1990s, to open markets, allow foreign investment, boost trade and liberalize film and television sales, has been a political one, made by national governments. It has not been forced upon them by technology, or by evil Americans. It has been a voluntary choice. But that also means that the choice can be extended, or it can be reversed.

Probably the biggest force both for progress and for regress can be found in the financial markets. If poor countries are to grow their way out of poverty, they will need capital from abroad to supplement their domestic savings. Thus it was that in the first half of the 1990s, when more and more governments began to permit it, the developing countries became a fashionable place to invest, so fashionable that they were renamed as 'emerging markets'. Between 1994 and 1997, the twenty-nine biggest emerging economies received a total of $655 billion in bank loans, bonds and cross-border investment in shares. Such money can ebb as quickly as it flows, however: in the subsequent four years, the same economies received only $19 billion in this way. With that sort of violent ebb and flow, it is not particularly surprising that there were so many financial crises during the 1990s. Money is welcomed when it floods in, but causes great instability when it floods out again.

It is also not surprising that not all countries have benefited (or chosen to benefit) from global integration, for not all will welcome the changes it brings. A recent study by the World Bank showed that twenty-four poor countries, home to 3 billion people (that is, half the world's population) have managed substantially to increase the role of trade in their economies over the past twenty years; on average, output per head in these economies grew by 5 per cent a year during the 1990s and the proportion of their citizens living in poverty declined. But the same study found that another 2 billion people live in countries that have become less integrated with the rest of the world rather than more. These nations include Pakistan, Afghanistan and much of the Middle East and Africa: the role of trade in their economies has shrunk, economic growth has been stagnant and more of their citizens are living in poverty. Such countries have not actually been hurt by globalization;

they have simply failed to take part in it, because their governments have chosen not to. They tend to be especially dependent on
income from exports of commodities, such as cocoa, oil and other
minerals, the prices of which fluctuate and the extraction of which
adds little value and thus does not command high wages. They are
also countries in which war and terrorism is most common. And they
are the countries in which the al-Qaeda terrorist network has found
most of its recruits.

*

What are the prospects that the recent success of those twenty-four
countries could spread to those other 2 billion people? On the other
hand, what are the prospects that the success of the twenty-four could
go into reverse? The experience of the twentieth century shows that in
the face of economic instability or of other threats to their own power,
governments can readily turn inwards, shutting their borders and
trying to impose their own direction on their country's economy. They
do not currently look likely to do so, for the reason already rehearsed:
that memories are still fresh of how bad life was behind closed borders.
But that could change.

There is another reason for optimism, however. This is the spread
of democracy during the past dozen years. Like globalization, it is
reversible. But it is probably harder to reverse than the opening of
borders, because of the press of popular opinion and of international
criticism.

Even in the rich world, democracy scarcely existed in 1900.
Although a very few countries had elections and thought of themselves
as democracies, including Britain and the United States, none had a
universal adult suffrage. Some men – including, in America, all black
men – and all women were at that time excluded. Although those
two countries gave women the vote in the 1920s, the rich world's
main democratic boom took place only after 1945, when Germany,
Italy and Japan joined the ranks of the democracies. Spain, Portugal
and Greece, members of today's European Union, did not become
democracies until the 1970s.

In the poorer world, post-independence India, famously the world's
largest democracy, was for decades the exception that proved an
authoritarian rule. Around the globe, democratic systems, freedoms

and accountability were the province of a small minority. In 1980, of the world's then 121 countries, only 37 had democracies, and those accounted for a mere 35 per cent of the world's population. But the 1990s saw a surge in the democratic direction. By 2000, according to a pro-democracy think tank in America called Freedom House, some 120 of the by then 192 countries were defined as having 'electoral democracies'. Those countries accounted for about 60 per cent of the world's population.

Intellectuals with a historical and melancholy bent might wonder whether this is cause for optimism at all: one of the rallying calls for both fascism and communism, the ideological scourges of the twentieth century, was the notion that democracies were terminally weak. Democracies certainly muddle their way through, trading interest against interest, rather than blazing a clear and exhilarating course. And, as systems depending on majority votes, they have particular difficulty in handling the views of large minorities. But democracy now exerts a powerful appeal, less because of what it can do than because of what it is hoped it will stop, namely the horrific, murderous clarities that in China, the USSR, Nazi Germany, fascist Italy, North Korea, Argentina and the Khmer Rouge's Cambodia have been associated with unaccountable authority.

Progress in the democratic direction is neither plain nor easy. Some countries that claim to be democracies have systems that are decidedly phoney, or at least incomplete. Freedom House's headline number of 120 'electoral democracies' includes a considerable list of countries whose citizens are far from free, in the true sense of the word. They hold elections, but still restrict freedoms in a number of ways. Freedom House's own rankings count only 86 countries as properly free. The optimistic way of putting this is that some countries are 'in transition' towards full democracy, and that a mixture of public exposure and private discussion by diplomats and politicians can help jostle them along that path. It will persuade them that ballot boxes may be necessary for democracy, but are far from sufficient: what is also needed is free speech and a free press; an independent judiciary; and, supervised by that judiciary, the impartial enforcement of the rule of law. Mexico, which in 2000 saw the election of a president from an opposition party for the first time in more than seventy years, is an example of a transition in progress, though it has been painfully slow. Indonesia has found it hard to establish proper judging and policing after decades of dictatorship came to an end in 1998, let alone a full set of legitimate laws and a clear-out of corruption. So has Russia, where opinion about President Vladimir Putin's democratic credentials has waxed and waned. Yet with help, patience and encouragement, it can be done. Some of the phoneys have been exposed. Peru, whose President Alberto Fujimori rigged his (unconstitutional) re-election in 2000, is one of them; fortunately he was then expelled, after corruption and other scandals involving his intelligence services, and Peru's full democracy has been restored. Haiti, its democracy supposedly restored by American intervention in 1994, is another phoney. So is Malaysia: its prime minister, Mahathir Mohamad, has abided by democratic procedures during his more than two decades in office (he has promised to stand down in October 2003), yet meanwhile has imprisoned his chief rival (Anwar Ibrahim) on trumped-up charges, has throttled the press and has suborned the judiciary. Zimbabwe's President Robert Mugabe, though a hopeful figure when he came to power in 1980, now uses violence and other intimidation to ensure that he wins all elections. Freedom House rated Mugabe's behaviour in Zimbabwe as the third most severe of its 'setbacks' for democracy in its 2002 report, after the 11 September terrorist attacks and the Israeli–Palestinian conflict. Iran is one of the most interesting cases, and the hardest to judge: it has a constitution, and an elected parliament and president; but ultimate power, most notably over the judiciary, the army and the police, is in the hands of unelected clerics, who are accountable only to themselves and, they say, to God.

Is this worse than no democracy at all? All these countries have more accountability with their limited dose of democracy than they would have without it. But the accountability thus gained is limited too. The trend towards world-wide pre-eminence for liberal democracy is young, and, like most youths, it is both vigorous and impressionable, eager and fragile. Even so, in the many countries that are not phoneys, the movement since 1990 has been firmly in the right direction. People seem to want democracy. Or, at least, they have in recent decades preferred it to the alternative.

*

Firmly in the right direction. That phrase encapsulates the optimists' view. To those who believe, rather, that the world is heading towards a calamity it doubtless reads like the most famous passage from Voltaire's satire, *Candide*: Dr Pangloss's claim that, however bad things may seem, 'all is for the best in the best of all possible worlds'. Or as the blinkered view of a pampered member of a Western élite, for whom the vast problems and privations encountered by millions, nay billions, of people can be waved aside with a generalization. Or perhaps as the latest conceited statement from a believer in the eighteenth-century Enlightenment idea that human progress is inevitable, that all problems are solvable by reason, and that mankind is forever at a new frontier of knowledge and improvement.

The case for optimism, tempered as always by paranoia, is indeed based on the view that the opportunity for further progress is there. The foundations on which higher living standards in the poor world can narrow the gap with the rich are in place, if in a tentative and immature manner. Markets have been opening, the world has been integrating. More governments are democracies, and have more or less secure institutions and the rule of law. Despite terrorism and international tensions, the world is broadly at peace, with America willing to provide sufficient leadership to avert the biggest threats to security, even if it can never be omnipotent or omniscient. Waves of technological development are splashing over the globe, in information technology, biotechnology and energy that promise to bring more improvements in productivity and new ways to reshape life, work, leisure and transport, mostly for the better. The opportunity exists for some really remarkable progress, for reductions in poverty and pollution, for conquest over more diseases, for even more improvements in living standards, all around the world.

But it is only an opportunity. It can be taken, or missed. Where the Enlightenment sort of optimism is surely wrong is in its presumption that progress is inevitable. It is doubly wrong if such optimism is based on the associated idea that mankind's knowledge of the world and how it works is getting ever deeper, and thus that problems always have ready solutions that have already been found. What the twentieth century showed, throughout its span, was that man's ability to take control of economic, social and political forces is severely limited.

And the biggest human, economic and even environmental disasters occurred when people came to believe that they had discovered all the answers to the question of what needed to be done.

Ideas of attainable human utopias, of the perfectibility of human nature and of human conditions, are not just a delusion but dangerous. They are a delusion because life is too complicated, too riven by competing desires, instincts and needs, to allow utopias ever to emerge. They are dangerous because they bring with them false notions of certainty, dogmas that drive people to demand that particular ideas and plans must be followed, and to back those demands with force.

After all, promises turning to dust and dogmas turning into disasters were big features of the century that has just ended. There are many works of philosophy or of literature that are emblematic of the twentieth century, but my choice is what might seem an oddly light-hearted one. It is a children's tale, *The Wonderful Wizard of Oz*, by Frank L. Baum. It is emblematic because it was first published in 1900, and because it is, in essence, a tale of false utopias. Dorothy travels along the yellow brick road to Oz, with the Lion, the Tin Man and the Straw Man, in the belief that the Wizard can solve all their problems. But he turns out to be a fake, using smoke and mirrors and trickery. The solutions to their problems actually lie in their own hands, rather than his. Mr Baum said in the introduction to his story that it was intended to be one 'in which the wonderment and joy are retained and the heartaches and nightmares are left out'. Yet by 1939, when Judy Garland starred in MGM's movie version, the real world had had heartaches and nightmares aplenty arising from wizards and claimed utopias, and worse were to come.

Some of them involved the very science that has laid the foundations of much of the human wonderment of today, and of the technological promise for the future. At the peak of nineteenth-century fervour, enthusiasts came to consider science as morally superior. There was no such thing as sin or evil, thought the most mechanistic scientists, just ignorance; in due course they would be able to transform man and control nature. In 1899 Ernst Haeckel, a German disciple of Charles Darwin, wrote a bestselling book called *The Riddle of the Universe*, in which he argued that science would soon solve all problems, and in doing so would eliminate war. With Hitler's gas chambers, Stalin's experiments in agricultural biology and those of the Japanese Imperial army in human biology, any moral authority that such zealots ascribed to science was buried with its victims. Science, it became clear, had no particular moral content: it could serve good, but could also bring evil.

Today, the authority of science and popular admiration for it are both again justifiably high. But no one should assign it moral superiority or certainty, particularly the scientists themselves, whether over the environment, or the origins of the universe, or the secrets of life, or anything else. Science is all about knowledge, but it is a knowledge that is constantly being tested and challenged by new theories and findings. Indeed, the most striking thing in this great age of scientific discovery is not how much scientists know but how little. Sir John Maddox, a long-time editor of *Nature*, a renowned scientific journal, mapped the frontiers in 1998 in a magisterial book, *What Remains to be Discovered*. 'What stands out', he wrote, 'is that there is no field of science that is free from glaring ignorance, even contradiction.' That may seem a damning judgement, but is not intended as such. Instead, it is meant to offer an inspiring challenge to tomorrow's explorers.

It may also help explain what, to many nineteenth-century scientists and even economists, might have seemed a puzzling feature of the early twenty-first century: the resilience of religious belief. After all, when Darwin published his ideas about evolution in 1859, it was widely feared that they would undermine the very foundation of religion. Together with affluence and education, they probably did. The genuinely devout are a smaller proportion of the population in all the rich, originally Judaeo-Christian countries, and fewer people in these now have well-formed beliefs about heaven and hell, or an afterlife at all. But religious observance and affiliation are nevertheless still strikingly high. In this, the United States is admittedly the most extreme case among the developed countries. In Gallup polls in the late 1990s, 88 per cent of adult Americans said that religion was either very important or fairly important in their lives, down surprisingly little from the 95 per cent who made that claim in 1952.

Some of the explanation for this is social rather than religious, and America's constitutional separation of Church and State may also be partly responsible. In Europe, where old-established Protestant and

Catholic churches were often tightly linked to governments, rejection of the old authoritarian structures after the Second World War also brought about rejection of established churches. In Western Europe, Church membership and attendance have declined sharply. However, even there, some revival can be detected in the past twenty years. And, as in the United States, the figures conceal a big transfer from older, traditional churches to new independent bodies. A similar movement has taken place in Japan. In all the developed countries there has been a burgeoning of 'new age' spiritualist beliefs of many kinds. Given the progress of science, the spread of material wealth and the growth of individual autonomy within Western societies, the surprise is how much religious observance there still is, rather than how little.

Those points about science and religion are worth keeping in mind for the next time someone says that we are living in a 'knowledge economy', a phrase that has been especially common during the past decade. To be told this is disturbing for two reasons: first, because it is outdated, in that the economic and social shift of emphasis from manpower to brainpower has been going on for more than a century; but second, because it is so inappropriate. Sir John Maddox's argument with regard to science also applies more widely: the most important knowledge that has been gained is of the scope of our ignorance.

Perhaps most of all, this applies to economics. Depressions have been created by over-confident economists and their followers, as have inflations, hyper-inflations and unemployment. The notion that economics is a science, in the sense that it can accurately map human behaviour and then predict and manage the consequences of a given action, is scorned in the common speech of most politicians and many economists. Yet the actions of those same politicians and economists when in government, both in the capitalist and the communist worlds, have often belied that scorn. Governments run their economies as though they could be certain about the outcomes, and have mostly been proved wrong.

What economists and all other policy-makers need most is humility – the same sort of humility that, in the rest of humanity, lies behind the resilience of religious observance. Calls to utopia are dangerous, but so are assumptions of omniscience in the face of social, economic and political complexity. That, in turn, is the case for the philosophy of liberalism: the belief in tolerance, freedom and experimentation rather than in the imposition of solutions from above.

The liberal presumption in favour of the market, of capitalism and indeed of freedom itself, is driven by intellectual humility: the acceptance that a process of constant experimentation, involving the freely expressed views and actions of millions of people, is likely to produce a better, more adaptable outcome than one involving a committee of economists, politicians, bureaucrats, businessmen or even journalists, drawing up a grand blueprint. This presumption is humble because it acknowledges the extent of our ignorance.

Liberalism involves, or should involve, an awareness that science cannot have all the answers, and that technological change will not inevitably make things better. Humbly, it should realize that there is no one right way to manage an organization, and no one right way to arrange social relationships, whatever a sociologist or psychologist may claim. Above all, the humble liberal has to be aware of a paradox: that when we think we have come up with a series of solutions to political or practical problems, the thing that should scare us most is the idea that someone might be able to assemble the power actually to implement them all.

Famously, Lord Acton, a nineteenth-century liberal, observed that 'power tends to corrupt, and absolute power corrupts absolutely'. What is generally remembered is the second half of that phrase, especially as the twentieth century had so many cases of the horror of absolute power. But the first half is, if anything, more important. And the point it contains, that holders of power will, sometimes consciously, sometimes unconsciously, exploit it for their own ends, lies behind the liberal's suspicion not only of government – even in democracies – but also of big business, trade unions, pressure groups and all others who accumulate power. Man is not perfectible, but neither is government or any other big group.

That is one of the biggest reasons why, along with the justified optimism about economic, social and scientific possibilities which we should take with us into the first decades of the twenty-first century, we must keep by us that winemakers' paranoia. Things can go wrong, not just because of the acts of chance or God that vex the viticulturalist, but also because of the many acts of man that, deliberately or in error, threaten our liberties and our freedom of choice, that are liable through false claims of certainty to send us in new and dangerous directions, even in the most mature democracies. Frank Baum's emerald city of Oz was shown to be full of humbug and false claims of certainty. In the end, the fact that many such humbugs were exposed towards the end of the twentieth century, and that liberalism then began to spread its influence more widely, is a good foundation for optimism about the twenty-first century. The hunt for humbugs is one of the basic purposes of journalism, the quintessentially paranoid profession. The hunt must go on.

Sources and
Select Bibliography

Many books, articles, websites and other statistical sources have been used throughout the text. I will firstly list general sources that apply to the whole book or to large parts of it, and then divide more specialist items according to the chapters to which they most directly apply.

General Histories

Boltho, Andrea, and Tonolo, Gianni, 'The Assessment: The Twentieth Century – Achievements, Failures, Lessons', *Oxford Review of Economic Policy*, vol. 15, no. 4 (Winter 1999, special issue on the twentieth century).

Brewster, Todd, and Jennings, Peter, *The Century*, Doubleday, 1998.

Briggs, Asa, and Snowman, Daniel, *Fins de Siècle: How Centuries End, 1400–2000*, Yale University Press, 1996.

Conquest, Robert, *Reflections on a Ravaged Century*, John Murray, 1999.

Davies, Norman, *Europe: A History – A Glorious Chronicle of the Full History of Europe from Kings to Peasants, from the Urals to the Faroes*, Oxford University Press, 1996.

De Long, J. Bradford, *Slouching towards Utopia*, forthcoming. Drafts can be downloaded from Bradford de Long's website, http://econ161.berkeley.edu/TCEH/Slouchtitle.html.

Evans, Harold, *The American Century*, Knopf, 1998.

Howard, Michael Eliot, and Louis, William Roger, *The Oxford History of the Twentieth Century*, Oxford University Press, 1998.

Kennedy, Paul, *Preparing for the Twenty-First Century*, Random House, 1993.

Keylor, William R., *The Twentieth-century World: An International History*, W. W. Norton & Co., 1998.

Mazower, Mark, *Dark Continent: Europe's Twentieth Century*, Allen Lane The Penguin Press, 1998.

Roberts, J. M., *Twentieth Century: A History of the World 1901 to the Present*, Allen Lane The Penguin Press, 1999.

Simon, Julian L., *The State of Humanity*, Blackwell, 1995.

Vinen, Richard, *A History in Fragments: Europe in the Twentieth Century*, Little, Brown, 2000.

Yergin, Daniel, and Stanislaw, Joseph, *The Commanding Heights: The Battle between Government and the Marketplace that is Remaking the Modern World*, Simon & Schuster, 1998.

Data Sources

Asian Development Bank, *Asian Development Outlook 2002*, Manila: Asian Development Bank, 2002.

Census Bureau, *Statistical Abstract of the United States 2001*, Washington DC: Department of Commerce, 2001.

Development Assistance Committee, *Development Co-operation 2001 Report*, Paris: OECD, 2002.

Economist Intelligence Unit, various country reports and forecasts.

Gwartney, James, and Lawson, Robert, *Economic Freedom of the World 2002 Annual Report*, Vancouver: Fraser Institute, 2002.

Inter-American Development Bank, *Annual Report 2001*, Washington DC: Inter-American Development Bank, 2002.

International Institute for Strategic Studies, *The Military Balance 2001/2002*, London: Oxford University Press, 2001.

International Institute for Strategic Studies, *Strategic Survey 2001/2002*, London: Oxford University Press, 2002.

International Monetary Fund, *Direction of Trade Statistics Yearbook 2001*, Washington DC: IMF, 2001.

—— *International Financial Statistics, June 2002*, Washington DC: IMF, 2002.

Maddison, Angus, *The World Economy: A Millennial Perspective*, Paris: OECD, 2001.

Office of the Secretary of Defense, *Quadrennial Defense Report September 2001*, Washington DC: Department of Defense, 2001.

SOPEMI, *Trends in International Migration 2000*, Paris: OECD, 2001.

Statistics Bureau and Statistics Center, *Statistical Handbook of Japan 2001*, Tokyo: Ministry of Public Management, 2001.

United Nations Food and Agriculture Organization, *State of the World's Forests 2001*, New York: United Nations, 2001.

United Nations Population Division, *World Population Prospects: The 2000 Revision*, New York: United Nations, 2001.

United Nations Statistics Division, *1998 Energy Yearbook*, New York: United Nations, 1998.

World Bank, *Global Development Finance 2002* (CD-ROM), Washington DC: World Bank, 2002.

—— *World Development Indicators 2002*, Washington DC: World Bank, 2002.

World Health Organization, *World Health Report 1998. Life in the 21st Century: A Vision for All*, New York: United Nations, 1998.

World Trade Organization, *WTO International Trade Statistics 2001*, Geneva: WTO, 2001.

Websites

www.epa.gov/airlinks AIRS, the US Environmental Protection Agency's database on air quality in American cities.

www.armscontrol.org Arms Control Association, an authoritative source for research and data on weapons control.

www.bea.doc.gov Bureau of Economic Analysis, US Commerce Department's website for statistics on GDP, trade and more.

www.ciesin.org Center for International Earth Science Information Network, based at Columbia University and includes statistics on environmental sustainability.

www.cns.miis.edu/index.htm Center for Nonproliferation Studies, Monterey Institute's premier research institute.

www.un.org/Depts/oip/ Office of the Iraq Program, UN's oil-for-food programme with details of sanctions and UN resolutions.

www.un.org/popin POPIN, the UN's Population Information Network, data and forecasts.

www.worldbank.org/poverty/ PovertyNet, for people working to understand and alleviate poverty.

www.unchs.org/programmes/guo UN-HABITAT, the UN's Human Settlements Program database including over 1,000 cities world-wide.

www.undp.org/poverty/initiatives/wider/wiid.htm World Income Inequality Database, poverty statistics maintained by the UN's Social Development and Poverty Elimination Division.

I. 20:21 VISION

Angell, Norman, *The Great Illusion*, Heinemann, 1910 (first published as *Europe's Optical Illusion*, 1909).

Easterlin, Richard A., *Growth Triumphant: The 21st Century in Historical Perspective*, University of Michigan Press, 1996.

Howard, Michael, *The Invention of Peace*, Profile Books, 2001.

Livi-Bacci, Massimo, *A Concise History of World Population*, Blackwell, 2nd edn., 1997.

Rummel, R. J., *Death by Government*, Transaction Publishers, 1994.

Sachs, Jeffrey, 'Twentieth Century Political Economy: A Brief History of Global Capitalism', *Oxford Review of Economic Policy*, vol. 15, no. 4 (Winter 1999).

Skidelsky, Robert, *The World After Communism: A Polemic for our Times*, Picador, 1995.

2. American Leadership

Bacevich, Andrew, *American Empire*, Harvard University Press, 2002.

Baily, Martin Neil, 'Macroeconomic Implications of the New Economy', Paper given at symposium sponsored by Federal Reserve Bank of Kansas City. 30 August–1 September 2001, Jackson Hole, Wyoming.

Blight, James G., and McNamara, Robert S., *Wilson's Ghost*, Public Affairs, 2001.

Center on Policy Attitudes, University of Maryland, *Program on International Policy Attitudes*. Various papers, notably Steven Kull and Clay Ramsay, 'American Public Attitudes to Fatalities in the Post-Cold-War period'.

Chace, James, *Acheson: The Secretary of State who Created the American World*, Simon & Schuster, 1998.

Dertouzos, Michael L., Lester, Richard K. and Solow, Robert M., *Made in America: Regaining the Productive Edge*, MIT Press, 1989.

Frankel, Jeffrey A., and Orszag, Peter R. (eds.), *American Economic Policy in the 1990s*, MIT Press, 2002.

Gaddis, John Lewis, *The United States and the End of the Cold War: Implications, Reconsiderations, Provocations*, Oxford University Press, 1992.

—— *We Now Know: Rethinking Cold War History*, Oxford University Press, 1997.

Haass, Richard N., *The Reluctant Sheriff: The United States after the Cold War*, Council on Foreign Relations, 1997.

Ishihara, Shintaro, and Morita, Akio, *The Japan That Can Say No: Why Japan Will Be First Among Equals*, Simon & Schuster, 1989.

Kennedy, Paul, *The Rise and Fall of the Great Powers*, Random House, 1987.

Kissinger, Henry R., *Does America Need a Foreign Policy?*, Simon & Schuster, 2001.

Lester, Richard K., *The Productive Edge: How US Industries are Pointing the Way to a New Era of Economic Growth*, W. W. Norton & Co., 1998.

Mead, Walter Russell, *Special Providence: American Foreign Policy and How it Changed the World*, Knopf, 2001.

Nau, Henry R., *The Myth of America's Decline*, Oxford University Press, 1990.

Nye, Joseph S. Jr., *Bound to Lead: The Changing Nature of American Power*, Basic Books, 1990.

—— *The Paradox of American Power: Why the World's Only Superpower Can't Go It Alone*, Oxford University Press, 2002.

Skidelsky, Robert, *John Maynard Keynes: Fighting for Britain, 1937–1946*, Macmillan, 2001.

3. Chinese Ambition

Becker, Jasper, *The Chinese*, John Murray, 2000.

Buruma, Ian, 'China and Liberty', *Prospect*, May 2000.

Fairbank, John King, and Goldman, Merle, *China: A New History*, Harvard University Press, 1998.

Gill, Bates, and Lardy, Nicholas, 'China: Searching for a Post-Cold-War Formula', *Brookings Review*, vol. 18, no. 4, Fall 2000.

Kristof, Nicholas D. and WuDunn, Sheryl, *China Wakes: The Struggle for the Soul of a Rising Power*, Times Books, 1994.

Ma, Ying, 'China's America Problem', *Policy Review*, no. 111, February 2002.

Maddison, Angus, *Chinese Economic Performance in the Long Run*, OECD Development Centre, 1998.

Miles, James, 'A Dragon out of Puff: A Survey of China', *The Economist*, 14 June 2002.

Segal, Gerald, 'Does China Matter?', *Foreign Affairs*, September 1999.

Short, Philip, *Mao: A Life*, Henry Holt & Co., 1999.

Ziegler, Dominic, 'Now Comes the Hard Part: A Survey of China', *The Economist*, 8 April 2000.

4. Japanese Vulnerability

Bracken, Paul, *Fire in the East: The Rise of Asian Military Power and the Second Nuclear Age*, HarperCollins, 1999.

Curtis, Gerald L., *The Logic of Japanese Politics: Leaders, Institutions and the Limits of Change*, Columbia University Press, 1999.

Dower, John, *Japan in War and Peace: Essays on History, Race and Culture*, HarperCollins, 1993.

Emmott, Bill, *The Sun Also Sets: Why Japan will not be Number One*, Simon & Schuster, 1989.

—— *Japanophobia: The Myth of the Invincible Japanese*, Times Books, 1993 (published in Britain as *Japan's Global Reach* by Century Business, 1992).

Hartcher, Peter, *The Ministry: The Inside Story of Japan's Ministry of Finance's Economic Power*, HarperCollins, 1998.

Posen, Adam, 'Japan 2001 – Decisive Action or Financial Panic', *International Economic Policy Briefs*, Institute for International Economics, March 2001.

Van Wolferen, Karel, *The Enigma of Japanese Power*, Vintage Books, 1990.

5. European Envy

Duchêne, François, *Jean Monnet: The First Statesman of Interdependence*, W. W. Norton & Co., 1996.

Grant, Charles, *Delors: Inside the House that Jacques Built*, Nicholas Brealey, 1994.

Hayek, Friedrich von, *The Road to Serfdom*, Routledge, 1944.

Jack, Andrew, *The French Exception*, Profile Books, 1999.

Layard, Richard, and Parker, John, *The Coming Russian Boom: A Guide to New Markets and Politics*, Free Press, 1996.

Marsh, David, *Germany and Europe: The Crisis of Unity*, Heinemann, 1994.

Messerlin, Patrick A., *Measuring the Costs of Protection in Europe: European Commercial Policy in the 2000s*, Institute for International Economics, 2001.

Pedder, Sophie, 'La Grande Illusion: A Survey of France', *The Economist*, 5 June 1999.

Siedentop, Larry, *Democracy in Europe*, Allen Lane The Penguin Press, 2000.

Thurow, Lester, *Head to Head: The Coming Economic Battle among Japan, Europe and America*, William Morrow & Co., 1992.

Young, Hugo, *This Blessed Plot: Britain and Europe from Churchill to Blair*, Macmillan, 1998.

6. Turbulence and Terror

Allison, Graham, 'Could worse be yet to come?', *The Economist*, 5 November 2001.

Buruma, Ian, and Margalit, Avishai, 'Occidentalism', *New York Review of Books*, 17 January 2002.

Butler, Richard, *Saddam Defiant: The Threat of Weapons of Mass Destruction and the Crisis of Global Security*, Weidenfeld & Nicolson, 2000.

Chanda, Nayan, and Talbott, Strobe, *The Age of Terror: America and the World after September 11th*, Perseus, 2001.

Huntington, Samuel, 'The Clash of Civilizations', *Foreign Affairs*, vol. 72, no. 3, Summer 1993.

Lewis, Bernard, *The Middle East: 2000 Years of History From the Rise of Christianity to the Present Day*, Weidenfeld & Nicolson, 1995.

Rashid, Ahmed, *Taliban: The Story of the Afghan Warlords*, Pan, 2001.

—— *Jihad: The Rise of Militant Islam in Central Asia*, Yale University Press, 2002.

Shawcross, William, *Deliver Us From Evil: Warlords and Peacekeepers in a World of Endless Conflict*, Bloomsbury, 2000.

7. Unpopular

Berle, Adolf, and Means, Gardiner, *The Modern Corporation and Private Property*, Commerce Clearing House, 1932.

Cantril, Hedley, *The Politics of Despair*, Basic Books, 1958.

Chandler, Alfred D., *The Visible Hand: The Managerial Revolution in American Business*, Belknap, 1977.

—— *Scale and Scope: The Dynamics of Industrial Capitalism*, Belknap, 1990.

Chernow, Ron, *The House of Morgan: An American Banking Dynasty and the Rise of Modern Finance*, Simon & Schuster, 1991.

Drucker, Peter F., *The End of Economic Man: The Origins of Totalitarianism*, John Day, 1939.

—— *The Concept of the Corporation*, John Day, 1946.

—— *The Unseen Revolution: How Pension Fund Socialism Came to America*, HarperTrade, 1976.

—— *Management Challenges for the 21st Century*, Butterworth-Heinemann, 1999.

Emmott, Bill, 'Everybody's Favourite Monsters: A Survey of Multinationals', *The Economist*, 27 March 1993.

Furet, François, *The Passing of an Illusion: The Idea of Communism in the Twentieth Century*, University of Chicago Press, 1999.

Graham, Edward M., *Global Corporations and National Governments*, Institute for International Economics, 1996.

—— *Fighting the Wrong Enemy*, Institute for International Economics, 2001.

Handy, Charles, *The Hungry Spirit: Beyond Capitalism: A Quest for Purpose in the Modern World*, Arrow, 1998.

Hertz, Noreena, *The Silent Takeover: Global Capitalism and the Death of Democracy*, Heinemann, 2001.

Klein, Naomi, *No Logo*, Knopf, 2000.

Oswald, Andrew, 'Happiness and Economic Performance', *Warwick Economic Research Paper*, no. 478, University of Warwick, April 1997.

Packard, Vance, *The Hidden Persuaders*, David McKay, 1957.

Sampson, Anthony, *Company Man: The Rise and Fall of Corporate Life*, HarperCollins, 1995.

Strouse, Jean, *Morgan: American Financier*, Random House, 1999.

Whyte, William H., Jr., *The Organization Man*, Doubleday, 1956.

Williamson, Oliver G., and Winter, Sidney G., *The Nature of the Firm: Origins, Evolution, and Development*, Oxford University Press, 1991.

8. Unstable

Bagehot, Walter, *Lombard Street*, Kegan Paul, 1873.

Bordo, Michael, Eichengreen, Barry, Klingebiel, Daniela and Martinez-Perla, Maria Soledad, 'Is the Crisis Problem Growing More Severe?', *Economic Policy*, April 2001.

Crook, Clive, 'The Visible Hand: A Survey of the World Economy', *The Economist*, 20 September 1997.

Delargy, P. J. R., and Goodhart, Charles, 'Plus ça change, plus c'est la même chose', *LSE Financial Markets Group Special Paper*, 108, January 1999.

Dow, Christopher, *Major Recessions: Britain and the World 1920–1995*, Oxford University Press, 1999.

Eichengreen, Barry, *Globalizing Capital: A History of the International Monetary System*, Princeton University Press, 1996.

Emmott, Bill, 'The Ebb Tide: A Survey of Global Finance', *The Economist*, 27 April 1991.

Friedman, Milton, *Capitalism and Freedom*, University of Chicago Press, 1963.

Keynes, John Maynard, *A General Theory of Employment, Interest and Money*, Macmillan, 1936.

Kindleberger, Charles P., *The World in Depression, 1929–1939*, University of California Press, 1986.

—— *Manias, Panics and Crashes: A History of Financial Crises*, John Wiley & Sons, 1999.

Malkiel, Burton Gordon, *A Random Walk Down Wall Street*, W. W. Norton & Co., 1996.

Minton Beddoes, Zanny, 'Time for a Redesign? A Survey of Global Finance', *The Economist*, 30 January 1999.

Shiller, Robert J., *Irrational Exuberance*, Princeton University Press, 2000.

Shleifer, Andrei, and Vishny, Robert, *The Grabbing Hand: Government Pathologies and their Cures*, Harvard University Press, 1999.

Skidelsky, Robert, *Beyond the Welfare State*, Social Market Foundation, 1997.

Soros, George, *The Crisis of Global Capitalism*, Litle, Brown, 1998.

—— *George Soros on Globalization*, Public Affairs, 2002.

9. Unequal (1)

Acemoglu, Daron, and Robinson, James A., 'Why Did the West Extend the Franchise? Democracy, Inequality and Growth in Historical Perspective', *Quarterly Journal of Economics*, vol. 115, November 2000.

Atkinson, A. B., 'The Distribution of Income in the UK and OECD Countries in the Twentieth Century, *Oxford Review of Economic Policy*, vol. 15, no. 4, Winter 1999.

Costa, Dora, 'Less of a Luxury: The Rise of Recreation since 1888', *NBER Working Paper*, no. 6054, June 1997.

Daedalus, 'On Inequality', *Journal of the American Academy of Arts and Sciences*, Winter 2002, special issue.

Keynes, John Maynard, 'Economic Possibilities for our Grandchildren', in *Essays in Persuasion*, Macmillan, 1930.

Russell, Bertrand, *In Praise of Idleness and Other Essays*, Allen & Unwin, 1935.

10. Unequal (2)

Cohen, Stephen P., *India: Emerging Power*, Brookings Institution Press, 2001.

Connors, Michael, *The Race to the Intelligent State: Towards the Global Information State*, Blackwell, 1993.

Jacobs, Jane, *Cities and the Wealth of Nations: Principles of Economic Life*, Vintage Books, 1985.

Landes, David S., *The Wealth and Poverty of Nations: Why Some Are So Rich and Some So Poor*, W. W. Norton & Co., 1998.

Olson, Mancur J., *The Rise and Decline of Nations: Economic Growth, Stagflation and Social Rigidities*, Yale University Press, 1982.

—— 'Big Bills left on the Sidewalk: Why Some Nations are Rich and Others Poor', *Journal of Economic Perspectives*, vol. 10, no. 2, Spring 1996.

—— *Power and Prosperity: Outgrowing Communist and Capitalist Dictatorships*, Basic Books, 2000.

Powelson, John P., *Centuries of Economic Endeavor: Parallel Paths in Japan and Europe and Their Contrast with the Third World*, University of Michigan, 1994.

Pritchett, Lant, 'Divergence, Bigtime', *Journal of Economic Perspectives*, vol. 11, no. 3, Summer 1997.

Ramesh, Jairam, *Yankee Go Home – and Take Me With You*, Asia Society, New York, monograph, 1998.

Rubinstein, W. D., *Capitalism, Culture and Decline in Britain 1750–1990*, Routledge, 1993.

Sachs, Jeffrey, 'A New Map of the World', *The Economist*, 24 June 2000.

Sala-i-Martin, Xavier, 'The Disturbing "Rise" of Global Income Inequality', *NBER Working Paper*, no. 8904.

Sen, Amartya K., *Development as Freedom: Human Capability and Global Need*, Oxford University Press, 1999.

Soto, Hernando de, *The Mystery of Capital: Why Capitalism Triumphs in the West and Fails Everywhere Else*, Bantam Press, 2000.

Wade, Robert, 'Winners and Losers', *The Economist*, 28 April 2001.

11. Unclean

Cairncross, Frances, *Costing the Earth: The Challenge for Governments, the Opportunities for Business*, Earthscan, 1995.

Cazorla, Marina, and Toman, Michael, 'International Equity and Climate Change Policy', *Resources for the Future, Climate Change Issues Brief*, no. 27, December 2000.

Club of Rome, *The Limits to Growth*, New American Library, 1972.

Easterbrook, Gregg, *A Moment on the Earth: The Coming Age of Environmental Optimism*, Penguin, 1995.

Flink, James J., *The Car Culture*, MIT Press, 1975.

Gore, Al, *Earth in the Balance: Forging a New Common Purpose*, Earthscan, 1992.

Huber, Peter, *Hard Green: Saving the Environment from the Environmentalists*, Basic Books, 1999.

Inter-Governmental Panel on Climate Change, *Summary for Policy-Makers: A Report of Working Group 1*, January 2001 *http://www.ipcc.ch/*

Jones, Daniel T., Roos, Daniel and Womack, James P., *The Machine that Changed the World: The Story of Lean Production*, HarperCollins 1991.

Litvin, Daniel, 'Dirt Poor: A Survey of the Environment and Developing Countries', *The Economist*, 21 March 1998.

Lomborg, Bjorn, *The Skeptical Environmentalist: Measuring the Real State of the World*, Cambridge University Press, 2001.

McNeill, J. R., *Something New Under the Sun: An Environmental History of the Twentieth-century World*, W. W. Norton & Co., 2000.

Ridley, Matt, *Down to Earth: A Contrarian View of Environmental Problems*, Institute of Economic Affairs, 1995.

Shogren, Jason, and Toman, Michael, 'How Much Climate Change is Too Much? An Economics Perspective', *Resources for the Future, Climate Change Issues Brief*, no. 25, September 2000.

Sloan, Alfred P., *My Years with General Motors*, Doubleday, 1964.

12. Paranoid Optimism

Brierley, Peter W., and Verwer, George, *Future Church*, Monarch Publications, 1998.

Dahl, Robert A., *On Democracy*, Yale University Press, 1999.

Davis, Bob, and Wessel, David, *Prosperity: The Coming Twenty-year Boom and What It Means to You*, Times Books, 1998.

Friedman, Milton, *Capitalism and Freedom*, University of Chicago Press, 1963.

Friedman, Thomas L., *The Lexus and the Olive Tree*, Farrar, Straus & Giroux, 1999.

Garbade, Kenneth, and Silber, William, 'Technology, Communication and the Performance of Financial Markets 1840–1975', *Journal of Finance*, June 1978.

Henderson, David, 'Changing Fortunes of Economic Liberalism – Yesterday, Today and Tomorrow', *Institute of Economic Affairs Occasional Paper*, 105, 1998.

Irwin, Douglas A., *Against the Tide: An Intellectual History of Free Trade*, Princeton University Press, 1996.

—— 'The United States in a New Global Economy? A Century's Perspective', *AEA Papers and Proceedings*, May 1996.

Keynes, John Maynard, *The Economic Consequences of the Peace*, Macmillan, 1919.

Kiplinger, Knight, *World Boom Ahead: Why Business and Consumers Will Prosper*, Kiplinger Books, 1998 (British edn).

Lutz, Wolfgang, Sanderson, Warren and Scherbov, Sergei, 'The End of World Population Growth', *Nature*, vol. 412, 2 August, 2001.

Maddox, John, *What Remains to be Discovered: Mapping the Secrets of the Universe, the Origins of Life, and the Future of the Human Race*, The Free Press, 1998.

Micklethwait, John, and Wooldridge, Adrian, *A Future Perfect: The Challenge and Hidden Promise of Globalisation*, Crown Business, 2000.

Sen, Amartya K. 'Democracy as a Universal Value', Keynote address at the Global Conference on Democracy, New Delhi, 14–17 February 1999.

Smart, Ninian, *The World's Religions*, Cambridge University Press, 1998.

Standage, Tom, *The Victorian Internet: The Remarkable Story of the Telegraph and the Nineteenth Century's On-line Pioneers*, Walker & Co., 1998.

Index

social protection
  Japan 85
  US 42–3, 44–5
socialism 154, 162, 238
software 166
Somalia 132, 133, 140, 238
  US deaths 47, 48
Sony 78, 84, 166
Soros, George 196
South Africa 136
South China Sea 74–5, 77
South Korea
  car industry 169
  central planning 155
  democracy 73
  economy 58, 237
  and Japan 93, 95
  living standards 224
  and North Korea 96, 138
  and US 27
sovereignty 50, 108
Soviet Union 12, 16
  Afghanistan 33
  central planning 109
  and China 65
  deaths 8–10
  economic isolation 20
  empire 132
  environment 252
  and liberation movements 151
  Second World War 156
  trade 106
  US foreign policy 31–2
  see also cold war; Russia
Spain
  defence spending 121
  democracy 289
  fascism 151, 156
  separatism 134
species extinction 249–50

Srebrenica 124
Sri Lanka 58, 127, 134
stability 183
Stalin, Joseph 9, 141, 151, 156
states of concern 34, 35, 36, 140,
  230
Steinbeck, John 182
Stepford Wives, The 164
stockmarkets see financial markets
Subaru 168
Sudan 125, 133, 138, 238
Suharto, President 72, 167
suicide attacks 125, 127–8, 144
sustainable development 244
Suzuki 168
Sweden 59, 105, 193
Symbionese Liberation Front 228
Syria 95

Taiwan
  and China 61, 69, 75–6, 95–6,
    138
  democracy 73, 74
  and Japan 64, 95
  Kuomintang 152
  living standards 224
  US policy 34
Taliban 33, 133, 144
Tamils 134
taxation
  cars 261
  and environment 268, 269
  and inequality 214
technology 80, 274, 275, 292, 296
  and capitalism 20
  and dictatorships 10–12
  domestic services 209
  and environment 264, 269
  and globalization 287
  and inequality 231–2, 283